CIA LIFE

10,000 Days with the Agency

CIA LIFE

10,000 Days with the Agency

Tom Gilligan

Intelligence Book Division, IEP
Boston, Massachusetts

IEP
Intelligence Book Division

Published by:
Intelligence Book Division, IEP

Library of Congress Control Number: 2003097642

Gilligan, Tom.
CIA Life : 10,000 Days with the Agency / Tom Gilligan.
Second Edition.
ISBN 0-9729659-1-2 (hardcover)
ISBN 0-9729659-2-0 (softcover)
ISBN 0-9729659-0-4 (e-book)
1. Gilligan, Tom. 2. Intelligence Officers — United States — History.
3. United States. Central Intelligence Agency. I. Title.

For Bonnie,
who raised five wonderful children during the
10,000-day journey in a peculiar career
with a sometimes impossible mate.

Contents

Prologue to Second Edition

SEPTEMBER 2003

POST COLD WAR TRANSITION

A DECADE AGO, as the Cold War with the USSR drew to a close, *CIA LIFE: 10,000 Days with the Agency* described the internal factors and external forces undermining the Central Intelligence Agency's ability to meet its responsibilities in Clandestine Collection, Counterintelligence, and Covert Action. *CIA LIFE* closed with a review of "Threats Facing America in the 1990s" that focused on the Agency's limited ability to deal with future supranational threats — of Terrorism, International Criminal networks, weapons proliferation, and nations that support Terrorism. *CIA LIFE*, finally, called for "a new CIA, one that is well led, well staffed and well used to keep the world's barbarians at bay."

Unfortunately, this post-Cold War renewal of CIA did not take place in the 1990s — and certainly not before September 11, 2001 — partly because CIA had gotten away from its core principles and because it had remained in the Congressionally-imposed straightjacket of the 1970s and 1980s. In addition, as *CIA LIFE* describes in detail, the Agency had become bureaucratically rigid as administrative managers had replaced real Clandestine Operations leaders who, in prior decades, made CIA one of the most innovative institutions in Government, not only in the realm of Scientific Intelligence (U-2, satellite reconnaissance, etc.) but also in Human Intelligence Operations (HUMINT) which ran the gamut from penetrating closed societies to running strategically important Covert Action Operations.

By examining the public record of the 1990s, one sees a series of intelligence failures in all major aspects of the work of the Directorate of Operations (DDO), the HUMINT side of the Agency. Underlying the inability to make an effective transformation to the post-Cold War world was lack of reflection on DDO capabilities in light of the new challenges identified in *CIA LIFE* and which, by the way, were well known to the political and intelligence leadership in Washington. Osama bin Laden did not suddenly come to life on September 11 and neither did Middle Eastern extremism, Hussein of Iraq, Weapons of Mass Destruction,

North Korean nuclear blackmail, nor the array of International Money Laundering and Narco-Terrorist networks. Why was America not able to act preemptively against self-declared enemies of the United States? Why was America's watchman, CIA, sound asleep in the watch tower as Terrorists planned their many attacks?

CIA MISSION FAILURES IN 1990S AND BEYOND

CIA DID NOT MAKE an effective internal transition to the post-Cold War world in terms of its Human Agent Intelligence (HUMINT) responsibilities in any of its three basic Clandestine Service missions:

Foreign Intelligence Collection (FI). The catastrophic Intelligence failure of September 11, 2001 stands as the single greatest military or paramilitary assault on America in its two century history — surpassing Pearl Harbor in human loss, dwarfing the Tet offensive in psychological setback for the U.S., and driving America further into recession by the extent of the economic dislocations. What does September 11 indicate on the effectiveness of the Central Intelligence Agency, which played such a strong and active role in winning the Cold War between 1946 and 1991 without another Pearl Harbor-like intelligence failure? Although the Terrorists alone are to blame for these attacks, they could not have succeeded in pulling off the several concurrent hijackings had there not been a systemic failure within the U.S. Intelligence Community, specifically within the CIA and the FBI. The Executive Branch did not know what it needed to know, and should have known, to prevent this massive, coordinated multi-target attack that took many months, several dozens of people, hundreds of thousands of dollars, and even Boeing 757 pilot training at U.S. flight schools to orchestrate.

Counterintelligence (CI): The CI disasters of the 1980s were surpassed in the 1990s in the spy cases of Aldrich H. Ames and Robert P. Hanssen whose treason revealed that the very Counterintelligence structures within CIA, and the FBI, had been penetrated thoroughly by the Soviet KGB and its successor organs. The American spy catchers, it turned out, were essentially under the thumb of the other side. So massive were the CI failures that more CIA senior officers would be officially reprimanded in the 1990s for Counterintelligence losses than in all of the previous four decades of Agency Operations. Internal weaknesses in Counterintelligence proved disastrous for U.S. Intelligence and, most directly, for the large number of executed Soviet agents who had placed their lives in the hands of the U.S. Government.

Covert Action (CA): U.S. Intelligence weakness after the Cold War continued to be reflected in the lack of flexible Covert Action options for recent U.S. Presidents, who have been forced to operate internationally with severely-limited capabilities. The weakened Presidents have continued to suffer the *either-or* syndrome that resulted directly from the Congressional 1970s/1980s assault on both CIA and the Presidency: America could *either* blow away its enemies militarily *or,* send diplomatic protest notes condemning this atrocity or that. In the 1990s, U.S. Presidents had less flexibility to deal with foreign threats than their predecessors — from Truman through Eisenhower, Kennedy, Johnson, and Nixon — who had a viable CIA to apply unconventional, covert force as and when required. The *either-or* limitation on Covert Action was quite in evidence during the Clinton Administration, which either a) took the military path of launching missiles (Iraq, Afghanistan and Sudan) and sending in U.S. troops (Haiti, Somalia and Kosovo) or b) did nothing meaningful in the wake of a series of al Qaida-sponsored Terror acts — including the 1993 first Twin Towers Attack, the Manila bombing in 1994, the Manila hijacking plot of 1995, the bombing of two U.S. Embassies in 1998, or the USS Cole bombing in 2000.

INTERNAL FACTORS AND EXTERNAL FORCES

THAT WEAKENED CIA

THE FACTORS, or pressure points, leading to CIA failures in the 1990s were both internal and external in origin. Internally, as *CIA LIFE* shows vividly, the Agency came out of the 1980s suffering from bureaucratic calcification due to a) the rise of management-and-budget bean counters who imported numbers games from America's declining manufacturing sector and b) the accession of in-house lawyers who made their living telling CIA Operations Officers what they were *not* allowed to do under this or that new regulation, Presidential Finding, or DCI Directive. Also, CIA senior managers by the 1980s had become very cautious following the anti-CIA attacks from Congress and from Justice. A fundamental internal problem for CIA was that it had gotten away from its own principles of sound clandestine Operations which resulted in the Aldrich Ames Counterintelligence failure which reads like an Intelligence horror tale.

Externally, the anti-Agency assaults of the 1970s and 1980s, which came from the Liberal Left in the U.S. Congress, managed to undermine secrecy itself, the bedrock of all clandestine Operations. Consider the insight of our first Congress which chose to punish Thomas Paine for publicly revealing a Covert Action Operation (that the French King had given secret aid to the American Colonies in the Revolutionary War). Contrast this adherence to principle (that of secrecy) with the 1970s Church Congressional Committee which released a public report describing in detail the U.S. Government's Covert Action Program for Chile from 1963 to 1973. That a Branch of Government can publicly compromise previously-secret Operations damaging to our foreign allies and our own nation's future capabilities defies understanding or explanation. It was unprecedented at any time or place.

In addition to making these disclosures publicly in the post-Vietnam witch hunt era, Congress purposely then set about to place a permanent damper on CIA future Covert Action capabilities by creating groundrules that were disabling. The principal casualty of the attacks was in non-paramilitary Covert Action Operations which, for all intents and purposes, ceased to exist as a viable CIA — read Presidential — capability from the mid-1970s Church Committee onward. Oversight by Congress thereafter meant that CIA could not run Covert Action programs and do so with the required secrecy. Terrorists read papers too and they enjoyed an open playing field for the post-Cold War years of the 1990s.

The weakening of CIA deprived Presidents in the 1990s of the ability to conduct foreign policy without having to rely continually and primarily on direct military force to protect U.S. security interests around the globe. Specifically, Congressional inroads into both the product and the process of the Intelligence Community, and Congress's misuse of the Budget and Oversight processes, weakened the Executive Branch of Government and added to American vulnerability. That Congress in this period became a stepping stone to CIA leadership shows just how far matters got out of hand in terms of separation of powers between these two branches of government.

What Is Needed to Build a CIA

for the 21st Century

WHAT IS NEEDED to make up for decades of anti-CIA Congressional assaults and internal decay? To begin with, CIA must itself start by identifying the gaps that exist between its current capabilities and future requirements affecting all three core Clandestine Service disciplines — FI, CI, and CA. Can an organization that has shown itself historically unwilling to reflect deeply on its own weaknesses and failures undertake such a review? Probably not without outside inspiration, although some organizations have been able to do so. For example, in contrast with CIA which continued on a HUMINT meltdown path throughout the 1990s and into the 21st Century, the U.S. Air Force began shortly after Vietnam to reflect on its own approach to future Scientific Intelligence requirements as they related to the mission of that branch of the Armed Services. Specifically, in the late 1970s, the USAF contacted Professor of Physics Reginald V. Jones of the University of Aberdeen in Scotland and sought his help for a new Joint Electronic Warfare Command getting set to launch an Intelligence countermeasures and deception program. The aging professor, and former maestro of *The Wizard War*, expressed misgivings that his WWII Intelligence experience would be all that useful against the modern technological problems the West then faced. He was told that the Air Force wished to begin its new Intelligence initiative by going back to *first principles of Scientific Intelligence* and wanted his help in making that examination. The return to first principles by the USAF paid off. Later, Professor Jones would be awarded the first R.V. Jones Intelligence Award by Director of Central Intelligence (DCI) James Woolsey for contributions both to Scientific Intelligence during World War II and, more recently, to USAF Intelligence. According to Major General Doyle Larsen, referring to Desert Storm: "as a direct result of his teachings...(the) Iraqi command and control system was rendered ineffective in just a few minutes. Reg Jones deserves considerable credit for a stunning victory, and I salute him for that achievement." First principles of Scientific Intelligence, which had enabled the Allies to defeat the German Luftwaffe in WW II, helped the U.S. Air Force two generations later meet the new threats they faced in Iraq.

FIRST PRINCIPLES

OF HUMAN INTELLIGENCE OPERATIONS

To UNDERSTAND and then meet the challenges of this age of fragmented Terror, CIA needs to return to first principles of Intelligence, the violation of which got the U.S. into the difficulties that Terrorists and other enemies so effectively exploited in the years before and leading up to September 11, 2001. As comprehensive as the changes may seem to be, a determined President can effect the needed changes and undo the damage that Congress accomplished in the aftermath of Vietnam by encroaching unconstitutionally on Executive Branch responsibilities in both Foreign Affairs and the Foreign Intelligence mechanisms needed by this nation, which found itself as the single democratic superpower in a thoroughly fragmented world. (If one needs any evidence that fragmentation followed the Cold War, just take a look at Yugoslavia under Tito and all the "nations" and forces that emerged when Communist systems collapsed across Eastern Europe.)

A First Principle: Presidential Primacy in Foreign Affairs

IN *CIA LIFE*, we saw how the Congress took advantage of the post-Vietnam period to encroach on Executive Branch responsibilities in foreign affairs, undermining much of what went into the National Security Act of 1947 through which President Truman and Congress created a viable central intelligence authority to prevent another Pearl Harbor. To return to the words of Senator Barry Goldwater, who served for years on both the Armed Services and Intelligence Committees and was an Air Force General in his own right:

> Congress wants preeminence over the executive branch. America is witnessing a classic internal struggle, a revolution going back to the constitutional foundation of the Republic. These are strong words but Congress has launched a powerful attack. That is why some basic understanding of American intelligence is important. This apparatus is now at the center of a battle at the highest levels of our national leadership.

The difficult job of leading America internationally has been made more difficult by the death of bipartisanship, a death made more stunningly visible as former President Clinton, even in war, travels abroad and lambastes his successor on international policy as no other President has done in the history of the country. Returning to first principles of our Constitutional Government would include restoring the comity that permitted Presidents to conduct American foreign relations — between elections at least — without partisan obstructionism from Congress.

A First Principle: Director of Central Intelligence (DCI) Selection and Role

PRESIDENTS have appointed several DCIs who caused significant damage to Agency effectiveness and U.S. security by the way they failed to lead, and in some cases mismanaged or abused, the Agency and its people, especially within the Directorate of Operations. Without getting into the matter of which DCIs so failed, it is critical to note that it is time that U.S. Presidents appoint individuals who meet the highest standards on international strategic experience and savvy, intellectual independence and balance, and who will make a long-term commitment to return CIA to excellence in the face of tough challenges abroad and chronic Congressional attacks here at home.

A concomitant of Presidential foreign affairs primacy established in the Constitution is that the President do more than use the CIA merely to his own advantage and term of office; he has an obligation to the American public to strengthen the institution itself by appointing a DCI who meets the highest standards set by earlier Presidents and who will improve future Agency effectiveness. History tells us that there are standards for excellence and first principles when it comes to making the DCI selection:

When Democrat President Franklin Roosevelt appointed Republican attorney and WWI hero William "Wild Bill" Donovan to lead American Intelligence in the Second World War, the President put the nation's survival foremost in making his choice. Just as Winston Churchill turned to superior British scientists to defend England in its "darkest hours," the wartime American President called on this nation's best and brightest to serve in the intelligence war against Germany and Japan.

Under President Truman, the senior military officers who served as DCI through the internecine Washington battles in the late 1940s and early 1950s (Admirals Sidney Souers and Roscoe Hillenkoetter and Generals Hoyt Vandenberg and Walter Bedell Smith) had the experience, status, and clout to win the turf battles against motivated FBI, State Department, and Defense Department opponents of any post-War centralized intelligence system they did not themselves control.

With the central intelligence authority firmly in place by 1953, President Eisenhower turned to CIA Intelligence professional Allen W. Dulles, who had the Operations and international experience to forge CIA swiftly into the world's foremost intelligence service in power, worldwide reach, and effectiveness.

To replace Allen Dulles after the Bay of Pigs disaster, President Kennedy appointed a man who would prove to be an exemplary DCI, Republican John McCone. DCI McCone would lead the Agency through the Cuban missile crisis where he singularly challenged conventional Intelligence Analysis, at that point pleasing to a Kennedy White House not looking for more bad news regarding Cuba, and pushed for a more complete investigation into why the Soviets had introduced ground-to-air missiles on the island. McCone's pressure led to locating the Soviet strategic missiles before they were installed and, therefore, operational. McCone's unique ability to play the role of chief intelligence advisor to the President was again evident in 1965 when, according to Richard Helms's book, *A Look Over My Shoulder*, McCone warned President Johnson and Secretaries Rusk and McNamara regarding Vietnam: "We will find ourselves mired in combat in the jungle in a military effort we cannot win, and from which we will have extreme difficulty extracting ourselves."

Obviously, DCI McCone had special qualities of intellect and character that made him a superb leader of U.S. Intelligence. His management genius shone through when he established a separate CIA Directorate of Science and Technology to carry the Agency and America into the arena of space-age Intelligence. McCone knew implicitly the unlikelihood that the Liberal Arts-dominant Clandestine Service could attract and manage the scientists and engineers needed in the arcane world of imagery, satellites, and signal intelligence. In sum, DCI McCone was a stellar strategic analyst. He was an independent individual with the moral fortitude to bring all news, both bad and good, to the President, He was a seasoned manager and accomplished leader who left a lofty position in industry to serve his nation as DCI. On the honor roll for leaders of U.S. Intelligence, John McCone would be up there at the top — right behind Medal of Honor recipient General William Donovan, that extraordinary man of thought and action who forged and led the OSS in WWII and had the vision to set the stage for CIA.

The litmus test for DCI appointment after Vietnam became political connectedness in Washington and, especially, the personal-political comfort level of the President in finding another reliable member of his team — a Postmaster General of sorts. The lowering of DCI selection standards has been CIA's and America's loss.

The 21st Century CIA requires a return to superior standards in DCI selection. It is not right that a President select an individual with only his own comfort level and term of office in mind. The President should meet the high standards of his predecessors in the 1940s, 1950s, and 1960s by selecting a DCI who will strengthen the Agency for the next generation of Intelligence problems the country will face.

With the intractability of America's present international threats and national survival at stake, it is time that DCIs be appointed (like the FBI Director) for a ten-year term of office. This would help insulate the country's Intelligence Community leader from the political machinations of those in Congress who act as though they were elected to conduct U.S. foreign affairs as well as direct foreign intelligence. One may recall Senator Frank Church from Idaho trying to ride his anti-CIA horse to the Presidency. He did not succeed in his personal political goals, but he surely succeeded in taking the Covert Political Action legs off CIA — in the end, indirectly costing many innocent lives around the world as the U.S. came to rely overwhelmingly on military force and war to deal with international threats.

A First Principle: Operations Leadership within CIA

THE DIRECTORATE OF OPERATIONS (DO) must be restored to excellence in its fundamental missions of Intelligence Collection, Counterintelligence, and Covert Action. The Deputy Director for Operations (DDO) must have earned that leadership position on substantive Operations and Intelligence grounds, not because of political connectedness and certainly not due primarily to high-profile visibility at either the National Security Council or with the Congress. The new DDO leadership itself must confront and resolve problems in each of the three key missions of that Directorate and do so by returning to first principles in each of the core disciplines:

Intelligence Collection (FI): Improved human-agent Intelligence Collection — as we explored in *CIA LIFE* — requires a change in the DO culture that, by the early 1990s, had come to place a premium on shallow beancounting as the way to advance careers, direct Field Stations, and measure Directorate progress. Recent public accounts suggest that matters have improved little in this regard. When President Clinton left office — just eight months before September 11 — the Operations Directorate was reportedly in very bad shape and the morale was very low. Since September 11, the Agency has been forced to draw upon many retirees and members of an earlier generation of Operations professionals to fight the Wars in the Middle East and South Asia.

Counterintelligence (CI): In CIA's first twenty-five years, Counterintelligence fell into the hands of individuals who bordered on paranoia and attributed superhuman powers to the Soviets. The next generation of Counterintelligence managers reversed matters so dramatically that they set the Agency up for the CI disasters of the 1980s and 1990s by walking away from elementary standards of operational security. According to insider Milt Bearden in his penetrating book, *The Main Enemy*, CIA managers — in the face of the series of unprecedented and unexplained Moscow Station agent losses — ruled out systematic investigation and polygraphing of all Agency personnel in a position to identify the many lost Moscow agent sources and could, in fact, have been KGB moles within the Agency.

Nor was there any justification for exposing all active Soviet Operations, both human and technical, to a substandard performer like Aldrich Ames, who ranked near the bottom in competitive evaluations and had failed badly in two overseas assignments, in Turkey and in Mexico. That this drunk and social misfit was then promoted to head Soviet Division Counterintelligence — after returning in disgrace from Mexico City — defies reason.

What can assure that we do not again go to extremes in re-building CIA's Counterintelligence program? We should be guided by CI first principles that historically have protected successful Intelligence Operations but were abandoned in CIA and FBI operations in the glorious numbers game years of the 1980s and 1990s. *Compartmentation* — an Intelligence first principle requiring one to insulate and isolate Intelligence Operations and sources from each other to avoid cross-contamination — was violated in both CIA and FBI to an extent calling into question the very professionalism and seriousness of the senior managers in charge of these national programs. Ames-Hanssen could do the damage they did for as long as they did only because their bosses failed to apply basic operational security standards taught in the first weeks of Operations Training.

Covert Action (CA): As a result of September 11, the Agency seems to have bolstered enormously its Covert Action Paramilitary capabilities according to all public accounts of the new boost in both Agency and Defense Department budgets for Special Paramilitary Operations. To take on the new challenges of this post-Cold War world, CIA must develop and use new Covert Action capabilities that are also political, economic/financial, and psychological/cultural. A purely military CA response to Terrorism will not be sufficient over the next generation.

What are the *Covert Action first principles* to be applied in the new War on Terror? I suggest that, because principles are principles, we not shift our standards just because the targets have changed or the Cold War is over. Rather, we should apply the *CIA LIFE* five litmus tests (see pages 227 and 228) used to assess Covert Actions in the Cold War: a) Does the Covert Action program or project support U.S. overt public policy? b) Is the CA necessary for overall success? c) Can operational secrecy be sustained, especially in light of Congressional oversight? d) Are the Covert Action means to be employed practical and sufficient? and e) Will the

Covert Action ends and means be seen as principled in terms of American values if and when they surface in *The Times*?

A First Principle: An Officer Corps for the 21st Century

A CRUCIAL national intelligence resource of the United States for the War on Terror is the Operations Officer corps of CIA which, when it succeeds, delivers the precious *Intentions Intelligence* that U.S. policymakers require to prevent future calamities along the lines of September 11. The assault on the Agency Operations Officers from the Congress, from anti-CIA lawyer-ideologues operating under the cover of the Justice Department, and from Left-leaning elites in the American media and academia persisted for nearly three decades and went a long way towards undermining CIA morale. With the external assaults presently suspended due to September 11, how can the Agency rebuild its badly-damaged and historically-abused Operations Officer cadre and its effectiveness be restored?

First, the Congressional *Sword of Damocles* should be removed from CIA where oversight has meant — after Chile, after Vietnam, after Central America, and after the Cold War itself — witch hunts against Operations Officers and CIA managers who ran programs displeasing to the American Left.

Second, a symbolic positive step would be for the President to grant a posthumous pardon for Richard Helms who, with respect to Chile, was caught up in a Congressional trap involving his obligations, under the National Security Act of 1947, that he honored more faithfully than other DCIs who gave away the store and were never prosecuted.

Third, because the next generation of Operations Officers will have to perform against the most challenging Foreign Intelligence targets the Agency has ever faced, Officer selection as well as foreign language and Operations Training all must improve profoundly for reasons described in depth in *CIA LIFE*.

Fourth, to retain such exceptional individuals for careers in Clandestine Operations, the CIA DDO Career Service must be transformed so that this elite group of Americans again form part of an elite service, one that does not treat them in the shabby ways of the past.

Fifth, modernization of the CIA Officer Corps requires that we approach this business as a marathon in the full knowledge that, on average, it requires about five years to take an individual from initial employment application through the hiring and Operations training process, a minimum six months of foreign language training and an initial two-year overseas assignment. On a macro basis, it means that we will be spending the next ten years — if we do all the right things outlined on selection, training, and career management in *CIA LIFE* — just filling critical existing holes in the organization. (Anyone in authority trying to get a grip on this issue had better ask all of the right questions because the current self-satisfied CIA administrative managers will make political Washington believe that things are fully on the mend now that they have a few hundred Operations Officer candidates in the pipeline. They should remember DCI Casey and how the bureaucrats left him bewildered at his inability to make changes in the Agency Operations Officer cadre during his six years as Director.)

Sixth, CIA's overseas personnel can no longer — relative to status, pay, benefits and retirement — be dead last compared to professionals serving in careers at State, NSA, or FBI. CIA overseas personnel merit retirement plans equal to the superior law enforcement formula used for FBI and, believe it or not, Members of Congress — neither institution of which has suffered as many fatalities in the line of duty, numerically or proportionally, as has the Directorate of Operations.

Finally, it is time that CIA Operations Officers, with appropriate safeguards to protect identities during active clandestine service careers, be Congressionally-commissioned as are U.S. Military Officers and State Department Foreign Service Officers. CIA's Operations Officers provide the essential cadre for directly combating Terrorism, a cadre whose Operations take place in the shadowy world between those of the Embassy diplomats and the battlefield warriors.

Why CIA Effectiveness Must Be Restored

THE POST-COLD WAR world America faces today is potentially lethal because of the twin dangers coming from Terrorism and Weapons of Mass Destruction — biological, chemical, and nuclear. The leaders who created the Central Intelligence Agency in 1947, also uncertain about the dangers the country then faced from a belligerent Soviet empire, placed the needs of the nation ahead of partisanship, personal rivalries, and bureaucratic competition. They set U.S. Intelligence on a successful fifty-year path leading to Cold War victory. America's present leaders must restore CIA capabilities and strengthen Operations Directorate staffing and effectiveness in the spirit of their late 1940s predecessors so that never again is there a catastrophic Intelligence failure on the scale of — or worse than — Pearl Harbor and September 11.

Preface

WE PARKED under a shady tree on a Washington side street and strolled two blocks to a chic restaurant, this former CIA superstar and I, and found two places at the long table in the private room. A few of the other "spooks" had already arrived and soon the seats were filled by Cold Warriors of the early CIA years, many of whom belonged to that illustrious alumni group, Veterans of the OSS. The lunch was just another get-together for men and women who kept memories and friendships alive by meeting regularly with other survivors of wars hot and cold. For me it was far more special because this was the day I was signing my retirement papers and taking voluntary early leave of the Central Intelligence Agency, where I had worked 28 years. My host was none other than David Atlee Phillips who also had gone into early retirement in the mid-1970s to defend the Intelligence service from its domestic foes. Because it was my last real day in CIA, and because I had just spent two years in the recruitment of new Intelligence Officers, the veterans asked about current hiring practices as well as my own reasons for early retirement. By the way the questions were framed, I could see that most of them had more than idle curiosity about the state of CIA. Some, in fact, displayed deep misgivings of people concerned that their former employer may have slipped since they left. For most CIA vets, the Agency was more than the place they had once worked; it was "The Company" but it had also been simultaneously their club, their school and even their family in a very poignant and durable sense.

I had two sets of reasons for leaving the Agency when I did, one personal and the other professional. At this lunch I spoke only of obvious personal reasons for getting out: I had just turned 50 and was now eligible to take early retirement, I had promised my good wife to take her home to New England, we had moved more than a dozen times in 28 years, the oldest four children had been jerked from school to school and we were now determined not to do that again to our fifth child. All solid reasons with which the veterans could relate, often in painful ways given the price paid by Agency families during the Cold War years. I did not even begin to discuss or reveal the professional reason; I saw no reason to inflict pain on those who left the active Intelligence arena and needed more to be uplifted than depressed. Phillips himself was in the last months of a brave but losing fight with cancer and I saw no good to be served in saying things negative. To one and all at the lunch that day the Agency had been and would always be a dear friend, an alma mater.

One might have thought as we entered 1988 that CIA must be riding high, having recovered from the low point reached during the Carter years. After all, Reagan had been President for six years and he was by temperament a friend of American Intelligence. Vice President Bush had been Director of Central Intelligence in the mid-Seventies. Certainly, it was not something that flashed before me as the New Year approached that left me feeling badly about the state of CIA as the Eighties were drawing to a close. It would take months more to sort out why I felt the way I did. When I completed that reflection I realized that it was as much what had been happening to American society in recent years as it was the situation at CIA that had left a hole in me. America and CIA were losing it. We were in a decline made more insidious by what we were doing to the next generation.

We were now in a unique period in the country's history when at every level the holders of power were squeezing out all the juices for themselves, leaving to the kids a national debt from which there is no escape, an economic structure that is noncompetitive internationally, retirement systems tilted in favor of those retired and soon retiring, banking and real estate industries that offer the young few opportunities for home ownership. From eighteen years of age, youngsters are burdened by long-term educational debts pushed on them with a carelessness and zeal that compares to the debt explosion of the Seventies in Latin America, except the kids are free to repudiate nothing. The CIA itself now has two retirement systems, one for the lucky who got in before 1984, and a markedly inferior model for the newcomers. I had considerable experience looking at the Agency and explaining it to others in my role as a recruiter. I knew that it was and would continue to be a necessary institution. But could it do the job that needs doing in the years ahead? I had concluded, several years before this lunch, that the Agency had so little Covert Action clout left as to make it laughable if that were not so deadly serious a matter for the nation and its leaders. To anyone familiar with CIA it would be no surprise that it would lose the war with the Communists in Nicaragua, that it would be unable to rescue any American hostages anywhere in the Middle East, or that it would fail in covert efforts to remove the drug-running thug, General Manuel Noriega, from power in Panama.

Why spoil, therefore, this polite nostalgic luncheon with dark but realistic talk about CIA and its sorry state. Better to be pleasant, enjoy the company and the meal, and then go back to New England to begin an entirely new life. But, just as these Cold Warriors had a hard time letting go, so would I, as I would discover in the months ahead. Within weeks I was jotting down notes and ideas with the thought of possibly doing an article. Within months I was outlining a book to help other Americans understand this creature called CIA about which much has been written on a sensational level and little has been written that is balanced. Going back mentally through the Agency portal in writing this book may also have been the one way for me to let go.

I left the lunch, said a final goodbye to Dave Phillips, and went out to CIA Headquarters to sign my retirement papers and then head home.

1

Getting Hired

NOTHING in my background or childhood suggested that I would want, or be accepted for, a career in Intelligence fresh out of college. When I applied in 1959 to what was then a very secret Central Intelligence Agency, the twelve-year-old spy organization had basically three kinds of people working in the business of Foreign Intelligence Collection (espionage or spying), Counterintelligence (spy catching) and Covert Action (secret action Operations). First, there were the educated, elite holdovers from the wartime Office of Strategic Services (OSS). These men and women were mostly of fine education and "breeding" and had been drawn to the world of Intelligence because they had some international experience or language skills prior to the Second World War. These elites, like cream in the milk bottles of pre-homogenized days, rose automatically to occupy virtually all top CIA management jobs in Washington and in the overseas Field Stations of most importance to this country. It was not by mere chance that such men as Dulles, Roosevelt, FitzGerald, Scott, Helms, Kirkpatrick, Bissel, George and King held positions of power virtually from the beginning of CIA in 1947. Given the times, the limited competition, their own advantages of education, and inherited Social Register contacts, these accomplished and connected men would have risen to high levels in any American profession. The second definable group of operatives came from first-generation Americans, also primarily of European extraction, who brought to CIA its original native-level foreign language fluencies. They brought also the toughness and cunning that survivors of displacement and war uniquely develop — something we see again in the refugees from Southeast Asia. The third, more amorphous group included those individuals hired after the outbreak of the Korean War in 1950, many of them WW II veterans, who had completed their education after returning to civilian life. These recruits were increasingly representative of American society as a whole and included few of the old Yankee elites or the displaced nationalities of Europe. By the late 1950s, the Agency had given up on the idea of hiring primarily by referral from the Ivy League, although that was still the preferred source for the Career Training Program, which was designed specifically to develop future leaders of the Clandestine Service and, therefore, the Agency. With the emergence of new nations and different field Station requirements that accompanied the decline of European colonialism, CIA needed a larger, sustainable influx of career officers than the Ivies could produce. So, the hiring net was stretched to include other colleges, although still mainly in the eastern United States.

As the Eisenhower Presidency came to a close, and as the country moved into what would be the turbulent 1960s, the Central Intelligence Agency at the stratospheric level was still very much a white, male, Protestant organization, but one that was a full decade into the process of broadening and "Americanizing" itself from below. This is not to suggest that CIA was then hiring enough Blacks, Hispanics or other minorities; it was not then and still was not in the 1990s. But by 1960 the tight fraternity in American Intelligence that resembled an English Men's Club had developed cracks, and a relatively unsophisticated, little-traveled Irishman from Boston was able to get himself hired into the Career Training Program for overseas Operations Officers.

The fourth of seven children of a Ford Motor Company factory worker and supervisor, I was born in the industrial city of Waltham, Massachusetts, which produced some of the world's best timepieces before Swiss-made watches displaced them in the early years after World War II. In 1943, we moved to an adjacent industrial town, Watertown, where I grew up. The Gilligan family did not really leave the Depression until well after the war — war production workers had faced frozen wages during WW II and seven children were a lot to feed and clothe. So, my older brother and I spent virtually every free day from the age of ten at nearby golf courses, earning a few dollars to help meet family living costs. The experience taught hard work and self-reliance, how to play golf decently, how to play cards and spit and how to swear and fight — not exactly what one thinks of when visualizing the American Intelligence professional. The Watertown public schools were sound and solid in those days, with a teaching staff that today would be the pride of any public or private school. Some of the country's best-educated people, especially women who had such limited professional opportunities, entered public education during the Great Depression. It was common even into the late Forties and early Fifties to have graduates of such colleges as Harvard and MIT entering the public school system for teaching careers.

Schooling did not rank very high on my list of priorities through junior and senior high school — in fact, it ranked well behind making some dollars for home and having fun with friends during and after school. Thanks to the excellence of the teaching, however, I somehow received along the way a decent grounding in the basics. But as friends planned for college at expensive New England institutions, I did not see how I could really afford a college education and began making plans to go into military service as one way of having something honorable to do after high school. I had joined the Massachusetts Air National Guard in my junior year of high school, at seventeen, and was scheduled on graduation to do thirteen weeks of Air Force Basic Training. My thought at that point was to join the Marines on graduation because of their gallant reputation in WWII and the Korean War. My oldest sister's boyfriend had in fact gone to Korea and, like hundreds of other eighteen-year-olds, died fighting at the once-remembered Chosin Reservoir. At this point my older brother, who would later serve as an officer in the USMC, paid my application fee at Northeastern University in Boston, one of the country's oldest cooperative education institutions, where students attend freshman year full time and then work their way through four years part time. I got accepted, went off to Air Force Basic Training in June 1955, and returned in early September to begin work on the assembly line at the nearby Ford Motor automobile factory for ten weeks. I entered Northeastern in November, by which time I had earned some tuition money for the first year and decided to major in Economics. The November term happened to include a large percentage of returning military veterans, something I still consider one of my better breaks in life. I had certainly worked hard to pay for this chance at college, but it was the example, competitiveness and determination of the returning Vets that gave me the stimulus to study hard, and I began doing very well for the first time since elementary school.

Another thing happened to me that fall which was to change my life immeasurably. Walking each school day across town to hitch a ride to college, I had begun eyeing this pretty young lady walking with her little sister to the local Catholic high school. She wore a school uniform, green of course for St. Patrick, and carried a school bag that seemed heavier than she was at the time. In those days, it took weeks or months to make the social breakthroughs our kids today seem to make in a single weekend. It was almost Christmastime before I had my first date with Bonnie Smith.

Bonnie grew up in Watertown, Massachusetts, the eighth of twelve children. The ages of the children ranged from fourteen to twenty-seven, and it seemed that every couple of months someone was getting engaged or married, having a child or getting one baptized, graduating from high school, college, law school or medical school. Bonnie's sister Virginia had entered the Dominican Convent fresh out of high school. The youngest member of the Smith family, Charlotte, had died in infancy with pneumonia but was still lovingly remembered on her birthday each year. The range of personalities was striking, and Bonnie tended to do those things expected of a child from the midst of the pack; being neither the eldest nor the youngest she quietly went about her chores at home and school. She sought in poetry and literature the solitude that was rare in a home with so much energy and activity. I was naturally outgoing, even aggressive. By contrast, Bonnie had a quiet air of mystery about her, one which would lead her exasperated mother to occasionally declare that "still waters run deep."

For the first year of our courtship I had no car and very little money. Dates consisted of a walk to town, where on winter evenings we had hot chocolate and toast, and the rest of the year a cup of coffee and a dish of ice cream. In keeping with the simplicity of the times, certain old-fashioned customs were scrupulously observed. I did the telephoning; I went to where Bonnie was working or waiting. I paid for the little treats. No matter how modest the circumstances, a date was a date and as the male I was expected to do the appropriate courting.

My most thrilling acquisition as a young adult was my first car, a prime-condition 1946 Pontiac with four doors, six cylinders, standard shift and ninety-six horsepower. It opened up whole new vistas. We could now travel an hour away to a sandy beach or get to a movie in the next town. The thought of going more than fifty miles never occurred to us, and in our three-and-a-half-year courtship we never once set foot outside eastern Massachusetts together. This was in marked contrast with our later married years, when we would travel from Massachusetts to Latin America as though that were the natural thing to do.

That previously-provincial Americans became international travelers was characteristic of the decade following World War II. This breaking away from the cocoon reflected the change of America itself from committed isolationist to reluctant world leader. As wary as the country continued to be about its new and expanded role in the world, those of us eventually caught up in the centrifugal process were exhilarated at the very idea that we might become part of something bigger than ourselves or our home towns. Yet, as Bonnie and I courted for forty-two months, the subject of where we would spend the rest of our lives never really came up. We were both seized with the joy and challenge of work and school and were living in the present for the most part. Any thought of the future was on our planned wedding in 1959. We were caught up in the Hollywood notion that after people get married they walk into the sunset and live happily ever after. Part of this confidence, which bordered on presumption, was bred in the 1950s, the American decade. It affected America as a nation and us citizens in all aspects of our society and lives. It certainly affected me as I looked to the future with the view that the world was full of possibilities and not limits.

I completed the first year at Northeastern and decided to take off a year to work and then transfer to Boston College because, in those days, the only students at Northeastern University who got decent co-op jobs were the Engineering students. The rest of us were working clerk-level positions at insurance firms and the like for sixty dollars per week, something I did for one term before deciding I would be better off back in the factory for a year. In the fall of 1957, I began as a full-time student and sophomore at Boston College, again in Economics. Like the overwhelming majority of B.C. undergrads in the 1950s, I was a commuting student.

The political atmosphere on campus in the late 1950s was becoming volatile. At Catholic, conservative Boston College it revolved around the issue of Communism. Even though Wisconsin Senator Joe McCarthy had already been censured by his U.S. Senate colleagues and discredited in America generally, there was among the Irish a belief that McCarthy had not been entirely wrong in his crusade against Soviet penetrations of the U.S. Government. The more conservative students were championing Arizona Senator, and later Presidential candidate, Barry Goldwater, whose *Conscience of a Conservative* capsulized the right-of-center message. The most reactionary of the student body were mesmerized by the conspiracy assertions of the John Birch Society, which was headquartered only six miles away in little Belmont, Massachusetts. A real liberal in those days was someone who favored Foreign Aid and supported continued U.S. membership in the United Nations. The 1950s liberal was just as likely after graduation to become a military or Intelligence Officer as any conservative on campus. The right and the left at the time were both pretty close to the center on the political spectrum. The extreme polarization of American political opinion was still a few years away, even though the campus political dialogue and differences were picking up steam.

My views on Economics and U.S. Fiscal Policy were rooted in Adam Smith, and I can remember my shock just a couple of years later when the new Kennedy Administration presented the first $100 billion Federal Budget. On the issue of Communism, I felt that the international threat was real and enormous, and had to be dealt with directly and with toughness by the leader of the free world, the United States. The so-called domestic Communism problem, I thought, was grossly overstated by the far right and pitted Americans against each other needlessly. For one thing, I respected the FBI and was confident that J. Edgar Hoover's Special Agents were on top of the American Communist Party problem, just as they had been successful in penetrating and taming the pro-Nazi groups at the start of World War II.

I recall my chagrin when a young man in my Economics class told me he was joining the John Birch Society which, at the time, was putting out nonsense that President Eisenhower had been a "secret Communist" and "agent of Moscow." That conversation took place the night of our senior prom at B.C. which Bonnie and I were attending as man and wife, having married the previous June. We always enjoyed going out dancing, and this night was a special treat because Bonnie was carrying our first child. But what I recall most vividly from that evening was trying to persuade my classmate that the John Birchers did not understand Communism. His response was to smile only, giving me that true believer's "I've-seen-the-light look," that was his gentle way of putting me off without telling me that I was a "dupe of the Commies" — which was how the Birchers dealt with all reasoned opposition. At that point I knew I was going off to join CIA a few weeks later, but I couldn't share that with any of my classmates. Some years later I would occasionally read my friend's name in association with the John Birch Society and I would flash back to prom night and my complete inability to convince one pal that extremism was not the answer to the Communist problem.

As unconcerned as I may have been on the question of domestic Communism at the time, I had nothing but total aversion for International Communism, specifically the work of the Soviet Union to subvert the weaker nations of the world. Of course, I had grown up seeing the Soviets subjugate Eastern Europe, assist in the takeover of China, support North Korea in the Korean War and win (it was rumored) a revolution in our own hemisphere — in fact just ninety miles off our own Florida coast. I also had heard my father talk at home about the pro-Russia types within the American labor movement during his own years of trade union leadership in the late 1930s and early 1940s. Just as the American intellectual and artistic community had been seized by what they perceived to be progressive, humanistic developments in Russia in the Thirties, some of this country's labor leaders looked to Russia for an answer to the problems of economic depression and social injustice. The rise of Nazi Germany strengthened that bond enormously, but the Russo-German pact between Stalin and Hitler threw pro-Russia supporters throughout the West into complete disarray as they tried to reconcile the irreconcilable.

At the level of the local union, in the factory itself, my father saw how Communist labor leaders pulled a 180-degree reversal once the ten-year Non-Aggression Pact was signed between Germany and Russia. Yet, when Hitler then invaded Russia itself in June 1941, Communists worldwide and within the United States did a second U-turn, calling for an all-out American labor effort to support Russia against Nazi Germany. This latter shift manifested itself in the labor movement by calls for a No-strike Pledge, so that America, not yet in the war, could continue uninterrupted production of war materials being shipped abroad under Lend Lease agreements. As President of his local union, my father was a delegate to national United Auto Worker (UAW) conventions, where the struggle was especially vicious between pro-Communists and anti-Communists. My father aligned himself with the latter group and was particularly distrustful of those auto workers who had gone to the Soviet Union in the Twenties and Thirties and assisted in the construction of car factories. This basic affinity for trade union affairs stayed with me through college, as did an abiding distrust of the Soviet Union. Much of what I would do early in my Agency career would rest on these two pillars.

In early 1959, I read an article in the adventure magazine *Argosy*, which I probably found on a bus. It told of the 1954 CIA overthrow of the pro-Communist Arbenz regime in Guatemala. I liked what I read. In late spring of my junior year I walked into the CIA Recruitment Office in Boston to inquire about getting hired after college. It is difficult in today's world, in which CIA has become a household word, to realize that only a limited cross section of Americans, mainly those involved in government or military affairs internationally, had even heard of the Central Intelligence Agency in the 1950s. In fact, mention the initials to someone back then and he would probably have thought it was a kind of trade union, such as the AFL or CIO. It was not until the following May, when the U-2 spy plane of Francis Gary Powers was shot down over the

Soviet Union, that CIA became known to most of the American public. The Agency itself told prospective employees very little about the organization or its mission, and the recruiter, a fellow who served in New England for a couple of decades, told me about the hiring procedures and the testing, nothing more. Realizing that CIA was active overseas, I felt a need to display some facility in foreign languages and signed up for Russian language in my senior year at B.C. Had I known better, I would have studied Spanish, partly because a single year of the more difficult Russian language would have little value for an Agency that attracted Russian linguists from U.S. universities and the military.

The CIA applicant process has changed little over the past several decades — I went through the same steps that I would put Agency applicants through many years later. I had to fill out a once-in-a-lifetime comprehensive application telling CIA my whole life history. I also had to take a written test designed to measure four skills or areas of knowledge. An intellectual aptitude test measured my competitiveness in verbal and quantitative skills. There was a test of my knowledge of contemporary international affairs. Foreign language learning ability was evaluated through construction and use of an artificial language. The artificial language ensured that all individuals were tested fairly, regardless of prior foreign language knowledge. Finally, part of the written test made a rough-cut, initial assessment of my general psychological suitability for the demands and stresses of clandestine Operations.

The night before the tests, I attended a Christmas party at the bank where my wife was working. The bank personnel had gone out to a private dinner; the spouses and dates were invited to show up after the dinner itself. I had very little to eat that day and all that was available to us after-dinner guests were some potato chips, peanuts and the usual array of alcoholic drinks. Drinking booze on an empty stomach, especially in concert with the cigarettes I puffed in those days, made me a very sick young man as my expectant Bonnie took me home that evening. I woke up with a miserable, dry, cotton mouth and the feeling that my chance of doing well in the eight-hour CIA exam at Harvard was pretty close to zero. The memories of that awful day would often flash before me years later when I advised many hundreds of young people to get a good night's sleep the night before our examination.

Always a good test-taker, I managed to get through the written test and was invited down to Washington for medical, psychological, psychiatric and polygraph ("lie detector") tests, as well as in-depth interviews with the Career Training Program officials. I continue to be surprised, in retrospect, that anyone like myself with no graduate school background, overseas experience or extended military service was hired at 21 into the country's top spy organization.

While I graduated "with honors" from Boston College, I really had managed to do only the required readings to pass examinations and more or less went through college like a commuter wolfing down a stand-up coffee and doughnut on the way to the morning train. During my junior year at B.C., when my factory savings were gone, I averaged more than sixty hours a week in "part-time" jobs while taking a full-time course load at school. I would go to classes, have a quick cup of coffee with classmates in the cafeteria, and run to one of three jobs I worked simultaneously that year. In the afternoons I swept out a building at B.C., the famous Gasson Hall with its clock-tower and the Eagle posted out front. For that I was paid a dollar per hour, twenty dollars a week towards my tuition. Each evening from 5:30 until 10:30, I worked at the Raytheon engineering facility fifteen miles away, where I ran what was called an Ozalid machine, duplicating blueprints in a stinky chemical-based process. On the weekends, I worked two ten-to-twelve hour days at a nearby country club as, of all things, a shoe shine boy, which netted me a pocketful of dollar bills each week in tips. It was good for perspective, humility and a sense of humor to be shining shoes where some of my B.C. classmates played golf under their parents' family membership.

If anything got me hired by CIA, it was probably my sheer determination and capacity for hard work brought on by necessity. Later, I too would look for signs of industry and hard work as I evaluated applicants, but I was also aware that undergrads now have more support and access to financial aid. They also get a deeper education than I was able to attain since I was working full time and commuting to and fro.

The studying I managed to do was invariably from 11:30 at night, when I arrived home after work and a quick coffee with Bonnie at her house, until 2:00 in the morning. I really lived from test to test. For me college life was something sandwiched in between a series of jobs and commutes. Yet, as near as this was to the drudgery of the assembly line, I dreamed too of working and traveling in foreign lands, of doing something meaningful in my life. For that opportunity I remain most grateful to those fine old gentlemen who ran the Career Training Program under the iron grip of the Director of Training, Matthew Baird, who answered only to Allen Dulles, Director of Central Intelligence. The program officers looked beyond my obvious shortcomings and education gaps, concluding that I would bring something to the Agency.

They made their decision certainly against the advice of at least one staff psychologist, as I was to learn a year later during the overseas Operations Training. It was the custom during our training course to have visitors come down from Washington, and for about a week the psychologists were there, observing training exercises during the day and mixing it up at the bar in the evening. Late in the week one of the shrinks got to talking with me. He had too much to drink and revealed something he ought professionally not to have done: he told me he had recommended against my being hired, and his explanation was purely in personal terms. He began a rambling explanation of how he and his wife had been engaged in a battle over birth control and he was really quite pissed at me, the Roman Catholic Church, at Jesuits, and my Catholic educational background, which he concluded was inappropriate for CIA Operations — if not for life itself.

The lesson for me was that it is next to impossible to insulate any hiring process from human foibles and biases. Happily for me, in those days especially, the assessments of the Psychological Staff were treated as mere opinions supplemental to the evaluations of the Career Training Staff. A thumbs down by the psychologists had none of the veto power it would come to have from the 1970s onward when, completely trau- matized by the defections and betrayals of CIA by its own people, the Agency reduced to zero its willingness to take a chance on an applicant not endorsed by all parties in the hiring chain.

Another lesson in the psychologist's performance at the bar was the insidious capacity of alcohol to compromise a person professionally and personally. In flight simulations, pilots are shown how impaired their judgment and reflexes become when they drink too much booze. In the same way, there is a fundamental incompatibility between alcohol and effective Intelligence Operations. Most boozers in this profession lose their agents and their families, and they wreck their own careers as well.

In late winter of my senior year of college, I was advised in a plain envelope that I had been accepted by CIA and would begin working upon graduation at the annual pay of $4,980. I would have to pay to move myself and my family to Washington, D.C. to begin training in early July. CIA has always been relatively Spartan in the treatment of its Operations personnel, and it was not out of character for some Agency miser to decide at the last moment that we should not report for duty until the fifth of July. In that way, the Agency could avoid paying us for the Nation's Holiday. That should have been a warning of the lean years that lay ahead.

Our son was born on that great Socialist day, the First of May, which happened to be the same day CIA's Francis Gary Powers crashed in his U-2 over Russia. On the sizzling 4th of July 1960 weekend, we got into our 1950 DeSoto pulling a U-Haul trailer, mattress and box spring tied to the car roof, and with two hundred borrowed dollars in our pocket headed southward toward Washington and a CIA career. South of New Jersey the temperature kept climbing toward and past 100 degrees, and my one vivid memory is of Bonnie standing up on an embankment holding our 8-week-old baby as I fed water and ice into the overheating radiator. We made it later in the day to Alexandria, Virginia, thanks to the car's old-fashioned temperature gauge which warned of impending boilovers. We moved into a rented one-bedroom apartment in a red brick complex where the summer air never seemed to circulate and the temperature never seemed to drop, even at night. I am convinced that marriages benefit by beginning modestly, providing a bit of the pioneering spirit that developed character in earlier generations of Americans. In any case, we were young, together, healthy, happy, and personally confident about the future, as was the country itself 15 years after WW II. Bonnie and I were about to embark on a 10,000-day journey in an Agency and career that would be more than your average nine-to-five job.

As new as all this was for me and my young wife, the business of Intelligence was hardly a recent calling; it had been employed throughout history by all surviving peoples and nations. Without tracing all Intelligence history, it is useful when reading or hearing reports suggesting that U.S. Intelligence agencies are a creature only of the Cold War to bear in mind that the oversimplification is inaccurate. It coincides with neither the American nor the Soviet experience.

2

U.S. Intelligence History

O NE DANGER in examining history is taking the view that events got started or took a dramatic turn when the observer first arrived on the scene. There are many watersheds in the history of men, nations and institutions, and the world of Intelligence is no different, but the tendency toward what I call myopic egocentricity affects virtually all of us. I have often tended to view 1960 as a pivotal year for American Intelligence because it was the year I first went to Washington. By then, of course, the American Intelligence experience was long and rich as we shall outline in this chapter.

The year 1960 was certainly an important turning point, however, but not just because I came on board the Agency. Besides the election of John F. Kennedy and the ending of the Eisenhower Presidency, important events were reshaping the relationship between East and West, between KGB and CIA, signaling the emergence of a new theater for the struggle between the superpowers. The Third World was moving fully to center stage, and the vacuum created by the postwar collapse of the European colonial system tempted the Soviets to fill that void wherever possible with Marxist regimes. In his Inaugural Address and in the earliest actions of his Administration, John Kennedy seemed to anticipate the battle that lay ahead. In fact, he launched the Peace Corps even before the ill-fated Bay of Pigs invasion of April 1961.

Yet, to understand the American Intelligence experience, it is not sufficient to begin at that point. How far, then, does one go back? To 1947, when the United States acknowledged publicly and formally that it was in a life-and-death struggle with the Soviet Union and passed into law the National Security Act to resurrect Foreign Intelligence capabilities summarily terminated in August 1945 as WW II came to an end? Or to Pearl Harbor itself, the Intelligence failure cited most often to justify the need for the United States to have a professional, continuing Intelligence capability in the modern age? Is the American Intelligence history of such recent vintage and merely a manifestation of the Cold War? Why should our open society have secret Federal

Government mechanisms and activities after the Cold War and after the national emergency?

These questions may fly in an undergraduate political science class here and there, but they belie the American historical experience entirely. Indeed, well before the Cold War and well before the 20th Century, America had a rich Intelligence experience that in the beginning involved those same key individuals who wrote our Declaration of Independence, Constitution, and Bill of Rights, thus laying the basis for the world's oldest continuous democracy and open society.

As early as September 1775, the Second Continental Congress set up "The Secret Committee" that received funds, and had broad authority as well as necessary confidentiality, to carry out activities associated with a modern Intelligence service. It engaged in the secret purchase of military supplies abroad, collected Intelligence on the location of such materials, covered its tracks by using foreign-flag vessels, and stole British stores of ammunition. This was no ragtag group of clandestine operatives; it included the most influential and responsible members of Congress. Among the Secret Committee members: Benjamin Franklin, Robert Morris, John Dickinson, Samuel Ward, and John Langdon.

Two months later, in November 1775, Congress took a further step and created the "Committee of Secret Correspondence" which was our first Foreign Intelligence agency. "RESOLVED, That a committee of five be appointed for the sole purpose of corresponding with our friends in Great Britain, Ireland and other parts of the world, and that they lay their correspondence before Congress when directed. RESOLVED, That this Congress will make provision to defray all such expenses as they may arise by carrying on such correspondence, and for the payment of such agents as the said Committee may send on this service." The first Intelligence Chiefs or Intelligence Officers of the new nation included Benjamin Franklin of Pennsylvania, John Jay of New York (and the *Federalist Papers*), Benjamin Harrison of Virginia, John Dickinson of Pennsylvania and Thomas Johnson of Maryland. The Committee ran a network of secret reporting sources as well as a communications system. It even had its own little navy. Secrecy was strongly emphasized and breach of it cost *Common Sense* author Thomas Paine his position as Committee Secretary. Paine erred when he publicly revealed that the French had begun providing covert support to the Americans before formally entering the war on their side. Even though the indiscretion occurred after France was already in the war on the Colonialists' side, Congress issued a public statement — and lie — that the French King had not so lent aid to the American side. (Contrast this with the 1980s Iran-Contra spectacle in which the U.S. Congress publicly exposed several nations that had provided covert support to the United States on the assumption it would remain confidential.)

The American colonists were rightly concerned also with Counterintelligence. Commander-in-Chief George Washington wrote: "There is one evil I dread, and that is their spies." He referred, of course, to those working for the British. Accordingly, a "Committee for Detecting and Defeating Conspiracies" was established, headed by America's first spycatcher, John Jay, who later served as America's first Supreme Court Chief Justice. One of the Committee's agents managed to infiltrate several Tory military units which lead to their capture. Another Counterintelligence agent became a courier for British Intelligence, successfully acquiring the contents of all dispatches sent from the British secret service Chief in New York through Canada and on to London.

Intelligence Collection was very extensive and, throughout the struggle for independence, America had reporting agents operating in London and key European capitals such as Paris and The Hague. These reporting sources were equipped with ciphers for encrypting their messages, addresses or letter drops for sending their information through a protected route, and cover names to protect their own identities. In many ways their skills were better developed than those of American operatives in the opening days of World War II.

While the Intelligence Collection and the Counterintelligence achievements of the new nation were excellent, its Covert Action accomplishments were even better. On the political action front, they courted secretly a Frenchman, converting Pierre Augustin Caron de Beaumarchais into an agent of influence who contributed enormously to the American cause and success in the war. On a tactical level, this author of *The Barber of Seville* and *The Marriage of Figaro* got French government funding in 1776 for a cover company for channeling key war supplies to the Colonists. To the King he wrote: "Your Majesty knows better than anyone that secrecy is the soul of business, and that in politics a project once disclosed is a project doomed to failure."

On a strategic level, he succeeded also in getting the French on the American side in 1778. That major coup, which later brought the French fleet to Yorktown for the War's final, decisive victory, was the direct work of Ben Franklin, who had arrived in Paris with two colleagues to seek French alliance in the war. Thomas Jefferson was originally to be part of that mission, but his wife fell ill and he stayed home. Simply,

America was sending its top Intelligence and political operatives to Paris because the stakes were so crucial. So was secrecy: "Secrecy shall be observed until further Order of Congress, and that until permission be obtained from Congress to disclose the particulars of this business, no member be permitted to say anything more upon this subject, than that Congress have taken such steps as they judged necessary for the purpose of obtaining foreign alliance."

The Spanish connection was second in importance to the French, and this political action target was approached in a number of ways and with considerable success. Early in the war, the Spanish Governor at New Orleans "privately" provided gunpowder from the "King's stores," enabling the Colonists to prevent British capture of Fort Pitt. Six tons of powder moved up the Mississippi River under the Spanish flag in 1776, three years before Spain itself formally joined the war on the American side. The next Spanish governor, Bernardo de Galvez, basically made New Orleans an open city for the Americans, letting them sell and purchase contraband and war supplies. At the same time, he provided both ammunition and money from his "very secret service fund" and seized British ships as smugglers. The American agent in New Orleans, businessman Oliver Pollock, served actively in Galvez's capture of Baton Rouge, Natchez, Mobile and Pensacola. He also went personally bankrupt funding the American revolutionary cause.

Special or paramilitary Operations were also carried out on both land and sea. Benjamin Franklin developed a system of "privateers" that included John Paul Jones's *Bonhomme Richard*. One of Franklin's delegation members in Paris arranged false documentation through the French Foreign Ministry so that a Covert Action volunteer could travel to England to engage in sabotage Operations. Before he was captured and hanged in Portsmouth, England, James Aiken brought about a suspension of civil liberties as he went about British port areas and warehouses setting fires with an incendiary device of his own design — a saboteur, Aiken met the same fate as the U.S. would mete out to the German saboteurs who were captured in the U.S. early in WW II.

The Colonists also carried out Propaganda Operations with excellent results, especially among the German Hessian mercenaries who were encouraged to desert. This policy was the direct result of a Congressional action setting up a committee "to devise a plan for encouraging the Hessians and other foreigners ... to quit that iniquitous service." Congress passed a resolution, believed to have been authored by Thomas Jefferson, had it translated into German, and disseminated it among the Hessians in leaflets disguised as tobacco packets. "Many hundred soldiers" defected from the British ranks. Franklin himself engaged in "black propaganda" by fabricating a letter supposedly written by a German prince demanding "blood money" for the high number of casualties among the Hessian mercenaries he had provided to the British from his own private army. The bogus letter urged the Hessian commander to let men die rather than be left as cripples, a ruse designed to destroy morale among the fighting men. Another Franklin fabrication was a letter purportedly describing the details of scalp-taking by Indian allies of the British. Scalps with certain identifiable marks were supposedly those of women who "were knocked dead or had their brains beat out." Not very subtle, Mr. Franklin!

The crowning Intelligence achievement of the War for Independence — in Covert Action and Counterintelligence — was clearly the deception operation run personally by General Washington in getting the British to conclude that he would attack New York and not Yorktown, thus creating the conditions for the capture of General Cornwallis and, in effect, the end of the war. Washington had led the British to believe the Colonists had forty thousand and not merely three thousand soldiers camped outside of Philadelphia. This has some of the same flair as the great World War II deception that had Hitler convinced the Allied landing in France would be at Calais and not Normandy. Washington fed disinformation to the British in New York by placing forged military dispatches in the British courier pouches as well as allowing his own couriers to be captured carrying misleading information. The decisive Battle of Yorktown was marked by several successful deceptions which left Cornwallis overestimating American strength considerably. James Armistead, a slave who had been given permission to join the American cause, crossed into British lines and was sent back across to the American side to spy for the British, or so they believed. He then went back with fabricated reports on the number of American troop replacements. For this and other Intelligence service Armistead was later granted his freedom by an act of the Virginia legislature.

The types of Intelligence Operations the Americans conducted were matched also in the variety of Intelligence techniques they employed. Clandestine communications have historically been the weakest link in all Intelligence activities; to be effective they must remain secret. The American revolutionaries employed secret writing (John Jay's brother, James, developed an invisible ink used by the first secret agent in Europe, Silas Deane), concealment devices for courier use, and coded messages to protect the messages from discovery. They employed cover and disguises with success as they entered British garrisons or crossed enemy lines. When the original hollow lead bullet for carrying messages proved poisonous to any courier forced to swallow it to avoid detection, the Americans proved their ingenuity by fashioning a silver bullet for the same purpose.

On January 10, 1781, the Department of Foreign Affairs, (predecessor to the Department of State) was formed "for the purpose of obtaining the most useful information relative to foreign affairs." The government assigned this new permanent organ authority to collect Intelligence and permitted its Secretary to correspond "with all other persons from whom he may expect to receive useful information." The first Washington Administration was also granted a Secret Fund for continued spying. Congress, aware that a formal peace treaty with the British did not mean that the dangers had ceased to exist, was correct. England was back at war with America within two decades.

War, it seems, has been the only event to inspire Americans to attend to their military strength and the need for accurate Intelligence on the secret plans, intentions and capabilities of foreign adversaries. In fact, through most of the 19th Century the new nation avoided foreign entanglements as President Washington had counseled in his Farewell Address. The Monroe Doctrine was not an acceptance of responsibility for leadership in the Western Hemisphere. Rather, it was a simple American way of telling the Europeans to stay away from the Americas. The U.S. did not want to get involved in Europe's perennial wars.

The American approach to diplomacy itself, even its staffing of the Foreign Service with wealthy volunteers at token salaries, exemplified a general lack of interest in international relations. With little more than the desire to be left alone, Americans had no interest in Intelligence Collection other than the natural flow of information to Washington as a by-product of official diplomacy. The Secret Fund was maintained but was diminished in size and significance over time.

In the American Civil War, the art of spying received renewed impetus as each side scrambled to gain information and take advantage of the ease with which spies could pass into enemy-held territory and blend in with the general population. Hundreds of spies operated in Washington and Richmond and made use of military passes to cross the fighting lines and carry information back to their superiors.

New technology aided Intelligence efforts on the military front. The telegraph, invented two decades earlier by Samuel Morse, provided long distance communications, even from the battlefield, where a "magneto" provided electric power without batteries. For the first time, Intelligence operatives used the now-familiar "message intercept" to spread disinformation, using captured telegraph equipment to mislead the enemy. Using aerial balloons for observation, "Professor" Thaddeus S. C. Lowe of the Union Army invented overhead reconnaissance. Realizing that the North had become reliant on balloon observation, the Confederate Army's Robert E. Lee ran a deception operation of his own at Fredericksburg, moving forces behind ridges and trees and into a position to score a decisive victory against Rhode Island's General Ambrose Burnside, whose balloonists had given him false assurances of enemy strength. The new science of photography, which played a major part in recording Civil War battles, also aided spies on both sides despite the severe technical limits that made it impossible to photograph moving objects.

The primary use of the cavalry was to collect information; its use in actual combat was relatively minor. The U.S. Army Signal Corps, formed just before the war by Major Albert Myer, used a system of flag signals that he developed while stationed in the Southwest, where he saw Pueblo Indians making use of signals to send messages in their war with other tribes. A young man from the South, E. Porter Alexander, had helped Myer develop that system; Alexander eventually became General of Artillery of the Confederate Army.

Each side, when not shooting each other's signalmen, was busily working to break the enemy's codes. Once, when the North broke the Confederate code, a New York newspaper exposed that success in a report "to the folks back home." The writer, and the newspaper itself, had not considered the obvious, that the Confederacy had agents in New York. The South soon changed its code, and General William Sherman claimed that the revelation cost the Union ten thousand lives.

To assure that the Confederacy did not receive the kind of European aid that had been valuable to the Colonists in the War for Independence, the Union ran both collection and action Operations in England, France and Mexico. As a result, the South remained isolated. No foreign state recognized it formally, although some clearly felt that a victory by the Secessionists would open opportunities for gains in Latin America, closed by the Monroe Doctrine in the early nineteenth century. When the Civil War ended, the military forces and Intelligence operatives were demobilized.

Until Pearl Harbor drew a reluctant nation into its second great war in just over two decades, the Twentieth Century saw America doing everything possible to remain disengaged from international affairs. A late entrant into World War I, the United States became involved only after it had become clear that the British and French could not end it on their own. The League of Nations, created to establish a mechanism for permanent peaceful resolutions of differences between nations, never did get to enjoy American participation. After the Treaty of Versailles was signed in 1919, the U. S. again wanted to attend to its own affairs and withdrew to fortress America. In the 1940 election, when Hitler's armies had defeated France and had the British against the wall, Franklin Roosevelt ran and was re-elected on a platform promising noninvolvement in the war.

Against such a fundamentally isolationist orientation covering a full century and a half, it is not at all surprising that the country would not start building an Intelligence service until it found itself again at war. Of course, throughout that extended period there were some wiser men who realized that isolationism was a luxury Americans could not afford. President Woodrow Wilson made a major effort to get the United States into the League of Nations, but Congress and the country as a whole wanted no part of it.

Similarly, FDR was aware quite early of the dangers facing the country from both Germany and Japan, but he too had to wait for Congress and the country to catch up with him. Meanwhile, he did what he could through Lend Lease, his own Covert Actions in both theaters of war, and through agents of influence to keep the British and Chinese afloat until America could play a more active role.

Though the attack on Pearl Harbor was the single event prompting the creation of a national Intelligence system, it took the leadership of two men to spearhead the development of a professional Collection, Action and Analytical service — President Franklin Roosevelt and New York lawyer William Donovan. The connection between these men would prove crucial for the wartime Office of Strategic Services (OSS) and, indirectly, for its successor organization, CIA. They established the principle that the central Intelligence authority worked under the President, and not under any department of government.

By the mid-1930s, both FDR and Donovan were convinced that the United States had to break out of its deep-rooted isolationism. For the next five years, Irish-Catholic Republican Donovan worked closely with WASP Democrat FDR, assessing developments in Europe by direct observation of German military actions as a neutral observer, all the while maintaining secret contact for FDR with British Intelligence.

Back in 1929, Secretary of State Henry Stimson had closed down the so-called Black Chamber, a joint effort of the State and War Departments that had been breaking codes and reading other nations' diplomatic traffic since World War I. Donovan eventually managed to overcome the enormous bureaucratic obstacles of the old-line Departments which wanted no centralized Intelligence organization — something that Donovan persuaded FDR was required. In June 1941, Roosevelt directed the creation of the civilian Coordinator of Information (COI), which was designed with British guidance and support. Donovan had used his legal experience to find Lend Lease loopholes by which FDR could provide destroyers to the British in 1940, circumventing Congressional approval requirements that would have been intractable. For their part, the British felt that helping the United States set up an Intelligence service would inspire the Americans to break out of the traditional U.S. isolationism that had resumed after WW I. Establishing an Intelligence service would be a positive step toward international cooperation, but there were only a few Americans who had even a minimal understanding of the business of espionage. Obviously, there had been considerable slippage since the American Revolution when the Colonists outperformed the British in the crafts of Intelligence Collection or spying, in Counterintelligence Operations, and in Covert Action.

Little known, even within the Intelligence profession, the COI spent most of its energies during the single year of its existence — it was dismantled on June 13, 1942 when OSS was created — wrestling with the twin tasks of sorting out its charter and attracting talented individuals to leave private, successful careers and enter the world of Intelligence with a fledgling outfit before America itself was even at war. During that year, the COI did establish a research and analytical capability that would be a cornerstone for later wartime OSS Operations. But bureaucratic opposition within the Government and U.S. Military prevented progress in the areas of collection and action. Once the U.S. entered the war, OSS paramilitary Operations took a full year to get underway because the formal agreement with the Military Services took that long to work out. Even though the nation faced deadly threats from both the Atlantic and Pacific regions, the separate military services were protecting their own turf. (It should not be surprising, therefore, that turf battles would again be dominant in the 1990s as America tried to deal with post-Cold War threats from international narcotics traffickers and international Terrorists. Bureaucracies and bureaucrats, like skunks, do not change their stripes.)

The declassification of the *War Report of the OSS* makes it possible to know in considerable depth what that organization did from 1942 until it was disbanded in late 1945. The OSS range of activities was broad and included espionage, counter-espionage, sabotage, propaganda, support to guerrilla or partisan groups behind German and Japanese lines and, at war's end, the gathering up of top German rocket scientists before they found themselves involuntarily on their way to Moscow. As broad as the operational charter may have been, however, the OSS had to deal with serious obstacles throughout the war besides those posed by the Germans and Japanese.

In the first place, lacking a trained or experienced cadre of Intelligence operatives from which to draw personnel, OSS had to find, recruit, test and train virtually all personnel from scratch. With a total corps of twenty-five thousand OSS bodies by war's end, the personnel challenge alone was of mammoth proportions. Most of 1942 was devoted to putting in the OSS plumbing both in Washington and in the field. The active operational years ran from 1943 through war's end — a mere thirty-two months. With national mobilization, however, the OSS had been able to tap into talent pools unreachable in peacetime. Arthur Goldberg, Arthur Schlesinger, Archibald MacLeish, Walt Rostow, Allen Dulles, William Casey, and movie Director John Ford were a few of the illustrious Americans whom General Donovan was able to attract into OSS.

In its earliest months especially, the OSS relied considerably on the British for training and technical support, a tremendous advantage for a new service with no experience on which to base its Operations. In time this dependency became another obstacle because the British kept the American organization, even with its enormous resources and potential, in a subordinate role until the landings at Normandy.

OSS faced opposition within American ranks as well. Major theater commanders, such as General Douglas MacArthur and Admiral Chester Nimitz, kept OSS "irregulars" on the periphery of the war against Japan. Latin America was the guarded preserve of J. Edgar Hoover and the FBI. Despite these considerable obstacles and the bureaucratic minefields littering the OSS path, the talented, imaginative and courageous men and women of this organization contributed significantly to the war effort wherever they were given an opportunity.

The OSS's most lasting contribution, however, was establishing the credibility, discipline and foundation for CIA itself. General Donovan strongly emphasized research and analysis as the starting point and final stop in the whole Intelligence process. Though he personally identified with the field personnel operating behind enemy lines — having tried several times himself to get into an active combat role — the lawyer in him required close attention to good scholarship. Classical spying, including the breaking of German and Japanese codes, yielded results critical to the success of the Allies.

Open source information read by scholars provided essential information as well, especially on Nazi Germany which recorded and published information that would be harmless in peacetime but very useful to an enemy in time of war. The breadth of OSS field Operations, especially its paramilitary and covert political work, would be reflected later in CIA.

OSS was also one of the first American organs to report indications of the Soviet Union's postwar plans to expand permanently beyond its own borders once the Americans demobilized. The Roosevelt and Truman Administrations were reluctant to believe that Stalin, who only four years earlier had allied himself with Hitler, would recommit Russia to worldwide revolution. This benign and flawed view was actively promoted within the American and British governments by secret, recruited Soviet agents. And, because no one wanted to take any steps that might provoke the Russians, excellent Intelligence opportunities to penetrate the Soviet government were lost. So, as America turned toward peace, OSS was disbanded — *within a month of Japan's surrender!* The so-called "Intelligence lesson" of Pearl Harbor had not been learned after all. Instead, it would take the cumulative transgressions of the Russians in Europe in late 1945 and 1946 to persuade America to create a central Intelligence authority. The Japanese attack on Pearl Harbor had exposed utter Intelligence disarray within the U.S. Government, civilian and military. Yet, America within 30 days of war's end was ready to put its head back in the sand. Ironically, it would be the Soviets themselves who would keep America from retreating back into isolationism.

How does the American Intelligence experience compare with that of the Russians? For one thing, the Russians in 1947 did not have to start all over again. Soviet Intelligence organs had continuously served the rulers of Communist Russia all the way back to December 20, 1917, when Vladimir Ilyich Ulyanov, known also as Lenin, signed the decree forming the "Extraordinary Commission to Combat Counterrevolution, Speculation, and Sabotage" (Cheka) under Polish Communist Felix Edmundovich Dzerzhinsky. Ruthless and cunning, Dzerzhinsky led the outnumbered Bolsheviks to consolidate power and conduct a terror campaign that effectively wiped out all organized opposition.

The Cheka, and its successor civilian organs down to the present KGB, should not be confused with Russian Military Intelligence (GRU) which has concentrated its energies on external enemies. The Chekists, the original group and the KGB, have traditionally made no such distinction between internal or external threats. They attacked all real or perceived enemies of the Soviet state — whether foreigners or Russian citizens, whether civilians or military personnel, whether KGB officers or GRU officers, whether innocent or guilty, or whether actively in opposition or only seen as potential threats.

The first groups to be systematically exterminated were the intellectuals and liberal thinkers who, in Lenin's estimation, would critique the new regime and undermine its public authority. The civilian Cheka moved to murder unreliable elements within the Red Army, men who fought bravely for the Russian Revolution, but previously served in the Imperial Army of the Czar. To assure that the remaining Red Army officers and men did not pose a threat to Lenin, Dzerzhinsky created the Special Department (Osobye Otdel, or OO), a system of political commissars, who were assigned from the highest level down to the platoon and had the authority to perform summary executions. OO's stationed themselves behind Soviet troops in battle and shot soldiers who withdrew from their position.

A system of identity documents effectively subdued the country as a whole, permitting the Cheka to identify and wipe out whole classes of people considered undesirable or potentially threatening to the Bolsheviks. The direct exterminations by internal security and Intelligence arms have been reasonably estimated at twenty million. That people trying to flee the country were simply murdered at the borders by Cheka troops makes it impossible to know with precision the extent of the bloodshed under Lenin and Dzerzhinsky. Such were the roots of Russian Intelligence, a heritage not only well understood by present-day Russian operatives, but celebrated on December 20 each year, the anniversary of the Cheka's creation.

The long arm of the Cheka also reached outside the country. Assassinations and disinformation/deception operations left the Russian exile community incapable of unified action or mutual trust on even an elementary level. The earliest overseas operatives lured thousands of émigrés back to Russia, where they were murdered. Lenin, who had been in exile himself before the Russian Revolution, knew very well the dangers posed by an active exile community, especially one that might conspire with other hostile governments to overthrow his Bolsheviks.

Dzerzhinsky knew the danger represented by imprisonment of political opponents; he had matured as a revolutionary during his own time in prison under the Czar. His solution: murder people outright rather than place them in prison where they can develop the accomplices and motivation to strike back.

The Chairman of the Eastern front for the Cheka wrote the following in the November 1918 edition of *The Red Terror*, the organization's in-house journal: "We are not waging war against individual persons. We are exterminating the bourgeoisie as a class. During the investigation, do not look for evidence that the accused acted in deed or word against Soviet power. The first questions you ought to put are: To what class does he belong? What is his origin? What is his education or profession? And it is these questions that ought to determine the fate of the accused. In this lies the significance and essence of the Red Terror."

The Cheka established a firm place within the Soviet system and, although the name would change several times in the next seventy years, it would prove over time to be the instrument that preserved and protected State power. In the power struggle following Lenin's death in 1924, only Felix Dzerzhinsky potentially blocked Stalin's ascension to the pinnacle of leadership in Soviet Russia. Conveniently for Stalin, Dzerzhinsky died under mysterious circumstances at an opportune moment for Stalin, who then succeeded Lenin without opposition. The former Communist Party bureaucrat, Stalin, then consolidated power with a Red Terror campaign of his own, one that in time contributed the bulk of the twenty million official murders.

Stalin's instrument of terror continued to be the internal security apparatus — whether it was called the Unified State Political Administration (OGPU) until 1934, The People's Commissariat of Internal Affairs (NKVD), and variants thereof from 1934 until Stalin's death in 1953. The Committee for State Security (KGB) was created in 1954. It was perilous to run afoul of the "security organs" as millions were to discover. It was a dangerous job also for its several Chiefs and their lieutenants. Stalin's choice to conduct the purges that began in 1934 was Genrikh Yagoda, who oversaw the carnage until he himself was executed in 1936 and replaced by Nikolai Yezhov. Rather than reverse the terror campaign for which Yagoda was ostensibly tried and executed, Yezhov unleashed a greater purge, which lasted until 1938 and his "suicide."

Under Yezhov, the purge included the Soviet military leadership, a response to Stalin's obsessive fear of Trotskyite and other conspiracies. As Intelligence historians Corson and Crowley point out in *The New KGB*:

"Three of the Red Army's marshals were murdered, all eleven deputy commissars of defense, thirteen of fifteen army commanders, 110 of 195 Division commanders, 220 of 406 brigade commanders, and tens of thousands of other officers were imprisoned or executed. The killings were on a scale much greater than that experienced by any army officer corps, of any nation, in any war."

It is estimated that 90 percent of the Generals and 80 percent of the Colonels were murdered and, altogether, the extermination of Red Army leadership totaled 30,000–35,000. The Soviets were equally thorough with "external enemies" as with "internal enemies" of the state, as the victims were inevitably labeled. After the Russo-German pact of 1939, the Soviets secretly murdered 15,000 of the Polish army's officers and senior enlisted men in the Katyn Forest massacre. It was carried out by the NKVD operating under Stalin's fellow Georgian, Lavrenti P. Beria, who would rule that organ until 1953. Beria had been brought in as deputy to the ailing Yezhov, who "took his own life" four months later. With the death of Stalin, Beria moved to consolidate his power, but he too was murdered under a directive from the Communist Party's Central Committee. In typical Soviet fashion, the event was papered over after the fact and presented publicly as an execution that took place after a trial. Several of Beria's top officials were executed as well: Colonel-General Sergei Goglidze, head of Far East Intelligence; General Vsevolod Merkulov (Minister for State Inspection); Colonel-General Bofdan Kobulov (Deputy to Merkulov); Lieutenant-General Lev Vlodzimirski (senior official in State Security); Vladimir Dekanozov (Minister of Internal Affairs in the Republic of Georgia and close to Stalin and Beria); and Pavel Menshik (former Minister of Internal Affairs in the Ukraine).

It is difficult to convey in writing the brutality of the Soviet security organs. Even a listing of the overwhelming statistics or a catalog of the names of real people falls short. It takes a single person, an Anne Frank if you will, to capture the horror of the murders. How could so many succumb to the executions, even those living in foreign lands whose summons to Moscow "for consultation" meant almost certain death to thousands in the 1930s?

Hede Massing, an American citizen who served Soviet Intelligence with her husband, Paul, tells of a conversation they had in Moscow in October 1937. They had been summoned back to Russia and were expecting to join the ranks of so many other foreign operatives who had been brought "home" to Russia for execution.

"A few days later there was a knock at the door and in came Yury Fischer. He was about fifteen years old then ... It wasn't long before we plunged into a political discussion. The main topic of conversation was, of course, the purges. Yury was a Consomol (Communist Youth), and imbued with the Soviet spirit, Paul said, 'Now Yury, you know that I'm a German revolutionary. You remember that I was in a concentration camp. Do you believe that I'm honest? Do you believe that I could do something against the revolution?' Yury said, 'Don't be silly, Paul, of course I believe in you! I know how honest you are. Why do you ask that? I know you could never do anything wrong. You are our hero — Vitya's and mine; we love you as much as our father!' 'All right,' Paul said, 'what would you say, Yury, if you were to come here tomorrow to our rooms and find that I had been arrested? You would be told that I am a traitor to the revolution; what would you think, Yury?' There was a long pause. Yury bit his lip ... It took him a long time before he finally said, 'Paul, if you are arrested, you are guilty'."

Such was the system which turned many well-intentioned people into creatures of the state, the Soviet State, abandoning all personal loyalties and values in the process. Hede Massing, by some deft maneuvers, escaped the purge and in time she broke altogether with the Soviets and even Communism. In the course of moving from Communist public activist to underground Soviet Intelligence agent, she got to know one of the Soviet's greatest spies, Richard Sorge, and a fair number of American Communists and Soviet spies in the U.S. Government — including Alger Hiss.

From the time of the Cheka until the modern KGB, the internal security organs have accounted for most of the murders. Soviet Military Intelligence has historically been apart from the executions and purges except on those occasions when its officers and field agents became victims of *Soviet justice*. The Chief Intelligence Directorate (GRU) of the Soviet General Staff ran the most successful spy rings against external adversaries of the Soviet Union, including the Sorge network in China and Japan before the war and the postwar Western military alliance. By the early 1960s, however, the GRU had been converted into an Intelligence arm clearly subordinate to the powerful KGB. The first major blow to the GRU came with the 1930s Stalin purge of the Soviet Military. Author John Barron points out that "hundreds of its ablest officers, including Director Berzin, perished in the mad purges, and the GRU never really recovered from this loss of talent. Demoralized and depleted, it performed miserably after the Soviet Union attacked Finland in 1939."

The GRU's wartime record was very good, principally because some of its external networks had escaped the Moscow purges, which were halted primarily because of the growing threat to the USSR posed by Germany and Japan. The next blow to the GRU came after the war and from within its own ranks when two of its officers were caught spying for Western Intelligence — Colonel Pyotr Popov, for six years in the 1950s, and Colonel Oleg Penkovsky, for two crucial years in the 1960s. Although the defections cost the head of KGB his position, the long-term result was that the KGB was placed in charge of security for the GRU as well. Finally, the KGB took advantage of its superior political clout to take over key GRU Operations, essentially converting the Soviet Military Intelligence structure into a support service for KGB.

While it took the Communist takeover of Eastern Europe after WW II to make the U.S. recognize the new struggle with the Soviet Union, the Soviets by contrast had figured things out considerably earlier than their wartime allies. In 1943, a year before the Allied armies came ashore at Normandy, Soviet Intelligence services had been re-directed to concentrate their Operations against the U.S. as the new *glavni vrag* (or "main enemy"), the country most important to Soviet Intelligence Collection and Covert Action. While America in the late 1940s was putting together its massive Marshall Plan, its new national security structure, and an array of military alliances to confront the emerging Soviet threat in the wake of the War, the USSR had previously positioned its own Intelligence operatives within both the United States and Great Britain.

In the U.S., the Soviets were able to steal critical atomic secrets. In Britain, they built on their penetrations of British Intelligence, which had been developed in the 1930s and served Soviet purposes undetected through the War. Ironically, the very lack of continuity in American Intelligence eventually helped protect it from direct Soviet penetration. Indirectly, however, Moscow monitored and neutralized some American Intelligence Operations in the 1940s and 1950s by exploiting their agents within British Intelligence, such as Kim Philby, who served in Washington in a liaison capacity with CIA.

The Soviet Union too suffered major Intelligence losses as it pursued its program to expand beyond post-War frontiers agreed to in 1944 with its Allies. The cynical reversals of Soviet policies, the publicized crimes of Stalin and the hoards of émigrés who fled Eastern Europe ended the Soviet capacity to recruit foreign intelligentsia, agents and supporters along ideological lines. The utopian Communist appeal had been exposed as a fraud. Nonetheless, this did not prevent the Soviets from making a major, concerted assault on the West, hoping to undermine the countries of Western Europe and Japan before their economies could be reconstructed and their political systems made viable again.

Anticipating and countering this Soviet activity was the major struggle in CIA's first decade. By the time the Kennedy Administration came to power in early 1961, the United States had, for all practical purposes, been successful. During the Administrations of Democrat Harry Truman and Republican Dwight Eisenhower, with the partnership of both the Executive Branch and the Congress, and through a complementary array of overt assistance programs and covert CIA Operations, the United States won the Cold War in all major theaters, with the exceptions of China and Eastern Europe. The outcome in China and Eastern Europe had been largely determined by events during WWII itself, as Chinese, Yugoslav and other indigenous Communists were maneuvered into the checkmate position before the West really understood that the Cold War was underway.

With the Soviets well aware by the late 1950s that they had no prospect of extending their power into Europe or Japan, they shifted their attention to the soft underbelly of the West, the underdeveloped world, which was in a state of disarray as the European colonial empires began to unravel. Soviet Intelligence, aware of the strategic value of many of these countries, geared up for rough-and-tumble struggle in the Third World. So did the Central Intelligence Agency. For both superpowers, the Cuban Revolution became a Cold War symbol as the Soviets tried to create "new Cubas" in Latin America, Africa, Asia and the Middle East. For its part, the U.S. tried to assure the world that Communism would not be allowed to spread in the Third World without American opposition — KGB-supported insurgency would be met by CIA counter-insurgency.

For some opinion makers in the United States, the Cuban revolution had been a confusing affair initially because of the breadth of support for the Castro guerrillas and the utter corruption of the Batista regime. It was well known that some of the anti-Batista fighters in the Sierra Maestra Mountains were Marxists. But there were also democratic elements within the guerrilla band and, until Castro himself ended the mystery some years later by revealing that he had been a Communist all along, the hope had been high that he was too much of a nationalist to fall into the Soviet camp. Dave Phillips, who within twenty-four months would be leading the Agency Psychological Operations to oust Castro, was under deep cover in Havana on January 1, 1959, when the

Cuban revolution succeeded in driving Batista from power. Phillips later recalled his feelings at the time: "Several days later I stood on a street corner as Fidel Castro marched into Havana. The crowds went wild. I applauded and cheered along with them ... Like so many Cubans, I was glad to see them."

Within months the Cuban government went about exterminating its democratic partners in a campaign reminiscent of the Dzerzhinsky program under Lenin in Russia. The Red Terror had come to Cuba as it had earlier visited retribution upon non-Communists in Latvia, Lithuania, Estonia, Armenia, Azerbaijan, Bulgaria, Poland, Hungary, East Germany, China, Czechoslovakia, the Ukraine — wherever the Soviet organs or their revolutionary pupils came to power. Castro turned on former comrades-in-arms with ferocity and a systemized brutality no less than that employed against members of the Batista regime. Batista, at least, carried out trials and executions in public. It took the United States several more months to acknowledge that yet another revolution had been subverted by Communists. The delay was a result of the enormous goodwill that had greeted Castro's victory in this country, not simply in the media but also among a broad cross section of Americans philosophically opposed to the Batista regime. Finally, America woke up to the fact that the Soviets now had a dangerous ally within our own hemisphere. Phillips and his family fled for their lives shortly after another American agent of CIA was executed in Havana.

Presidential candidate John F Kennedy, in the decisive 1960 debate with Vice President Richard Nixon, used the Cuba issue and charged that the Eisenhower Administration was quiescent in the face of Communism in Cuba. Ironically, the island nation would occupy center stage within JFK's 1,000-day Presidency, which was marked most dramatically by two Cuban events, the Bay of Pigs invasion of April 1961 and the Cuban missile crisis of October 1962.

Reflecting back on that period, I am struck by the fact that the issue of Cuba and Communism was not, as far as America was concerned, a clear-cut liberal-versus-conservative issue. Liberal Democrats at the time were in one important respect more consistently anti-Communist than their conservative Republican colleagues. Republicans, even in the 1960s, were inherently more isolationist than the Democrats, whose internationalist orientation was more in harmony with an activist, even an interventionist role for America in the world. Despite the tendency for pundits to link the Cold War to the years of the Eisenhower Presidency, it was under Truman that the Marshall Plan was launched, that the North

Korean invasion was challenged, and that Greece, Iran and Austria were wrested from Soviet control. The Republicans between 1953 and 1961 stayed a course set by Secretary of State George Marshall on June 5, 1947, during a Commencement Address at Harvard University. It would not be until the 1960s, again under a Democratic President, that new initiatives would be launched in Latin America with the Alliance for Progress and then in Southeast Asia with Green Berets and, still later, the use of conventional military forces.

In 1960, against the backdrop of thirteen years of Cold War, it was an exciting time to be joining the Central Intelligence Agency. Even though I had only a very general idea of the parameters of the conflict then taking place between East and West, between KGB and CIA, it was clear that a great struggle was underway, one that would have an impact on America and the world at large. To participate directly in that battle on the side of freedom was both an honor and a thrill. To be selected as a member of CIA's silent warriors made me feel lucky indeed. For me, for the Agency, for the Federal Government, for the Congress and for the country as a whole, this was clearly a battle of right against wrong. We were not trying merely to hold Soviet aggression in check; there was still the faint glimmer of hope for some of us that non-Russian peoples within Eastern Europe and even the USSR might be liberated from Cheka domination and the Red Terror.

3

Getting Started, Getting Trained

HEADQUARTERS for CIA in northern Virginia is a modern office building opened in 1962 as the final official act of fired Director of Central Intelligence Allen Dulles, removed by President Kennedy after the Bay of Pigs debacle. The building was doubled in size in 1987 by William Casey in a futile effort to bring the Agency under one roof. Since its humble beginnings in 1947, CIA now needs more than two dozen buildings in Virginia over and above the main Headquarters to house its numerous personnel.

Back in the summer of 1960 when I first arrived for work, CIA was housed in temporary, barracks-like wooden structures in the vicinity of the Mall and Reflecting Pool between the Washington Monument and the Lincoln Memorial. These modest buildings had been built during the War and bore innocuous names such as Alcott Hall, Barton Hall, Quarters Eye, Buildings J, K, L, and so forth. A short distance away, near the State Department, the Agency continued to occupy some small, pleasant buildings where the OSS headquarters had been located.

The simplicity of CIA's Washington offices during its first fifteen years was in keeping with the aura of clandestinity then considered appropriate for the nation's Foreign Intelligence service. It helped mask the raw power of the organization and its leadership in the 1950s, when U.S. Senator Joseph McCarthy came out second best when he tried to carry his witch hunt into the world of CIA, as he was doing with considerable success over at the State Department. The truly wealthy do not need to flaunt their fortunes and the genuinely powerful do not need to broadcast their strength. CIA was never more vigorous than in the days when it outwardly looked so modest.

Arriving at CIA on modest terms, with barely enough cash to carry us through to the first paycheck, I was happy to learn that a Federal pay raise meant I was starting at $5,135.00 per year — a full five dollars a week higher than originally offered. As a newly-hired Operations Officer candidate, I joined a new class that consisted mainly of individuals who were planning to serve in the Clandestine Service, or spy side, of

CIA. There were a few candidates for careers in Intelligence Analysis, primarily scholarly individuals with advanced degrees and excellent academic credentials who were more soft-spoken, reflective and gentle than those of us hired for Operations.

My Operations classmates were, with few exceptions, three to five years older than I. Two were female. Most of the males had served in the military. There was one Black but no Asian-Americans, Hispanics or Native Americans. None of us knew the first thing about Foreign Intelligence as a craft or profession, although a few had some tactical Military Intelligence experience. It was necessary, therefore, for the Agency to get down to basics and teach us some things that today would be known by most applicants. For example, we received an overview of the Soviet Union as a strategic threat. For those of us who had not majored in Soviet Studies, this was the first look we had at our principal adversary.

I remember my impatience at spending my first weeks in CIA sitting in class reading and being lectured on the National Security Act of 1947, on the role of Intelligence in policy formulation, on the responsibilities and structure of CIA's several offices. My internal urge was to get on with the business of espionage, sabotage and whatever other arts I would supposedly need to go out and confront America's enemies. This was before James Bond had surfaced to color the spy profession in brilliant hues, but I certainly had a somewhat romantic view of Intelligence nonetheless. And here I found myself tied to a chair for weeks, learning about policies, procedures and organizational plumbing! I must admit it almost drove me crazy waiting for something exciting to happen. At the same time, the Agency itself was waist deep in Covert Action all around the globe. Even those of us in training could sense that energy from the Operations Officer speakers who came in to address our class and who knew that most of us would be out in the field soon enough.

When the Washington classroom phase of the training was completed, my class headed out of town for the training in clandestine Operations. It was early fall of 1961. The Pittsburgh Pirates were winning the National League Pennant and would go on to beat the New York Yankees in the World Series. I remember that Series well because one of my car-pool mates was from Pittsburgh and took our money as the Pirates, scoring far fewer runs, managed to squeak out a World Championship. The other major news story that autumn was the Presidential campaign, which had Democratic Senator John Kennedy going against Republican Vice President Richard Nixon. Again the car pool divided along sharp lines and, again, the guy from Pittsburgh came out the winner as he picked Kennedy to come out on top.

Most of us were married and, for several months, we departed from home each week, usually on Sunday evenings, and returned on Friday evenings. The clandestine Operations Course was conducted some distance out in the Virginia countryside at a CIA training site known as "The Farm" that is under cover to this day despite having been exposed time and again since the 1970s by disgruntled former employees. The Agency cover fig leaf was relatively intact when those of us in Operations Course class OC-10 went through our training. CIA cover at the time was relatively solid for both CIA employees and for Agency mechanisms. The unraveling of cover on a wholesale basis was still seven years away. As a young officer new to the business of Intelligence, I was not conscious of just how fortunate we were at the time to enjoy decent cover protection. Our assumption was that such was the natural order of things for those working in secret Intelligence.

We assumed, further, that the threat to CIA cover and Operations would be posed primarily by the KGB and not, certainly, by fellow Americans. Our final, unfounded assumption was that American law would protect our cover because those given access to organizational secrets had signed Secrecy Agreements that held them accountable for their actions should they violate that trust. So much for assumptions! My classmates and I in OC-10 were to enjoy real cover, real anonymity for about the first 20 percent of our careers. After that, it would become thinner and thinner until the fig leaf had been reduced to a tea leaf.

The setting for our training in espionage was, overall, very good. We were sufficiently removed from the rest of society to learn what former DCI Dulles called the "craft of Intelligence" in a world simulating a real country. The "live problem" exercises had been written to permit the Trainee to learn the ropes by playing the role of Operations Officer. The instructor staff worked both ends of the live problem. One instructor would play the role of the foreign field agent and one of us Trainees would have to run that agent as though we were operating against a genuine overseas Intelligence target. Another staff instructor would play the role of senior CIA Station officer and would guide the Trainee in the running of each operation. Both instructors were then in a position to evaluate performance of the Trainee, one primarily on the quality of operational planning and the other on how well the Trainee performed in dealing with the field agent or source. Some of the Trainees had more facility than others getting into the live problem and playing the roles spontaneously and well. A little theatrical "ham" went a long way in making the training exercises work out.

The instructor staff in 1960 had an interesting mix of Intelligence experiences and personal backgrounds. Especially in its first two decades, there was no pattern distinguishable in the backgrounds of the instructor staff that was as striking as the individuality of the men themselves. Very clearly, no mold or template was being employed for the selection of Operations personnel in the beginning years of CIA. There was some significant variety as well in the Intelligence experience of the instructors. Some of the older men had served in OSS in paramilitary roles. War heroes and brave men all, they had little of the kind of Intelligence experience that we would need in our own careers when paramilitary Operations became a specialized activity of full-time officers, former Green Berets, Navy Seals or Army Rangers who concentrated on counter-insurgency. We were being trained as Operations Officer generalists. The staff included some professional training officers, some of whom had field experience in Operations and some who had never served overseas or seen a clandestine operation or agent. Finally, there were some Operations Officer instructors who had served abroad recently and run the kinds of Operations we were going to face in our own field assignments. Most of the latter were in Training for a single two-year assignment and went back to the field immediately afterwards. They had decided it would be more fun to be out in the woods harassing Trainees than pushing paper at Headquarters.

The training itself dealt substantially with the three main missions of CIA's Clandestine Service. Collection of Foreign Intelligence, known as FI, was, is, and will always remain the workhorse of the Agency. U.S. Presidents want to know what is happening around the world, so we spent a considerable amount of time learning how to recruit and acquire information through the use of secret agents or spies. The Operations requirements varied. An agent may have to attend a meeting, let's say, of his or her country's Communist Party Central Committee, and come back to the CIA officer and report what was decided. In that case, no special spy gear is needed because the agent merely reports what was said in the Party meeting and the Operations Officer takes notes, which serve as input for an Intelligence report written back at the CIA field Station. But even in such a simple scenario, the CIA officer and his Communist Party contact must be certain that they are not seen together. Neither can they securely use telephones to call each other to set up a meeting or to pass information. The training, therefore, addressed the critical matter of Clandestine Communications — which can run the gamut from personal agent meetings in an out-of-the-way safehouse to using exotic impersonal electronic means for transmitting information, signals, or instructions.

An Operations Officer must be trained in the various Clandestine Communications techniques and must have the good judgment and common sense to apply them judiciously according to the security situation of the agent. Some overseas CIA recruited agents run the relatively small risk of public embarrassment; other agents risk their lives and their family welfare if caught spying. Some countries have a benign security climate; others are positively perilous. It makes no sense applying the most extreme of spy techniques or *"tradecraft"* when the risks of discovery are low to nonexistent. A simple meeting arrangement along a dark street might be perfectly appropriate for passing a document or report. In other cases, CIA expends many thousands of dollars and employs hundreds of hours to work out one secure contact for passage of information. CIA may draw upon America's most advanced technology to protect a spy and the Agency Operation. The training, therefore, is meant to help develop the kind of sound judgment and the flexibility that will be useful for the Operations Officer's whole career. In one assignment, the officer may have to expend enormous energy and thought protecting Operations. The next tour abroad might well be operationally simple from the security standpoint. In the same assignment, he may be handling cases of substantially different risk, complexity, and value to CIA.

We had to learn how, where and under what circumstances to run agent meetings. We had to learn how to use basic spy gear such as cameras that can be used to "case" a building or military installation or how to copy documents that may have been pilfered from a government office. We learned how to copy keys for use in surreptitious entry. We learned surveillance by working in teams that followed instructors around nearby towns and tried to spot them conducting a clandestine act or meeting someone of Intelligence interest.

Some of the training, as one might expect, reflected OSS days and had little specific applicability in the world we would be facing. We learned about cross-border Operations that were employed in WW II to transport agents in and out of Nazi-occupied France, Holland, or Yugoslavia. We were sent away from the Farm on field exercises to sketch military or industrial targets. Overall, the emphasis on FI agent Operations was sound, even though we were not taught all of the techniques we would need in our careers. This was a course in basic spy techniques, again what we call "tradecraft." Specialized training was available later if an Operations Officer needed to learn electronic communications, audio Operations, or such exotics as locks-and-picks to open doors or counter-surveillance for running agents behind the Iron Curtain, as the Soviet Union and Soviet-controlled Eastern Europe were called in 1960.

The second important mission of the Agency is Covert Action, known as CA. When I joined, CA was primarily concerned with Covert Political Action, not the paramilitary or sabotage Operations employed in WW II. In the 1950s, the Agency had been involved in Paramilitary Operations in Korea, the Philippines, Southeast Asia and to an extent in Guatemala, where the leftist government of Jacobo Arbenz was basically frightened from power by some well-orchestrated CIA Psychological Operations. The Paramilitary heyday of CIA lay ahead, in the Administrations of Kennedy and Johnson. It was in Covert Action Political Operations where I felt the most challenge. There, I could see not simply the role of reporting on the world but, additionally, the opportunity to change it for the better. What better result of an Intelligence career can one aspire to than protecting freedom and blocking the KGB program in a tangible way?

We learned about the CIA-KGB "fronts war" that had been taking place in Europe and Japan in the 1950s. The battle for freedom, as President Kennedy acknowledged in launching the Alliance for Progress in Latin America and the Peace Corps in all regions of the globe, had shifted to the underdeveloped world. The 1959 World Communist Party Congress in Moscow had declared explicitly its intention to turn up the Marxist revolutionary heat in those areas. CIA Political Action Operations would certainly be needed to counter the Soviet threat. Unfortunately, few of the instructors had any solid experience in such CA Operations. Most were what were called FI Officers, collectors of Intelligence by trade and disposition. Few Covert Action officers at the time were in training assignments. Most such Officers were serving overseas in Covert Action programs or were supporting Covert Action activities from the Washington end.

Covert Action officers tended to be a different lot altogether from their FI Intelligence Collection colleagues. The CA officers were far less conventional in dress, work habits, and even thought processes. They tended to cut corners bureaucratically and shoot from the hip when dealing with risk and operational security. Their expense reports tended to be screwed up. Many sported facial hair — maybe even a waxed moustache or a goatee. They had imagination, flair and sometimes positively wacky ideas. Not content to accept the world as they found it, they visualized how to make it a better place. Whereas the FI officers in another incarnation may have been FBI or military officers, the CA officers would have been journalists, academics or writers. Maybe even revolutionaries, in the right time and place.

The third Clandestine Service mission is Counterintelligence, or CI, which in its most basic sense is spy-catching. It can range from the protection of CIA's own Operations and organization to the much broader defense of the U.S. Government and American society from the activities of hostile Foreign Intelligence services. First and foremost for CIA, that has meant the Russian KGB and GRU. But the CI charter and responsibility go beyond these two obvious targets. They include all Foreign Intelligence services trying to penetrate or damage our government including the several internal and external Intelligence services of the Cubans, Chinese, North Koreans, and the Eastern Bloc, as well as the services of a large number of nations not overtly hostile to the United States. "There is no such thing as a friendly Intelligence service" is the view of most Counterintelligence professionals. Given the Soviet success in penetrating all Intelligence services around the world, one has to assume that even a cooperating Foreign Intelligence Service has leaked information to our foes. Harold "Kim" Philby, who penetrated British Intelligence for the Soviets, was not an isolated case.

Our training in CI was relatively thin given its basic importance to the organization. For one thing, by 1960 the Counterintelligence mission had developed into an activity that was bureaucratically insulated from the rest of the Clandestine Service. A special CI unit at Headquarters had taken charge of that responsibility, and most of the Counterintelligence cases were being handled out of the CI Staff, supposedly on grounds of high sensitivity. To be sure, more than in FI or CA, it was essential that all of the various threads in a CI operation be pulled together in one office. CI is a painstaking process and demands more the temperament of an archivist and historian than that of an FI recruiter of reporting sources or a CA orchestrator of coups.

From the standpoint of career progression, CI offered much less opportunity than the flashier sides of the business. It also had within itself a natural core of paranoia much against the grain of most Americans but quite compatible with those coming out of totalitarian systems where trust can be a deadly luxury. Americans pride themselves on their openness, a quality of virtually all Operations Officer Trainees hired through the Career Training Program. To have a "CI mind" meant that one had been spooked into seeing Soviet Intelligence hiding behind every tree and every operation.

One CI-oriented instructor introduced Trainees in alias to his wife, suggesting that he somehow did not feel she should be entrusted with even that basic knowledge of Agency business. One CI joke suggested that if an Operations Officer got too carried away with his suspicions and security concerns, he would be assigned to an office where he would look through the Sunday *Times* in search of "secret coded messages of enemy agents." As a result of becoming isolated from the mainstream of operational business, of being left out of the training of new officers and, finally, of taking on the aura of the ridiculous, Counterintelligence became a very bent arrow in the CIA quiver. In time, the Agency, the Government and the nation would pay a very high price for that development.

Some training problems took us into the towns outside the Farm and we were grouped in three-person Operations teams. I was fortunate to be on a team with two older Trainees who gave this younger member a helping hand. Each had served in the military, and one was a graduate of Annapolis, with four years as an active duty Intelligence Officer. Each would go on to an illustrious career and serve as the Station Chief in a major field installation.

The OC-10 training class had a remarkable array of individuals. A few, like me, had never been outside the United States except through the pages of a book. Several, on the other hand, had significant overseas experience, having lived abroad with Foreign Service parents or in overseas American business families. A half-dozen or so had served abroad with the military, primarily on Okinawa with the Marines. There may have been about 15 percent from the Ivy League or elite small colleges, but most had gone to school at less notable institutions. I can recall about a third with very solid foreign language skills. One class member was so good at learning languages that he used this skill as a part-time job, studying one language after another until be passed fluency tests, which brought him CIA monetary awards for several languages simultaneously. One excellent Russian speaker made headlines a few years later in a spectacular espionage case that was a great CIA success while it lasted. And one vocal anti-Communist, in time, resigned from the Agency for the specific purpose of doing military service in Vietnam, where he "could get paid to kill North Vietnamese." The great majority of my class would serve full careers in the Agency. Approaching thirty years after the formation of our class, close to half were still working for CIA.

Just as the 1950s and 1960s were so different for American society, our training class also seemed to be very different from the next class that followed us into the Agency. For one thing, although we did not take very seriously what we called the "Mickey Mouse" part of training, we gave respectful if minimal compliance with such things as morning physical training. Most of us had already been through basic military training and knew that our formation as Clandestine Service officers had nothing to do with push-ups or sit-ups. Our long-term health certainly might, but not the specific business of Intelligence. Yet, OC-10 went along with the early morning nuisance and saw to it that a quorum at least showed up for the daylight drills — anything to satisfy the Office of Training hierarchy, which took all things large and small very seriously.

After we graduated, along came the next class, OC-11, which was a group that challenged the system in ways that almost caused apoplexy all the way up the Training chain of command. The OC-11 Trainees refused to show up for the mandatory daily physical training. They had the temerity to turn around a night escape-and-evasion exercise and capture the instructors instead. The senior training managers, fearful of losing face, overreacted and fired three of the Trainees for conduct well short of sedition. I mention this only because, in seeing the way the country's youth went through a metamorphosis in the 1960s from compliant adherents of the system to outright rebels, I often mused that the first manifestation of that shift may well have been buried within CIA, in the break between OC-10 and OC-11. I was similarly struck by the rigid, even brittle, way the managers dealt with the challenge. They fired three extremely promising young officers when they should have examined the training instead.

I recall how unaware I was of the matter of civil rights. I was unaware in the sense that I hardly noticed the segregation in rural Virginia until it was too obvious to miss. One car-pool mate was Black, and for several months we traveled together a couple of times a week on the way to or from our homes and the Farm. It was a ride of close to four hours and invariably we would stop for a drink or some snacks at a roadside stand or country store. We would all usually pile out of the car and pick up our goodies. Our Black classmate, meanwhile, always remained in the car. It was quite some time before I realized that he stayed in the car because he would not be served. No one did anything about this matter, and I don't recall even a conversation that might have let him know that we thought this was wrong. We certainly were not about to go out picketing and get arrested. The irony is that this Black officer went on to serve his country courageously and with distinction overseas, protecting those who would not serve him a coffee here at home.

The most memorable incident in my training occurred in November 1960, when DCI Allen Dulles made one of his periodic trips to the Farm for an evening with his Trainees. In a fatherly sort of way, he really did consider the Operations Officer Trainees his own. After dinner that night, we gathered in a lodge in the woods where the DCI did what he liked best, spinning yarns of his time in Switzerland in World War I as a Consular Officer and in World War II with OSS. He told the familiar story about having passed up a meeting with none other than V. I. Lenin on the eve of the Bolshevik victory, supposedly in favor of a tennis date. Dulles biographer Leonard Moseley reports that Dulles in fact had a date with a young lady — far more forgivable than missing the Russian Revolutionary over a game of tennis. Nonetheless, the next day Lenin was on his way to the Finland Station and the course of history was radically shifted. Would a meeting between Lenin and Dulles have changed anything? Probably not. More than likely, Lenin had in mind the transmission of disinformation to the American Government; it is unlikely that Lenin was interested in becoming an immigrant to the U.S. Regardless, for the rest of his long professional career, Dulles tended to have an open-door policy for all kinds of individuals, something that paid dividends for him during wartime service with OSS and later as Director of CIA. It gave him a titillating after-dinner story, one that conjured up the illusion that, for a frivolity, Dulles had missed a chance to change history — clearly, the spymaster was a master storyteller.

He lost his composure, however, at what took place next. When the time came for questions, one of our brasher and outspoken classmates, from New York City of course, asked the DCI whether President-elect Kennedy would be firing Dulles or keeping him on as head of CIA. This stunned "the old man" and he mumbled something appropriate about serving at the pleasure of the President. Secretary of State John Foster Dulles, Allen's brother and Eisenhower's key foreign policy architect, would be replaced of course. There was some thought that the Director of Central Intelligence would enjoy the protected status accorded FBI Director J. Edgar Hoover and be spared removal in the political transition that was taking place. Intelligence, after all, was supposed to be nonpartisan or at least bipartisan, as was American law enforcement. It was no secret that Allen Dulles wanted to stay on. The evening came to a close and the DCI flew back to Washington. We made jokes that the protagonist from the Big Apple could plan on being assigned to the world's hell holes if Dulles indeed remained, but figured that we had heard the last of the matter.

Some weeks later, when the decision was made by President Kennedy that both Hoover and Dulles would be staying on, a phone call came down to the Farm from the DCI's office: "Tell that young man that the Director is here to stay." For the time being at least, CIA was to enjoy the leadership of a great and remarkably-prepared man, one who would continue to set a standard of leadership that would be met by few of his successors.

As we neared the end of our training our minds became increasingly preoccupied with our placement within the Deputy Directorate of Plans (now Operations), the original and purposefully-bland euphemism for the Clandestine Service to which almost all of the class would be going for their careers. Three classmates resigned near the end of the training or shortly thereafter, returning either to more lucrative business opportunities or academia. The rest of us were about to be assigned to a geographic "Area Division" — Latin America, Far East, Europe, Middle East, Africa; etc., where one would serve the bulk of his future career.

A few were assigned to the worldwide International Organizations Division (IOD), which ran the Covert Action Operations spanning the globe and, like the activities of the Soviets, spread beyond the confines of any single geographic Area Division. The Communist worldwide subversive threat was by design and in practice truly international; early in CIA's existence, consequently, Agency leadership saw that a parallel international program was essential to meet, counter and neutralize the Russian-led effort. It was primarily in this special Division — with its psychological, political, labor, student and cultural Operations — that the Agency's most notable liberals were active. It was in this Division, headed in the early 1950s by Tom Braden (*Eight is Enough* author and Pat Buchanan's adversary for years on television's "Crossfire"), that Cord Meyer headed the Cold War battle through Radio Free Europe, Radio Liberty and a host of organizations that countered Soviet-supported fronts.

Cord Meyer had been a witch hunt target of Senator McCarthy in the 1950s and, DCI Dulles, to his credit, had refused to be cowed by the malicious campaign of the Wisconsin Republican Senator. As a young man in 1942, Cord Meyer had left Yale, joined the Marines, served in the Pacific as a lieutenant and was badly wounded in combat. Recovering from his wounds, he took part in the establishment of the United Nations, working under State Department Official — and Soviet spy — Alger Hiss. Seized by postwar idealism, Meyer later joined the World Federalists, which had a vision of world government that was premature, to say the least, given the power of the nation states at the time. In the late 1940s, Meyer struggled with Stalinists for control of the American Veterans Committee, a first-hand experience in the tenacity of the Marxist-Leninists. This lesson prepared him for the role he would play in battling the threat posed by the programs carried out through the International Department of the Soviet Communist Party, the KGB, the Eastern European Intelligence services, and a multiplicity of Moscow-controlled front groups — from the World Peace Council to the World Federation of Trade Unions and a host of others.

Having completed my Operations training in early 1961, and aware that a smattering of Russian language would not be attractive to the Division concerned directly with Soviet Operations, I engaged in the process that would match me up with my next, permanent assignment. For some of my classmates the decision was only a formality because they were already destined to serve in areas that would draw on their previous overseas experience, in-depth language skills, or specialized academic studies. An officer hired into the Agency with considerable skill in Chinese or Japanese was almost certainly slotted for assignment to the Far East Division. For many of us, however, there was no such compelling logic, and our assignment seemed more like a crap shoot than scientific selection. The pal from Pittsburgh spent one afternoon rolling on the barracks floor, half laughing and half crying, because he was being sent to South Asia. There was not a thing in his background, wish list or temperament to suggest that part of the world. Yet, that is where he would begin what would become a spectacular Operations career, one that would have him serving later in his career as Chief of Station in the most important country in the Soviet Bloc.

Although a good faith effort was made to match us to our first personal preference, the final word on assignment was CIA's, as each of us clearly understood. The Agency was then, and has remained, a disciplined outfit that is neither fully civilian nor military when it comes to career assignments. Someone has to serve in very underdeveloped areas where living conditions, sanitation, health facilities, and overall respect for the human person are very low. There are, obviously, only so many job possibilities in Western Europe, although that region appears on hundreds of employee requests for assignment overseas. I would have a chance to serve in Europe a decade later, but my start was to be in Latin America where Castro was busy stirring up discontent, guerrilla activity, and revolution. What made the choice appealing was that I was going to be working in Covert Action, a dream come true.

4

The Bay of Pigs

THE CHERRY BLOSSOMS were blooming on the trees surrounding the tidal basin in Washington as I arrived at Headquarters in the Spring of 1961 to discuss my new assignment to the Western Hemisphere Division (WHD) — later called Latin America Division (LAD). April is an especially fine time of the year in the nation's capital, as schoolchildren and other tourists arrive in busloads to visit the monuments and museums during their post-winter vacation week. Barely twenty-three years old myself, I felt on top of the world. I had completed the Operations Training Course, been accepted in the Western Hemisphere Division which was churning with activity, and I could now begin setting the stage for assignment abroad. Bonnie was expecting our second child in midsummer and, having no idea what lay ahead, was as supportive as ever as I began my career as an Operations Officer.

The Kennedy Administration, still on its public-relations honeymoon, dominated the news, introducing on the national scene names that would vis à vis Vietnam become household words. Robert McNamara had become Secretary of Defense after a career with Ford Motor Company. Dean Rusk was in charge at State. Robert Kennedy, formerly of Senator McCarthy's Committee Staff, was Attorney General. Former Illinois Governor and perennial Presidential candidate Adlai Stevenson was made Ambassador to the United Nations, which had evolved into little more than a bully pulpit that was marginal to the core foreign policy programs of the U.S. The ideal of the U.N. as a major instrument for peace, as originally envisaged at its inauguration in San Francisco in 1945, had given way to the reality of unilateralism. In the first fifteen years of the Cold War, Presidents had come to rely on CIA as the instrument for unilateral political action.

The Agency's secrecy offered advantages over adversaries and no immediate need for public accountability. There was the added advantage of CIA's reputation for getting things done without foot dragging — something the old-line departments of government always did. Getting things done, no public uproar, the advantages of surprise, operational secrecy — with these CIA traditions and the accompanying mystique, the new Administration moved ahead with the plan to invade Cuba and depose Fidel Castro twenty-seven months after he had come to power. The basic plan had been constructed during the final months of the Eisenhower Presidency. Richard Nixon had remained passive in the famous television debate when Kennedy berated the Eisenhower Administration for inaction on Castro. Actually, the Agency under Ike was busy in Cuba, busy in the Dominican Republic conspiring with coup plotters bent on ousting the tyrant Rafael Trujillo, and busy all the way over to Africa where Patrice Lumumba was presenting a threat to pro-Western elements in the Congo. Kennedy had inherited an activist government, and after winning the November election, he was bequeathed the Cuban invasion business which Eisenhower, whose health was fragile, had put on hold until he left office.

As the Cuban invasion date approached, those of us in training heard rumbles that something was going to happen. Officers visiting the WH Division sensed that a major move against Castro was about to be made. The memory of CIA success in Guatemala in 1954 was very much in the air. The U.S. was not going to accept a Soviet beachhead in the Western Hemisphere. The Monroe Doctrine was not dead.

Even though there was a great deal of confidence about Cuba, no one in the Agency underestimated the worldwide threat we were facing from the Soviet onslaught. Southeast Asia was beginning to receive increased attention from the Agency, even though two years earlier Eisenhower had responded to North Vietnamese invasion threat by putting the Marines on Okinawa on ships headed for the area. The direct invasion threat was averted, but the flow of insurgents into South Vietnam continued steady and strong. In Africa, meanwhile, the copper-rich region of the Congo was bordering on chaos. Latin America was experiencing increased Marxist guerrilla activity in a dozen countries. In northeast Brazil, the U. S. was growing alarmed over a broad and growing peasant movement that was reminiscent of Mao Tse Tung's Chinese Communist revolution, which had succeeded barely twelve years earlier. The view that all of these crises were connected, part of a single web of international subversion, was broadly accepted at the highest level of our government and publicly as well.

The Soviets lent credence to this perception by providing overt encouragement and support to the national liberation movements and by making continual public pronouncements in favor of worldwide revolution. Stalin had left the scene in 1953 and the formal structure of the Comintern had been dismantled even earlier, but no one in power in Moscow had stepped back from the historic pledge of extending the Russian Revolution to all nations. Again, the 1959 World Communist Party Congress had reconfirmed that pledge publicly. A steady stream of young revolutionaries from the Third World were being trained in guerrilla warfare by the Soviets and their surrogates, showing that the pledge was not mere rhetoric. So, even though it was implicitly accepted that the Cuban problem would soon be resolved to America's satisfaction, CIA had plenty of work to do in other parts of the underdeveloped world. Intolerable poverty and exploitation, widespread corruption, collapsing colonial empires, explosive population pressures from high birth rates and dropping death rates, and the structural weaknesses in international trade and Third World internal economies — all signaled societal instabilities that provided advantages to the Marxist and guerrilla revolutionaries working for Moscow.

As young Cold Warriors, it was our job neither to perpetuate the exploitation of people nor to promote social justice throughout the world — CIA is neither the Mafia nor the Boy Scouts or Red Cross. CIA's role was to neutralize the Soviet KGB and other international Communist subversive efforts and, in doing so, to buy time for the underdeveloped world to construct the systems and structures of the kind that had permitted Western Europe and Japan to escape the Communist gauntlet. Removing the Cuban threat in America's own backyard was seen as the first step in that process for the Kennedy team which campaigned in the 1960 election for a hard line against Castro.

As the radio news reports advised that a landing force had arrived in Cuba, those of us not involved directly in the operation assumed things were going well and that the island would be liberated soon from the Communist yoke. Many democratic Cubans who had fought against Batista, and with Castro, had been executed by the Communists already or had fled the island. Here was a chance to reverse the tide and do what had not yet been achieved in Eastern Europe. We did not know what had been going on in the Cuban invasion planning where last-minute changes and decisions were making failure inevitable. Cuban exile Brigade 2506 landed on Monday, April 17, 1961; by Wednesday it was over. In the interim it was becoming increasingly clear even to those of us outside the Cuban Operations Group that a disaster was in the making. Some felt that the U.S. would intervene directly. Instead, defeat was accepted by the Kennedy team.

The instant analysis within the corridors of the Agency was that the disaster was a direct result of Kennedy's last-minute cancellation of essential air strikes, which ceded air superiority to the Cuban Air Force, as skeletal as it was. Rumors suggested that Adlai Stevenson, incensed that he had been used unwittingly to sow disinformation within the United Nations, was instrumental in persuading the President to trim the operation back. Some felt the fatal flaw occurred when the site of the invasion was switched in early April from a desirable location to the isolated Bay of Pigs, a poor choice from the military standpoint.

Over at the White House, blame was cast in the direction of the Agency. There were suggestions that CIA had forecast a popular uprising of the Cuban people. The President publicly accepted formal responsibility and then appointed a group to investigate the Bay of Pigs, placing his brother Robert in charge. Within months, DCI Allen Dulles and his Clandestine Service Chief, Richard Bissel, were both replaced.

The Bay of Pigs disaster set the tone for the Western Hemisphere Division as I arrived there. After the invasion debacle, the atmosphere was anything but spiritually uplifting. The halls were full of grim, hurried people who, after working for weeks on a crash basis, had been soundly defeated. There was confusion over the extent of the losses as some held the faint hope that anti-Castro fighters may have made it safely into the swamps or out to sea. Yet, very few managed to do so. There was a new respect for Castro who, unlike Arbenz seven years earlier in Guatemala, could not be scared from power, even by a fighting force of 1,500 men backed directly by the United States. Within the Agency, people seemed oblivious to the inherent contradiction of sponsoring a "clandestine invasion" of another country — an oxymoron if there were one. CIA's earlier successes in Iran, Guatemala, and the Philippines had fostered an overconfidence that prevented cancellation of the Cuban enterprise when the foundations of the invasion were weakened for reasons of public policy. The can-do spirit of the Agency, bred by the success of the Cold War, had not succeeded this time.

At the working level, however, there was little suggestion of deep reflection on how things had failed except for occasional finger-pointing at political figures outside the Agency. Nor was there much attention to the big picture and how the U. S. Government would now deal with Castro. The immediate concern — as it would be fourteen years later in the halls of the East Asia Division as Vietnam collapsed — was for the agents who had not escaped or been confirmed as casualties or prisoners. I entered a Division fraught with the kind of tension that surrounds the aftermath of a mining accident. When I arrived that spring to begin a fifteen-year stint in Latin America Division Operations, I had no idea that this failure would be a turning point in Agency history. Certainly, before Bay of Pigs, several major CIA Operations had not worked out. But, within CIA, information concerning failures had been so closely held that those planning the invasion of Cuba probably knew little or nothing about what had happened eleven years earlier in Albania.

According to Chapman Pincher, several hundred Albanian exiles, who had been trained and armed by CIA, infiltrated Albania in 1950 in an effort to overthrow the Hoxha regime. Some three hundred Albanian exiles were killed in ambushes that were arranged by the Soviets and probably included Soviet troops as well. A similar fate befell Eastern Europeans and Ukrainians who infiltrated their homelands in the same period. All had been betrayed by Soviet agent Harold "Kim" Philby of British Intelligence when he was Coordinator of Operations in his liaison role with CIA. Within the Intelligence communities and governments of the U.S. and Allied Powers, these events were carefully held and protected from public disclosure. Nor did the Soviets and their Bloc partners publicize these events even when they came out on top. The Western nations wished to avoid embarrassment and erosion of morale; the Soviets and their subordinate Communist regimes wanted no public suggestion that the West was willing to train and arm insurgents to fight within the Soviet frontiers.

The tendency for adversaries to cooperate in keeping hostile paramilitary and Intelligence Operations secret was deeply ingrained until 1960 when, quite out of character with the way these things had been handled before, President Eisenhower took public responsibility for sponsoring the Francis Gary Powers U-2 flight that crashed in the USSR. This public blowing of cover stunned the Soviets who, aware of twenty prior overflights of the USSR since 1956, anticipated no U.S. public acknowledgement. Had Eisenhower kept quiet, the Eisenhower-Khrushchev Summit Meeting would likely have continued on schedule and U-2 pilot Powers would have been handled in a low-key manner. Once America took responsibility publicly, the Soviets canceled the Summit and chose to put on a dog-and-pony show including a public trial of the downed airman. There obviously was no ability to put protective coating around the Bay of Pigs fiasco, even if one was desired. In fact, the public nature of the debacle and the direct damage done so early in Kennedy's Administration deprived CIA of the special status it had enjoyed during the Truman and Eisenhower years.

For me, the invasion disaster was a very sad affair, especially when I heard stories of the chaos of the operation and the heroism of the anti-Castro Cuban Brigade lost on the beaches and the CIA pilots and Maritime Operations personnel lost out at sea. But I was looking at the affair principally in political terms, lamenting that Eisenhower, who had successfully led the greatest invasion in the history of warfare at Normandy, had not been in charge when this relatively modest affair had been executed. I had none of the Intelligence or Operations background at the time to appreciate that, from a Covert Action standpoint, the invasion of Cuba made no sense at all. Neither did it make any sense for an organization composed primarily of civilian political science types to be directing something as technical and inherently militaristic as an invasion from the sea. Hadn't the Marine Corps spent the better part of four years doing just that sort of thing in the Pacific in World War II?

I did not spend much time dissecting the Bay of Pigs affair and what it would mean for me in my next assignment. I was glad that I had not been involved and had been spared the turmoil that struck men like David Phillips, who recalled in later years that April 1961 was the saddest month of his very full life. He wrote of the invasion aftermath: "On awakening I tried to eat again, but couldn't. Outside, the day was sheer spring beauty. I carried a portable radio to the yard at the rear of the house and listened to the gloomy newscasts about Cuba as I sat on the ground, my back against a tree. Helen came out of the house and handed me a martini, a large one... Suddenly my stomach churned. I was sick. My body heaved. Then I began to cry."

One moment, the CIA Cuban Operations people were upright and swaggering in step. Then, they seemed collectively stooped and shuffling as they made their way around the corridors of the Agency. Such was the transformation brought on by defeat.

"Failure is an orphan," President Kennedy reminded the nation as he spoke of the failed invasion. In the rest of Western Hemisphere Division after a few days there was little talk about Cuba. Those not working on Cuban Operations were getting on with their own Operations made more critical because Castro Communism had not been excised in one surgical strike. Castro's survival against the onslaught of the "Colossus of the North," as he called us, was bound to perk up his supporters and draw more adherents to the Communist-led revolutionary movements in Latin America. For most of the 1950s, the Chinese Communists had been calling the United States a "paper tiger." In Kennedy's April 1961

Bay of Pigs debacle — as again would be the case fourteen years later with the April 1975 fall of Vietnam to the Communists — the Maoists would seem to be vindicated once again in that claim.

5

Preparing for Assignment Abroad

FOR THE NEXT eighteen months, I was busy preparing for my assignment to Latin America, a process beginning when I reported to the Branch responsible for a volatile part of the region. This Branch oversaw Operations in a country I will call El Dorado, then under considerable Communist pressure and considered one of the main and promising Soviet and Cuban country targets in the region. My assignment to El Dorado had been approved in the Division, and I had to do a number of things to prepare myself and set the foundation for what was going to be an extended tour of duty under "deep cover" or Nonofficial Cover, as it is known in CIA. Known as NOCs, Nonofficial Cover Operations Officers operate overseas outside official installations, posing usually as businessmen or scholars. They do not have the diplomatic immunity enjoyed by Operations Officers working out of U.S. installations under Official Cover.

My assignment as an NOC Officer to El Dorado had the support of my first real boss within CIA, a wonderful lady with a special talent in the field of Covert Action. Like many of the first generation of Agency Operation Officers, she had a distinguished record in WW II, having entered German-occupied France with OSS. Gifted in languages and well educated, she operated in German-occupied France despite her wooden leg. In 1961, when we first met, she was a senior Branch Chief responsible for the Covert Action program in three countries. She had a reputation for being a highly competent Covert Action manager.

She and I never discussed her wartime service, not because she was unwilling to do so, but because time was always at a premium and our concern was El Dorado in 1961, not what happened in France in 1944. She looked very much like an English school marm in her middle years when I knew her and, with her native French, she must have blended in nicely with the French population during the War. I never asked and never got a chance to ask about that service. By the time I came back from overseas some years later, she had retired. A new assignment often meant that paths would not cross again. Like a lot of young, aggressive Operations Officers, I tended to put off developing social relationships whenever there was a job to be done; I let a good many relationships evaporate over time. Also, going under deep cover meant that I could not legitimately keep up correspondence with Agency colleagues either in the field or back in the States. Eventually, I fell into the habit of putting off contacting old colleagues in the belief that when my life settled down I would catch up on all that socializing. Well, when I finally reached that point my first boss had died, and I never did get to hear about what she had done in the War.

The personnel staffing of Area Divisions in 1961 reflected different factors. To Europe Division went many of the Eastern elite who had been schooled in that region and many of the CIA ethnics (Greeks, European Jews and a smattering of Scandinavians). Working in the Far East Division were children of missionaries to China and former servicemen who had been stationed in the Orient. The Middle East Division attracted children of oil industry executives who served in that area and, generally, were the more adventurous officers in the Clandestine Service. Some of the adventurers also headed to the Division responsible for Africa, which had few American antecedents to draw upon beyond the slave trade of centuries earlier. This latter region offered the most immediate potential for career advancement and attracted some of the more ambitious officers.

The Latin America Division also had an identifiable staffing pattern. It included the turf controlled during World War II by the FBI which did an excellent job neutralizing Nazi agents in the region. When CIA was established — with active opposition from FBI's Hoover as well as the State Department and the Military Services — the FBI had to relinquish Intelligence responsibility south of the border. Many FBI officers in that area went to work for the Agency and brought with them their experience and many of their WW II reporting sources. They made CIA exceedingly thorough in its coverage of Communist Parties in Latin America but relatively narrow overall when it came to Covert Action, compared to other Area Divisions that had been battling Soviet-supported front groups. This was to Castro's advantage as he targeted the region for revolution. Latin America Division drew on Covert Action officers from other areas, especially Europe and the Far East, and on younger officers who displayed an interest or aptitude for the "fun and games" part of the business. My own appetite for CA, therefore, had a lot to do with my own assignment. I later could only blame myself for serving initially under NOC cover, a mistake that played a large role in shaping my Agency career.

In those days, CIA sent a fair number of first-tour officers abroad under some form of academic cover. This move had to be made early enough so that the officer could credibly play the student or researcher role. NOC had the advantage for the Agency of getting officers overseas more quickly than waiting for an opening in the limited number of official cover positions we enjoyed around the world in military and diplomatic facilities. Deep cover also allowed officers to learn foreign languages and politics in a more concentrated and authentic way. Finally, it added an extra operational dimension and capability to the CIA field Station. Even though the NOC officer was clearly an American — there was usually no change of identity or nationality — he did not move in American diplomatic circles and could learn and do things an American official could achieve only with difficulty and risk.

The overwhelming majority of Operations Officers, at the time, had not served under deep cover, and it was clear that NOC service enjoyed a mixed reputation. To many, it was a very inefficient way to conduct Operations because the NOC officer had no direct access to official communications, could not see Station files, and had to be handled or supported by a busy inside Station officer who could be doing better things than hand-holding an Operations Officer under deep cover. Yet, deep cover service had a certain classic flair that appealed to those of us with a yen for the intrigue of true clandestinity. The closest thing to a real spy, not merely a runner of spies, it was along the lines of the Soviet deep cover officers known as "illegals" who change identity, citizenship, family history, status in life and sometimes even their spouse to serve the KGB or GRU. Colonel Rudolf Abel of the KGB, who was captured in the States for spying and later swapped for U-2 pilot Francis Gary Powers, was a Soviet illegal.

One of the most famous illegals in the history of Intelligence was Soviet agent Richard Sorge, who served in Japan with distinction before being caught and executed during World War II. An officer of the GRU, Sorge had originally recruited Hede Massing, who served in New York and was instrumental in the eventual conviction of Alger Hiss. Sorge developed his journalistic cover in Germany and served in China in the 1930s, moving to Tokyo when Stalin became increasingly concerned with the military threat posed by Japan. Attaching himself to the German Embassy in an advisory capacity, Sorge became privy to Japanese war plans, including the planned attack on Pearl Harbor (which the Soviets elected not to share with the Americans). His stock with Stalin — who otherwise viewed overseas operatives as having been turned against him by Trotskyites and other enemies — was so high that Soviet troops were moved from Asia to Europe to battle the Germans based on Sorge's reporting from Tokyo. This was a remarkable Intelligence coup and, from Japan, Sorge contributed enormously to the defense of the Soviet Union in what they call "The Great Patriotic War." His reporting made a decisive difference in their ability to hold back the Germans at Stalingrad. In later years, Sorge came to be recognized as the great master spy — he acted with aplomb and he paid for that success and courage with his life.

The story of Sorge, and other spy lore, inspired Operations Officers to serve abroad as NOC officers, away from the comfort and protection of diplomatic sanctuary. Encouragement for deep cover service came from Agency managers, who told Operations Trainees that a new day had arrived for NOCs; CIA was going to do it right for a change. The head of the Clandestine Service spoke of planned special retirement credits and incentives (which never materialized) for those working outside the overseas Stations as NOC officers. Anyone could see that official cover limitations were damaging our ability to cope with the expanded threat we were facing. We were so obviously in need of deep cover officers that it made sense the Agency would clean up its act and take the NOC business more seriously. With childlike faith in the common sense of the leadership, I not only agreed to deep cover service but was pretty much a volunteer. But, first, I had to be prepared for the Operations and situation I would be facing in El Dorado.

The Soviets and Cubans, as well as their local cohorts in the Latin America area, were working their penetration and subversion programs on several levels, depending on the local situation. Where it was possible to do so, they worked through legally-established Communist Parties and other organizations such as trade unions to expand their influence. If the Communist Party was declared illegal and suppressed by the government authorities, an underground party was established, and the Communists worked through labor, university, peasant and religious organizations. When the repression of the government was so pervasive that it eliminated all opposition political activity as well as the social action of churches and service organizations, the stage was set for the Marxists to train and support armed insurgents. They had the flexibility to adapt their activities to the local operating conditions and political climate. They managed also to exploit several avenues to power simultaneously in certain countries. While working through a legal Communist Party, for example, they also buried members secretly in university circles and supported guerrilla groups operating in the countryside. The lack of dogmatism was one of their greatest assets because it meant that they had a whole range of options open to them, both regionally and within a single country. It was in good part why the Marxist-Leninists under Stalin had been able to outmaneuver in Russia the more ideologically-rigid Trotskyites. It was why the CIA, in turn, had to be flexible in meeting the Communist challenge as broadly as required, including in the field of labor.

Based on open source information and on our own Intelligence coming out of the region, we knew that the battle for control of the labor movements was in full swing in Latin America. This was true in El Dorado. There is, of course, a fundamental incompatibility between a free and democratic labor movement and any totalitarian system. Unions are not free to operate in the USSR, or in Cuba since Castro came to power. The Communist pattern is to use the unions or the labor movement at large to create the conditions for achieving power, and then discard or suppress them afterwards. It was not enough, however, that I have a general historic comprehension of labor. I had to acquire sufficient expertise to be able to run Labor Operations on the same terms that the KGB was doing in Latin America and had been doing for several decades — clandestinely, and without the hint of American involvement. If they were subverting the labor movement at night and in dark alleys, CIA would lend its countervailing support at night and in dark alleys. Fighting fire with fire, as the saying goes.

Latin America Division offered little in this regard. Covert Action as an operational discipline was in relative infancy compared with LAD's solid Collection (FI), and Counterintelligence (CI) programs. It had even less direct experience in Labor Operations, which were viewed as esoteric activities of specialists working under Cord Meyer in the International Organizations Division (IOD). So, to get ready for El Dorado, I was assigned to IOD. This group of heterogeneous operators funded the radio stations that broadcast news and hope to the Soviet Union and Eastern Europe and ran the programs that competed directly with Soviet front organizations throughout the world, which the KGB funded and controlled primarily through the World Peace Council, (headquartered in Prague to mask the controlling Russian hand). Unlike the more conservative Area Divisions, IO Division operated across national borders and other artificial barriers that mean nothing to Communists, guerrillas, Terrorists and drug traffickers. The freedom from territorial and normal bureaucratic constraints freed the IOD Cold Warriors to take the battle to those sectors in which the Communists blended so naturally and with such relative success — in labor, among peace activists and university students, with left-inclined intellectuals, journalists, and politicians. Freedom from old ideas and old habits marked Meyer's operators as they had fought and won the Europe and Japan rounds of the Cold War in the 1950s.

In IO Division, if someone had an imaginative idea or program, there was usually a way to find support. Each time the Soviets ventured out of their Eastern European turf to conduct a phony international youth festival in the West, they got driven back by IOD. Excepting for Communist strongholds in French and Italian labor, democratic forces by 1960 were victorious in the industrialized nations of Europe, in good part due to the Covert Action of Cord Meyer and IOD.

What was striking from the perspective of American politics — especially the subsequent developments within America in the 1960s — was that these IOD Covert Action professionals were both effective anti-Communists and the most concentrated group of liberals in the Agency, if not the government. That fact taught me, by disposition on the conservative side of the spectrum, an enduring lesson: the masters of subversion and intrigue, the Soviets, have seldom been beaten by right-ists anywhere on this planet. The forces that have been most successful against them on a sustained basis have been centrists and left-of-center liberals who compete on the same playing field as the Marxists for the allegiance of workers, women, peasants and students. American labor leaders never caved in during the Cold War or *détente;* they supported to the end Poland's Solidarity. By contrast, American capitalists have fallen all over themselves getting to Moscow (or Beijing) in search of business, beginning by inducing President Franklin Roosevelt in establish diplomatic relations with the Soviet Union in 1933 in hope of expanded trade, which never materialized. In the 1970s, it would be American industrialists who strengthened the Soviet military machine by care-lessly handling trade and technology. Anything for a buck, sometimes, in corporate America!

I learned about Labor Movements and about Labor Operations in a program that had three facets: I studied the Agency's own Covert Action Labor Operations throughout the world up to that period, especially the ones that applied to Latin America. I then engaged in a rigorous program of academic study, compressing a twenty-four month program into twelve months. Finally, I got hands-on Labor Operations experience under the auspices of the IO Division.

During this same period, I managed to study Spanish to the point where I established a solid foundation of grammar and vocabulary before departing for El Dorado. I was still a long way short of professional fluency, however, and would face many months of struggle and hard work before reaching the point where my Spanish skill matched the requirements needed for my work.

Meanwhile, Cuba was the focus of attention again, not only in the hemisphere but around the world, as the U.S. and the USSR squared off in the October 1962 missile crisis. In terms of stakes and high drama it made the Bay of Pigs affair seem minor in comparison. How close did the world come to nuclear war? There are as many theories as there are views on the Cold War itself. Had Kennedy flinched before Khrushchev's tirade when they met in mid-1961 in Vienna, three months after the Bay of Pigs fiasco? Kennedy himself explained Khrushchev's hostile attack: "I think he did it because of the Bay of Pigs...he just beat the hell out of me. So, I've got a terrible problem. If he thinks I'm inexperienced and have no guts, until we remove those ideas we won't get anywhere with him. So we have to act."

In the same tirade in Vienna, the Soviet leader ranted and raved about Berlin, talked about missiles flying, and six weeks later built the Berlin Wall against the terms of the Four Power Agreement between the USSR, the U.S., England, and France. This too went unopposed by Kennedy and very likely led Khrushchev to conclude that he could get away with placing strategic missiles in Cuba, shifting the balance of power significantly. Vienna, Berlin, and Cuba were Khrushchev's dominoes.

Kennedy, meanwhile, had come out of Vienna determined to pick his own spot to challenge the Soviets: "Now we have a problem to make our power credible, and Vietnam looks like the place."

Each in his own way miscalculated. Khrushchev was ousted two years after the October missile crisis, which had the appearance of a Soviet defeat. Kennedy's choice of Vietnam, as "the place" to demonstrate American will, would prove a miscalculation as well.

The Cuban missile crisis is said to have contributed to the shift of emphasis from Human Agent Operations to Technical Collection Operations. The U-2 overflights had brought back documentary proof of the missile construction, the "smoking gun" that exposed the Soviet ruse for what it really was. Thus began a tendency at the highest levels of the government and Intelligence Community to fall into the erroneous and simplistic view that Human Agent Operations were no longer needed.

Certainly, Technical Collection systems have irreplaceable strengths worth the billions of dollars they cost to develop and employ. Two other types of Intelligence activity in October 1962 played a significant role in that confrontation and its resolution on terms not requiring the U.S. to accept Soviet offensive missiles close to our coast. First, CIA Human Agent Collection was instrumental initially in alerting the United States to the construction of missiles in Cuba, and Colonel Penkovsky's reports on the Soviet ground-to-air missile characteristics gave the U.S. what it would need to take them out in a surgical air strike, if necessary. Just as important was the informed judgment and analytical ability of DCI John McCone, who concluded correctly that the Soviets must be putting in the tactical ground-to-air missiles for some specific reason; so, he kept pushing for more Technical Collection until strategic missile construction sites were located.

In the end, Soviet strategic missiles were removed from Cuba, and an agreement was reached that averted military conflict. What had been a Soviet Intelligence analytical failure — their conclusion that Kennedy's weaknesses regarding Bay of Pigs/Vienna/Berlin Wall meant they could place the long-range offensive missiles in Cuba with impunity — almost got them into a shooting war with the U.S.

The world did not come to a fiery end that time. So, I continued on my plans to depart for El Dorado, having been buried more deeply under cover by CIA than regular Agency employees. All CIA records of me were expunged from the official Clandestine Service personnel system and placed in a restricted office. I was heading out into the cold.

6

Assignment in El Dorado

BONNIE'S ARMS were loaded with diaper bags, baby formula bottles and our new son, Stephen, as we descended the airplane stairs for the beginning of what would be almost four years in El Dorado. I was carrying two children myself, three-year-old Tommy and two-year-old Julie. The early morning sun hit our tired eyes as we walked quickly toward the airport terminal building and out of the winter chill. It was a clear June day, early winter in the Southern Hemisphere.

We learned right away that life in El Dorado was not going to be overly comfortable. Our hotel was modest; our cover status required that we avoid the better hotels used by diplomats and businessmen. Our government allowance was meager, so we had to buy one meal for the children and split it between them. After over twenty-two hours in transit we were all exhausted, and Bonnie put the children to bed. Then she and I reviewed what we needed to do to deal with the local health situation. We could not drink the city water and had to use bottled water even to brush our teeth. Vegetables that had not been cooked, such as lettuce and tomatoes in salads, were likely to be contaminated by amoebas and a multitude of other microbes found in fecal matter that made its way into the antipasto. So, we had to avoid a variety of fruits, vegetables, ice cubes and seafood to steer clear of dysentery, El Dorado's number-one killer of small children. With three children under four we were not about to be careless in this regard. After several days of looking, we found an old furnished home with a yard full of beautiful plants and flowers behind a high wall. Throughout the underdeveloped world there is a direct correlation between economic status and the height of walls. The brick barriers capped by broken glass serve to protect property and to keep the children of the well-off from mixing with the children of the street. This is necessary only in early childhood. Later on, the fortunate children will look right past the unfortunate, as though the latter do not exist.

We soon got a sandbox for the children and placed it under some nice fruit trees. They could play there on sunny days, but the El Dorado winter was harsh. As soon as the sun went down, the house itself became very cold and damp. Living without central heat was a new experience and, as this would prove to be an especially cold winter, we bundled the children each evening into their snowsuits and put them to bed. Bonnie and I would then sit down to dinner in front of the space heater in the living room, invariably finding our tea or coffee cold before we could finish. It was so cold and damp that our only recourse in early to mid-evening was to get into bed ourselves; it was just too cold and damp to sit in the living room and read or listen to Bonnie at the piano. Before long, Bonnie was expecting again, illustrating the correlation in the underdeveloped world between birth rates and cold houses. El Dorado had a bumper baby crop the following summer.

During the day, of course, I escaped many of the inconveniences of underdevelopment and Bonnie was left to deal with them pretty much on her own, pregnant and managing three very active youngsters who were intrigued by the new world they had entered, with new hiding places, strange foods and people speaking to them in a different tongue. I had prepared hard and long for this assignment, and as soon as the basics of food, clothing and shelter had been met, I plunged into my work. I had been sent under deep cover not merely to survive physical hardships.

This first overseas assignment began at a time when the CIA Station in El Dorado was deeply involved in a Covert Action Election Operation. The Station itself was considered one of the most effective overseas Stations because of the range of its coverage of the Intelligence targets. A myriad of U.S. Government departments and agencies abroad are actively engaged in collecting information that will help the U.S. Ambassador and Washington decide policy and actions in each country where we have a diplomatic presence. The great bulk of information is collected openly and innocently. CIA's particular responsibility is to acquire protected information purposely hidden from the U.S. and which can be gathered only through secret or clandestine sources, spies if you will. As a deep cover officer, my job was to become as familiar as possible with the political dynamics of the country and the developments in the field of labor, where the pro-Soviet Communist Party of El Dorado had been actively working for a full forty years before my arrival.

The International Department of the Communist Party of the Soviet Union had a hand in El Dorado labor a quarter-century before the creation of the Central Intelligence Agency. There was little danger, therefore, that we were being premature in our concern. We knew they had been active a very long time; in fact, Soviet Intelligence agents were operating in the area with secret writing communication capabilities as early as the 1930s. All surface indicators suggested also that the local Communists and their Socialist allies were very much in control of the leadership of the country's trade unions. Not so clear were the depths to which the Marxist grip permeated the whole of the labor movement, including the grassroots unions in the country's strategic sectors. My assignment was to measure and assess that penetration and to identify covert options for challenging the Communists in ways that would be meaningful and sustainable within CIA's reasonable capabilities. At the time, of course, America and the Agency still believed that we could change the world, so there was little conscious thought about limits.

This was a great challenge for a very young man, and I had no difficulty finding the motivation or energy to go at the task with all of my being. I could have been working instead in some very large Station where I would be doing such necessary but basic chores as servicing post office boxes and the like for the first tour abroad. Instead, I was a member of a fairly small Station, by European or Asian standards, and involved in Covert Action at an interesting time in El Dorado's history.

The ideal operating posture for a field Station is to have a balanced program that covers all assigned targets and has resources devoted in a more concentrated way to the highest priority problem areas. Agents penetrate key political parties, hostile foreign embassies and groups outside the political mainstream, such as the local Communist Party, Terrorist groups, and so on. A CIA Station tries to strike a balance between Intelligence Collection and Covert Action, assuring also that it protects its own Operations with Counterintelligence safeguards. I was aware of this ideal balance from my training in CIA Headquarters.

The ideal Station program, however, tends to dissolve rather rapidly when it faces a major Covert Action program such as a national election operation. That kind of program commands the attention of senior Station management to the exclusion of the remainder of the Operations. Almost immediately, it was clear to me that the El Dorado Station was concentrating on the volatile national political situation. The thrust of its work was to discover what was happening with political parties and Presidential candidates, and the impact of these developments on the voters who would be going to the polls on a specific day in the following year. What happened beyond that election was, for the moment, of little concern to CIA. What happened within the country's infrastructure such as labor was of no concern — unless it related to the national election. Think of approaching a farmer whose barn is burning next to his house and imagine his response if you tried to sell him a roof. In the same way, no one cared about labor unless it had an election dimension.

Seeing the sense in this approach and adjusting to it was my first lesson in the real-world application of my training. It was also practically helpful because it gave me some time to develop a feel for the country and a reliable data base on which to build a pragmatic Covert Action program. Getting to know what is real and what is fantasy or outright deception is crucial, and too many policies and Operations have been constructed on weak or nonexistent foundations. The labor situation in El Dorado was so confusing that sorting out motives, policies and possible approaches was essential to a successful operation.

The Popular Front forces of the Marxist Left were trying to hype their power in the field of labor to achieve political legitimacy and create the impression that they alone represented the workers and socially-conscious middle class professionals. The centrist forces, especially the Christian Democrats, were continually emphasizing the gains they were making in the country's trade unions. Other anti-Communists in the labor field were aligned with similarly-inclined international organizations; though weak in El Dorado itself, these forces made use of funds from abroad to generate publicity suggesting strength and legitimacy.

It was relatively easy, therefore, to fall into the trap of seeking and finding information that supported preconceived views or wishes. Most supporters of one political force or another were inclined to do just that; before departing Washington I had read numerous reports that presented the labor situation entirely differently depending on the orientation of the writer or his organizational affiliation. Fortunately, the Latin America Division and the El Dorado field Station were relatively free of bias. Historically, intellectual detachment and honesty have been critical strengths of CIA. Pressure to view or present the world in a particular way is rarely applied. Objectivity has broken down mainly on those occasions when the Agency has become a major actor in a Covert Action program. At no time in my career was I pressured to report a certain way, even when my information ran counter to the view of the senior level. I was given the latitude and the resources to go about my job and get a handle on the labor problem.

Before departing for Latin America, I had met a senior officer in Washington who had worked on Soviet and Communist labor in the

Far East for several years. He had helped identify young and dynamic labor leaders, who had the necessary courage to challenge the very aggressive Communists, and he had provided covert assistance in the form of funds and guidance to these democratic labor leaders. By the time he returned to Headquarters, the Agency Operations had succeeded to the point that the Communists were reduced in strength and no longer able to threaten the political stability of that key Asian nation. I listened carefully to his advice. Rather than start in an action mode, he said, I should go out and get some reporting sources in El Dorado. From his own experience, he knew that defining the problem or challenge was the first key step, and penetrating the labor sector in a data collection role was critical.

A great strength of CIA that distinguishes it from other collectors of information is that it has recruited reporting sources called "agents" who respond to CIA direction — they do what they are asked or told to do and not what they feel like doing. Agents allow for disciplined collection or action; they make predictability possible; they are essential to Intelligence professionalism; without them we have an unguided vacuum system sucking in all kinds of material without discrimination.

My first real agent, a good one in many ways, had been recruited before my arrival in El Dorado. "Miguel" was, in Intelligence parlance, a "principal agent" with sufficient cover, mobility and talent to handle sub-sources who reported to him but did not necessarily know of Agency involvement or sponsorship. My agent, Miguel, both collected information and often acted on it. In other words, he combined roles the Agency usually likes to keep separate. This dual, and sometimes conflicting, function could be dangerous for CIA. Fortunately, Miguel was not our only source of information.

I met with Miguel in safehouse meetings because his situation would have been compromised if he were seen with an American. My own cover allowed me to meet all kinds of people in El Dorado, but not a labor activist with Miguel's high public profile. We met two to three times a week in the evening hours or during lunch when the local populace generally stopped work for two hours. All meetings with Miguel were prearranged, but the local security situation did not demand that we use fancy spy techniques or communications gear. We merely had to make certain that we were not observed together, and the best way to accomplish that was to rent an apartment in the city in a building that had multiple entrances and exits. This I managed to do through a local realtor, who assumed that I was looking for a pad to meet with a girlfriend, as was often the case with local businessmen. Meeting a male in such an apartment could draw attention to a safehouse, however, because of the general disdain in Latin American countries for homosexuality. Fortunately, my safehouse was located in a very large building where people tended to be indifferent to their neighbors because many of them were concerned only that they not be caught with another man's wife or girlfriend.

It became very clear in time that Miguel's value as an objective reporter suffered enormously from his own involvement in the labor movement and from his dreams, which colored his perceptions and his reporting. Given a choice, I will always work with the dreamer; I tend to be optimistic by nature too. At the same time, you have to be painstakingly diligent to keep from getting caught up in the enthusiasm of such an individual. Early in our relationship, I found myself accepting Miguel's explanation of the situation in El Dorado labor. He did not underestimate the strength of the Marxist forces nationally, but he did point to some individuals and organizations that he said could effectively challenge and defeat the Communists if they received our support.

As a CIA Covert Action officer, I was pleased with this information. I was convinced that if the Agency at least matched the material support the far left received from the Soviets and Cubans, the democratic forces were bound to win. After all, who would choose bondage over freedom? But, as I learned, the situation was more complex. What I did not appreciate at the time was that the Agency's wins in Europe and Asia were facilitated by the historical table-clearing of the Second World War. Even the Communists had to start from scratch in those areas not conquered by the Soviet Army. In Latin America, by contrast, the Communists had penetration roots in labor stretching back decades; essentially, CIA was the newcomer, not the KGB.

Miguel's Covert Action role soon began to take precedence over his role as a source of labor information. Through Miguel, we provided his labor contacts financial support and encouraged them in the national political election to get behind the Presidential candidate selected for secret support by the U.S. Government. "Our man" won an impressive victory. The electoral support of Miguel's labor contacts had very little noticeable effect on the election, but it helped Miguel expand his influence in labor by identifying him as a source of tangible support to non-Communist labor leaders. In time, he became a force in the labor field, so we made plans, after the election and the victory euphoria had subsided, to see how far Miguel could challenge the Marxists on their historic turf — in the fields, factories and mines of El Dorado.

Despite all the countless hours spent with Miguel and the support being channeled through him to non-Communist labor elements, I found in my second year that I was not a great deal closer to having a firm fix on the labor situation. Certainly, from reading several papers a day and moving about the capital city and surrounding region as an interested academic, I had come to know the names of the principal players and organizations. But, if I wanted to have a substantial effect on the labor situation and not just engage in the game of passing out American taxpayer dollars, I would have to dig deeper. How could the Marxists be displaced unless we knew where they were vulnerable and where they were not? I needed solid information, and I soon found and recruited two new sources to help me collect data to start filling in the blanks that Miguel, in a perpetual activist mode, never seemed to fill. One of the new labor sources was a government functionary with direct access to official labor files and information. The other was a social activist working within the central office of a major labor organization and who had access to the files and the leadership. I met both of them during my first year in El Dorado, as I conducted my academic cover research.

Well into my second year, then, I began doing what I should have done on arrival or even before I was sent to El Dorado as a Covert Action officer — I began pulling together a very serious and comprehensive study of the El Dorado labor situation. I wanted to use the examination to identify targets for covert Operations, especially in union elections in which we could funnel covert support to help non-Communists take over leadership from the Marxists. Good research tends to be painstaking and tedious; secret research goes very slowly. The sources, each working independently and without knowledge of the other, gathered the information at odd hours when they could be assured they would not be disturbed or discovered. They had to write down large amounts of data scattered throughout carelessly-maintained government and union files. The Xerox had not yet come to El Dorado. They then had to deliver the information undetected to me, an American with no ostensible reason for having data that constituted a wiring diagram of the country's trade union movement. For both sources I had to arrange discreet meetings for the passage of data from them to me and payments in cash from me to them for their time, the risk they took in working secretly with the Agency, and to complete their transitions from colleagues to agents. An agent, like an employee, accepts direction, is expected to perform a specified service, and is compensated for the effort and final results.

Does the payment or acceptance of money or its equivalent mean that an agent is categorized now as a mercenary, an unprincipled individual who rents himself out to the highest bidder and whose central motivation is based in venality? Is every agent a whore, so to speak, held by the Agency in low regard because a payment may be made as part of the arrangement? Not by a long shot. Like the rest of humanity, some agents will not take a dime; some are greedy through and through. Spectacular Intelligence sources who directly contribute information of national significance to the United States may be paid handsomely, be resettled with a new identity, and have their children's education paid by CIA at expensive universities here or in Europe. Other agents, depending on what constitutes a living wage in their country, may be working for as little as a few thousand dollars a year. Most of the time, an agent cooperates with an Intelligence service for more than one reason; it may be the character and persuasiveness of the recruiting CIA officer or some other intangible that has nothing to do with the dollar. Each of my agents was paid and each also exhibited a strong aversion for the thought that his country might succumb to the Marxists. I recruited them based on the latter but I also saw to it that they were compensated as a way of motivating them to spend evenings poring through dingy files when they could have gone home to their families.

One reason CIA needs scrupulously-honest Operations Officers is that most espionage and Covert Action work is done on a cash basis. The clandestine agent is paid in local currency. Often, there is no signed receipt. In the El Dorado election operation, we had paid huge sums of cash to our action agents; those funneling money to the Presidential campaign staff had to use shopping bags. I was channeling pretty sizeable amounts each month to Miguel quite apart from the election campaign. Carrying large amounts of currency was risky, of course, and I had become attuned to the problem shortly after arriving in El Dorado. As was my habit growing up, I carried my own cash in my wallet in my rear pants pocket. It was only a short while before my naiveté proved costly; sure enough, I was fleeced one evening as I rode a standing-room-only bus. Fortunately, my loss was entirely personal. I was already in the habit of carrying Agency-related materials inside my shirt, including the official funds that I carried for the agent Operations. I had lost my own hundred dollars, almost a week's pay, but not Uncle Sam's five thousand, which was tucked away safely next to my liver.

I learned then and there to be a little more cautious with my own possessions, but my overriding fear was that somehow I would lose something related to CIA Operations. The fear of professional humiliation would have been painful, but, more importantly, the security and safety of a vulnerable local agent could be the result of any loss or theft. That I was serving under deep cover outside the official community added to this sense of insecurity. I could not return after each agent meeting to the safety of the CIA Station and lock sensitive materials in guarded vaults. Most of the time in El Dorado, I had more Agency money in my possession than I could justify as an academic, and often I had reports or other written materials that could compromise my local agents. Security was a serious matter, and I developed physical security habits that endured throughout my career. Paranoia had become a professional necessity, as had endurance; NOC life had serious disadvantages for me and my family.

The emotion that comes to mind when I recall the service under deep cover was the sense of isolation and loneliness, of being "out in the cold" with partial and occasional feelings of being part of the larger team. Although I would eventually spend seven years or 25 percent of my career outside the official family as a deep cover officer, it was not a condition that was natural for me or for most Intelligence professionals.

One of the recurring myths about the spy business, fostered often by CIA officials who never left Washington, is that people in Intelligence have a *passion for anonymity,* that they prefer the solitary life, as in James Fenimore Cooper's *The Spy.* The myth suggests that CIA Clandestine Service officers have no problem at all serving in the silent service of their country, never to be recognized or to be publicly acknowledged, even in death. This is nonsense. The members of CIA's Clandestine Service are as strong a collection of people in need of recognition as any group in or out of government. For reasons of professional necessity, they are prepared to eschew public credit or recognition. It is a mistake to think, however, that they do not care who gets to be Division Chief or Station Chief, who gets promoted and who gets credit for a successful operation, who gets to sit next to the DCI at a dinner, or who gets to eat in the seventh floor executive dining room at CIA Headquarters.

CIA people do a lot of spectacular things around the world with only limited, controlled credit going to the operators. But the organization is not an order of monks, and deep cover service that takes place away from the Station proper and the American flagpole, runs against the grain of most Agency officers. For that reason, the NOC career track has had the highest resignation rate within the DDO Career Service, which historically had one of the lowest attrition rates in government. Of the several young officers from my training class who went abroad under Nonofficial Cover, all but one came back inside or resigned after the first tour. They had felt unconnected. The several personal and administrative irritants of being outside proved far less decisive than the psychological need, largely unmet under deep cover, to be and feel like part of something. For very sound reasons, CIA does not hire loners. Intelligence is very much a social business, and Intelligence Officers are by nature social animals.

Professional support, including good operational guidance and good feedback, helps the NOC Officer make a better contribution to the Station program as well as feel like part of the Station team. My first inside officer in El Dorado would meet me for substantive sessions and he freely shared the direction of the Station program, his own work, and how I might be able to help. He lived and breathed the El Dorado political situation, and no one at the time had a more comprehensive understanding of its political dynamics, players, and problems.

For things administrative and personal, on the other hand, he was an unmitigated disaster — for himself and for anyone unlucky enough to rely on him for support. It wasn't that he didn't care; he just happened to consider the substantive Intelligence and operational matters so much more important than the administrative nuts and bolts that he habitually neglected the latter. "Minor" matters such as getting paid, receiving medical insurance support, and getting reimbursed for official expenses were hit or miss. He would usually show up for scheduled safehouse meetings, but he was generally anywhere from a half-hour to two hours late. He would take notes on scraps of paper, napkins, and brown paper bags, later having difficulty deciphering his own scribbling. When he finally departed El Dorado after performing well in political Operations, envelopes with cash reimbursements were found throughout his cluttered safe drawers and no one knew to whom they belonged. "Say, Tom, does the figure $134.75 ring a bell? Maybe that one is yours." Oh well, you seldom find a person who does everything well, but God help the deep cover officer depending on an inside officer who is a walking administrative nightmare.

Bonnie, meanwhile, had her own problems to deal with. Her days were long and lonely, isolated from the Agency Station personnel, outside of the American business community, and thousands of miles away from her own family. Had we not lived in the Third World, some relatives may have taken the time to visit us, but El Dorado was not a place to which middle class Americans would ever consider going on vacation in those years.

Bonnie concentrated on household chores for the most part, which kept her busy but did not relieve the sense of being out there by ourselves. I was gone all day into the evening, some days getting home for lunch but more than likely arriving home at 9:00 or 10:00 PM as I attended to Agency business. Bonnie had to shop every day due to the limited refrigeration and quick spoilage of most foods. The shopping itself took her to several stores, each specializing in some single thing such as meat, vegetables, bread and so on. Not having a car, she would walk to the local stores and then come home by cab or bus if the bundles were too heavy.

All vegetables had to be soaked in iodine tablets to kill bacteria and to avoid dysentery. We weren't always successful. Our oldest daughter Julie came down first with the worst case and, for the few months it lasted, we used every available medicine and home remedy and juggled her diet to keep her from dehydrating. One evening, Bonnie found a lump in Julie's stomach, and the following week she was hospitalized for a hernia brought on by the severity of the diarrhea. The surgery, performed in a local hospital, went well and for the next month Bonnie had to keep her in a stroller during the day to slow down her activity and prevent the surgical wound from opening.

After a few weeks in the country, Bonnie became ill, and she too was ordered to bed while three active children roamed the house under the erratic care of our live-in maid, a young, unsophisticated girl from the countryside who required careful watching lest she give the kids a witch's brew or other home remedy of questionable value and safety. The high infant mortality rate, almost entirely from dysentery and poor sanitation, was above one in ten. A critical dehydration stage could be reached within twenty-four hours once diarrhea began. The two months Bonnie had to remain in bed for uncontrolled bleeding was the longest such period in her life, and the doctors tried every locally-available medicine to get her better. None worked. Finally, a doctor sent away to the States for a medicine that had her back to health in a week.

Being on the outside as NOCs, we were not in a position to get special help from the Station and, very soon, Bonnie began wondering what we were doing out there unprotected with three little children and no one to turn to for help. For reasons of cover and security, the Agency cannot intervene to help officers under deep cover in most medical and other emergencies.

Our first Christmas season was tough. Bonnie felt very lonely for home, for the crisp winter feeling of New England, for English-speaking radio and neighbors, but particularly for her Mom and Dad, who were getting on in years. Bonnie was struggling to pick up some Spanish to reach a survival level. I had managed to get a foundation in Spanish before we left the States, but Bonnie had not had a single class of Spanish, which made her life a genuine struggle. Try discussing the merits and desirability of surgery on a small child when you have only a smattering of Spanish and the local doctor's English is limited to "Good day, how are you these day (sic)?"

Even shopping for the kids was a chore because the toys were poorly crafted and used paints and parts that were a safety hazard and more expensive than we could imagine or afford. Early in our second year, Bonnie bumped into some English-speaking women while out at the supermarket and learned about a local American women's club. Through me she met a few wives of my El Dorado social contacts but had little in common with them. Most came from well-off families and spent their time grooming themselves, shopping for clothes and frivolously socializing. Unlike American mothers, the local ladies tended to leave the raising of their kids to maids, and someone like Bonnie who took care of our children, was considered uninteresting and backward. Her new American friends were, for the most part, from the business community, and many had spent as many as two or three decades living outside the United States. Initially, she was relieved to be in touch with women who shared her background, but in time she had to limit her American contacts because of my own cover limitations.

After the better part of a year without a car, dealing with everyday problems and even medical emergencies on the public transportation system, Bonnie reached the end of her rope and told me we had to have a car or she was going back to the States. A small European car in those days sold for about $6,000, and an American car for four times that amount. So, there was no way we would be able to buy one on our own. Our annual salary was only about $7,500. Bonnie was also getting wise to our lack of diplomatic status or protection; everyone else in the Station had a personal car they could sell at a huge profit as well as a government car they used for their official activities. To make matters worse, the wife of my inside contact came by one evening and tried to talk her out of her demand for a car. Bonnie continued to raise hell; twenty-five years old or not, she knew we were being poorly treated and I was just too wrapped up in my work to see that I was being a sap. Within forty-eight hours we had the funds for a car and finally got some freedom to get around town and live a little more normally as a family away from home.

Towards the end of her pregnancy, the local doctor told Bonnie she would not need his services at delivery, only the help of a midwife. Again my otherwise gentle Bonnie drew the line and demanded that he be in the hospital when the baby arrived. Her unyielding stance was rewarding: Elizabeth was born with the umbilical cord wrapped twice around her neck, and it took a great deal of skill to prevent death or damage as the doctor dealt with the complications of her delivery.

With four children under five, two of them in diapers, we decided to move to a newer but smaller home before the next winter, so that we would have central heat and a telephone — two basic amenities in the States that had become luxuries for us in El Dorado. Getting away from the first house allowed us to escape a permanently-fluid septic system that never behaved in the rainy season and often left us without flushing capability. I have been without lights, without heat and without water, but I can say in all candor that being without running or flushing water is the worst of all conditions.

If life's quality had diminished for us, it was nothing compared to the poverty around us in El Dorado. There were poor people and beggars all over the city, and in the evenings poor women and their little children frequently rang our gate bell, asking for bread or milk or a coin or two. One of the regular visitors had children about the same ages as ours, and even though Bonnie and I would sometimes wonder how we had gotten into our own fix being outside as NOCs, it took a simple ring of the front bell to remind us how fortunate we really were when we looked at the rest of mankind. Our maid would go crazy — the poor are not too sympathetic when it comes to their own sometimes — as we warmed up some food and gave them a meal and some clothes.

One especially-cold evening, Bonnie gave a shivering four-year-old boy a very nice winter jacket. A couple of nights later they were back, and the boy was shivering as before, with no sign of the jacket. Bonnie asked why he was not wearing it. The mother said she was "saving it for Sundays" but my guess was that the old man at home had peddled it for a bottle of wine or two. It was very common in El Dorado for the men to barter U.S.-supplied milk for wine. We never did see that jacket again, though the family kept coming back.

Our own children remember little of El Dorado; the oldest was under seven when we returned to the States. Bonnie cared for them extremely well; she knew the health hazards and, at the expense to her own freedom, spent the better part of four years raising the children herself. Not a very liberated thing to have done, but I was grateful to come home with all of them healthy and well, and I give all the credit to Bonnie, who wore out two medical paperbacks diagnosing illnesses, often before the doctors themselves.

The children's education was excellent. They sat in a one-room, three-grade school where an English lady taught them in a pleasant but no-nonsense atmosphere. Their most vivid recollection from El Dorado was the poor children coming by the gate of our home, conning the kids into handing them their toys. Ours also engaged for the first time in conspiracy, colluding to pour into the planter the terrible-tasting powdered milk. At their young ages, life itself seemed simple, and they returned from El Dorado on the old-fashioned side compared to children in the States, where events were churning as the Sixties got into midstream.

As Americans living abroad we had our own distinctive social problems. But as a CIA NOC I added to the complexity of a family living in a foreign country. We always had to be conscious of my cover. The single greatest threat to a CIA officer's cover does not come from the KGB, but from other Americans. Their intent is not malicious, however. Our unparalleled concern for occupation as the determining factor in measuring status and self-worth drives us to probe our fellow countrymen about their professional positions. When Americans talk about a "successful" individual, they usually mean a person who has risen in a profession or organization and, very probably, accumulated a good deal of material wealth in a short time. That is why the tenth high school reunion is such a drag and why the thirtieth can be so much fun. After three decades, people generally have attained a more wholesome and realistic view of life.

Non-Americans tend not to question what we do for a living unless we raise the subject ourselves. By contrast, meet an American anywhere in the world, under any circumstances — in bathing suit on the beach — and that fellow American wants to know right away where you work or what you do for a living. He wants to measure the new acquaintance right away against the yardstick of occupational success to determine whether it is worth the time and trouble to cultivate him. Is this a possible client? A competitor, maybe? Is this younger person doing better than he? Does this older person need a new sales manager? After seven years under deep cover and three more running a deep cover program, I can testify without hesitation that only Americans do this, one reason I am sure why unemployment is next to death in its psychological impact on Americans. But, when trying to live abroad with less-than-perfect cover, the last thing an Intelligence Officer wants to run into on an operational mission is some fellow American homing in right after the handshake and chipping away at his cover story.

The solution for CIA, of course, is to make the cover as substantial as possible, even though perfect cover can be arranged and afforded in only a very limited number of cases. Nor do you always want thorough, perfect cover. Allen Dulles, had he been blessed with excellent cover in Switzerland in World War II, would never have penetrated the German general staff, and the German volunteer spies would never have been able to find him. Perfect cover also results in low productivity, which runs entirely at odds with another fundamental American (and CIA) tendency and weakness: our need to produce tangible results, not merely in this year but in this quarter.

We Americans are basically too impatient for the long-term "sleeper" Operations for which the Soviets and British are famous. More often than not, when Agency management has been inspired to take a long-term approach to some intractable problem (be it Nonofficial Cover, Counterintelligence, Counterterrorism or Counter-Narcotics Operations), along comes some beancounting manager two or three years into the activity who makes a name for himself by pulling the plug and showing how hard-nosed and cost-effective he can be. It is crucial that we be aware of the kinds of tendencies we Americans have, as we conduct Intelligence Operations. It takes a great deal of resolve, and even special effort, to go against our own nature. Some things we cannot do, or at least cannot do well, because we are what we are.

The inconvenience and difference of being under Nonofficial Cover was perhaps most apparent when we went through the process of getting the required local identity card, an internal document issued to assist in law enforcement and internal security. It was a tortuous process no diplomat would tolerate. The bureau that issued the identity card was located not far from downtown, in a working-class neighborhood of El Dorado's capital city. Bonnie and I got ourselves and the children up, fed and dressed so we could catch the 6:45 AM bus that would connect with another bus to get us to the identity card office by 8:00 AM by which time one had to be in line to be processed on that visit. After the line reached a certain length, officials told all latecomers to go home and come back again some other time.

Our children were three years, two years and ten months old when we began the identification process, so it was a real juggling act just getting them on the bus and into seats or on our laps for the long bus ride across town. Well, we made it on time into the identity card line on the first try, and we moved along this line for two hours before we were finally given some forms to fill out, were photographed, paid the fees and were told to return in two weeks for the next steps in the process. Meanwhile, we had alternated holding the baby, changing his diaper, and getting the older two to and from the bathroom. We left the bureau, caught a bus home and arrived in the early afternoon. The kids needed naps and we each needed a stiff drink.

Two weeks later we got the children up before dawn, went through the same logistical game and got back to the bureau before the eight o'clock cutoff. This time, we still did not get our cards. Instead, we had to sign the cards under the pictures for ourselves and the children and have our fingerprints placed on the back. Why couldn't we get the ID cards on this day? They had to be laminated and that required yet a third visit by all of us to sign for receipt of the completed cards. So, home we trekked, wondering whether the special NOC officer premium pay of 10 percent — $750 per year and taxable — had been designed just to cover this identity card process. Two weeks later, it was up again before dawn, a stroll with three kids to the corner, a trip across town on the bus, and another wait in the line. Over an hour later, it was our turn and we went to the window. Bonnie was holding the baby; I had a grip on our other two little ones who, by this time, had lost all interest in waiting rooms and identity-card lines.

I gave our names, expecting the lady to give us the cards and keep us in compliance with El Dorado law, as all good NOCs must do. (It is okay to get caught for espionage, but a NOC should not have problems over an administrative screw up.) The lady didn't bat an eyelash. Gilligan begins with G, Senora Eugenia took care of all Gs, and this day she was out sick. "You'll have to come back next week," the lady said, calling for the next number in line. Wait a minute! Why couldn't she get them from the files? "Because all of Sra. Eugenia's work is locked in her desk and no one is allowed to touch it." It took yet another trip to get the ID cards needed for driver's licenses and a multitude of other registrations and processes for schooling, opening bank accounts, registering at hotels, and the like.

By contrast, our inside Station personnel had excellent homes, telephones, central heat, imported American cars, which they sold every two years for profits of $15,000 to $20,000 (more or less $100,000 to $125,000 in today's money), a commissary subsidized by the U.S. Government and that brought in American groceries (local corn flakes turned to mush as soon as hit by the milk, making our children cry or gag or both) and use of the official mail to receive presents and clothes from the States or order items from catalogs catering to overseas diplomats. To make things worse for the NOCs, the basic administrative support we received from the Station was appallingly bad. It delayed getting me money for an operational car, even though there was no cover problem whatsoever. El Dorado citizens saw all Americans as rich enough to buy a car. Because the Station did not tell me what our housing allowance was, we rented a substandard place when we could have gotten a house with telephone and heat right away.

My inside contact kept my administrative situation murky. The Agency even came out with a much-needed dental plan that we did not hear about until after the closing date for registration. When Bonnie was ready to begin taking Spanish lessons at the local language institute, we asked for the same reimbursement for which inside Station wives were eligible. We were told that, for that particular program, "we were not part of the Station" as though deep cover spouses did not need to communicate in the language of the host country. (Some years later, when I was serving as Senior Training Officer for the Clandestine Service, I was able to get the Agency Language Program adapted to guarantee Agency-paid foreign language instruction for the spouses of all personnel going overseas, whether inside the Station or outside under Nonofficial cover).

The inside officers were making tens of thousands of dollars at the end of their tours, sufficient to make large down payments on homes back in McLean, Virginia, and we were struck more than once that greed at times knows no limits. Diplomats not only sold their cars at huge profits, sometimes twice in a four-year assignment, but they also sold off all their household goods and even used clothing at inflated prices of two to five times the original prices. The windfall profits overseas personnel made in the late 1940s and the 1950s created an unfortunate mindset back in Washington; it would take almost two decades for the Washington-based administrators to realize that things had changed markedly for the worse. By the late 1960s, CIA Officers were not living in the better homes in town; they were scaling back to very modest homes and eventually would find themselves in modest apartments, as is the case in most cities in the world.

Greed sometimes took on absurd dimensions. My inside colleague, while preparing to leave the Station, offered me a chance to buy a used American swing set. By then, we had four children and were pleased at the prospect of having a swing set in the walled-in yard of our second home. The swing was not in the greatest condition; a Sears catalog special, it had originally cost around thirty dollars and had served five children for three years of fairly tough use. The price offered to us colleagues: "Only one hundred and fifty dollars." We passed on the swing set but did buy some American baby food from them for our new infant, stunned that a fellow Agency officer departing with tens of thousands of dollars in profit from car and furniture sales could be so venal. Within 24 hours, our daughter was violently ill; the baby food, which had been brought by them from an assignment three years earlier in Central America, was rancid and had caused food poisoning.

The few professional complaints I had (besides my inside contact's administrative laxity and habitual lateness for meetings) had to be balanced, then, against the Agency's poor support of outside personnel serving under deep cover. A few years later, when I was in charge of all deep cover personnel in Latin America Division, I remembered my prior experiences. One of the nicest things ever said about me officially was in a performance appraisal written six years later in another overseas Station and was meant as a criticism: "This officer is too sympathetic to the Nonofficial Cover personnel with whom he works." Should one wonder why?

At the risk of being sexist, I would note that if reincarnation is the way things work and I come back in a future life as a deep cover officer, I will make one demand only: make certain that my inside Station contact is a female. Women in the Agency (and in general in society, I believe) tend to be more considerate of others, more nurturing, less self-centered and more inclined to take a few minutes to jot down a note for a colleague than their male counterparts. This is particularly true with regard to the aggressive males CIA hires as Operations Officers and who, for the most part, have little patience for any activity that does not directly contribute to their own professional goals or careers. Hand-holding a deep cover officer who may need a little attention is viewed by most of the guys as a waste of their precious time. By contrast,

CIA females have shown more patience and balance, making them far better at working with deep cover personnel.

My second inside contact, who arrived as I was in my third year under NOC, was an administrative gem, a thorough and competent Operations Officer who turned things around and made the last half of my tour, compared with the difficult beginnings, a genuine pleasure. One problem for me was that this officer had increasingly grown skeptical about Covert Action Operations in general, as a result of his experience in two prior field assignments in Latin America. His problem did not at all seem to be broadly philosophical, or concern the rightness of CA. Rather, he seemed to feel that it had become a big charade, an end in itself wasting a great deal of energy and resources.

As a result of his waning interest in Covert Action, I pretty much defined my own responsibilities and ran my own operation. I went about the business of seeing whether we really could make a dent in the Marxist control of El Dorado's labor movement, relying heavily on a study I had completed after about a year's work and which was disseminated to the official American community there. The study showed that the Communists and Socialists controlled most unions in strategic sectors of the economy. Essentially, their forty-year program had solidified their grip on El Dorado labor. The study showed also that Marxist hegemony at the local level was much more extensive than we had once believed. In keeping with the broad view of those involved in the political elections, U.S. Government attention had been focused on labor at the national, political level. That the Communists' power was equally compelling at the factory level was not good news. For one thing, it meant that no single action, no quick fix, would solve the labor problem created by almost a half-century of Communist effort, training, sacrifice and support from Moscow.

At the time, the Johnson Administration was increasingly turning its attention from the Kennedy Administration's commitment to Latin America to the growing problems in Southeast Asia. As this change spread throughout the government, the Agency showed signs of lessening its commitment in the region. The first Operations to go were Covert Action Operations known as "nation building" activities that required many years of commitment and were not as readily defined as, say, an election, which you either won or lost in a short period of time.

Using the labor information that had been collected and verified independently, we channeled funding support through Miguel to non-

Communist union leaders in local elections where past voting patterns suggested there might be an opening to displace the Marxists. Over time, it became clear that we were making little headway; we would need a decade or so to begin to have any substantial effect on El Dorado labor. With almost all inside Station Operations Officer assignments running two to three years, on average, it would be impossible to bring any such program to a successful conclusion within the tour of duty of those responsible for Station Operations management.

We were out of gas in El Dorado just as we were exhausting our capabilities in other parts of the Third World in our attempt to make the kind of profound social and structural changes that had been so successful elsewhere in the world. In Europe and Japan, we had been successful but it was clearly the overt strength of America that had been the driving force. CIA's covert contribution supplemented the overt effort by neutralizing the destructive efforts of the Soviets' clandestine organs. In El Dorado, the U.S. Government had no such strong overt program beyond the ineffectual pouring in of AID money from the top, an approach which swelled the host government national bureaucracy in the capital city. Such U.S.G. funds had little trickle-down effect and seldom got to productive parts of the El Dorado economy to increase output and improve general living standards.

By late 1966, the Station concluded rightly that there was little sense in continuing a clandestine effort in the field of El Dorado labor. Someone likened what we were attempting to trying to heat up a cauldron of water with lighted matches, one at a time. The job was too big and the Covert Action instrument too small. Similar conclusions were being reached around the rest of Latin America and, by the time I completed my El Dorado assignment and returned to Washington in early 1967, the earlier Headquarters support for such Operations had all but disappeared. Within Latin America Division, there was a renewed ascendancy of the Operations Officers who were either indifferent or cool to Covert Action. The Agency was, in a sense, getting back to basic FI Collection Operations and trimming its own sails.

This in good part reflected the orientation and preference of Richard Helms, who ascended to the DCI position in June 1966 after a career in CIA that had him serving only in Headquarters and removed from the major Covert Action programs that had produced both spectacular career ascents and abrupt flameouts for the CA Warriors. Helms saw himself as a "prudent professional." As disinclined as he was to promote CA, it would be CA that would nail him seven years later.

The other Area Divisions, with one exception, were also pulling back from CA. The exception was Asia Division which, by 1967, was totally embroiled in trying to help win the unwinnable War. Since the French were defeated at Dien Bien Phu in 1954, Vietnam and eventually Laos and Cambodia had been kept in a basic state of equilibrium, or low-intensity conflict, to use the more recent academic buzz word, by CIA and a relatively small band of paramilitary officers.

As Defense Secretary McNamara, under Presidents Kennedy and Johnson, expanded American Military involvement and converted it into an overt war, logic suggests that possibly the Agency's clandestine involvement in Southeast Asia might lessen. Instead, CIA expanded its commitment of people and resources so that Vietnam became in time the largest overseas Agency program. During the Johnson Administration period especially, Government employees either supported the Vietnam War effort fully, and without question, or faced professional dismissal or oblivion. DCI Helms probably had no more appetite for that theater of Operations than he had for Covert Action in general. But, being the career survivor that he was (CIA had been his only real job), he knew what happened to DCI John McCone. McCone was forced out because he had brought to the Vietnam War the same perspicacity and integrity he had displayed at the time of the Cuban missile crisis — again he challenged conventional Washington wisdom, this time by suggesting that the bombing of North Vietnam was not working. Although there was widespread knowledge within the Agency that Southeast Asia was "going down the tubes" — the most commonly used expression at the time in the CIA halls and cafeteria — CIA institutional support for the War continued unabated.

With Covert Action otherwise in decline within the Area Divisions, the Agency in early 1967 still had its array of CA programs being run by IO Division. Within sixty days of my return to the States, that would all change and, when it did, I was glad to be out of El Dorado. The radical-leftist U.S. magazine, *Ramparts*, published articles that blew the cover of International Organization Division's support of the international democratic student movement through funding of America's National Student Association. This might have been a single, isolated embarrassment if the Covert Action Warriors had been as diligent with tradecraft as they had been resourceful in their operational programs, which still stand as a credit to CIA's defense of freedom. The *Ramparts* flap was spurred not by the KGB or the GRU. Instead, our own *New York Times* and *Washington Post* went searching for other loose strings that would unravel the whole fabric of IO Division's Operations. The Soviets could not have done a better job.

I earlier alluded to their operational weakness, namely the tendency of the Covert Action Warriors to cut corners in their haste to run Operations. This time, rather than building solid protective insulation, or *compartmentation*, between the dozens of CA Operations being conducted around the globe, IO Division linked them all through the U.S. foundations that channeled CIA funds to the various anti-Communist organizations — some leaders of which were unaware that they had been living off Clandestine Service money for years. Inattention to operational detail, and sheer laziness, compromised dozens of organizations, hundreds of foreign agents, and even deep cover officers like me who had been funded through the identical foundation as some high-profile anti-Communist front.

I departed El Dorado weeks before the IOD cover collapse took place, and I was relieved that I had not come back to the States with my cover fig leaf on fire. As it was, our return trip was a delight after five years under Nonofficial Cover. We flew to a neighboring country and jumped on an American steamer, which hosted several dozen passengers as it moved principally cargo between the United States and Latin America. Two weeks at sea was a great way to unwind; no phone calls or Operations or clandestine meetings to worry about. The days when one could travel officially by boat were numbered, and I was determined that Bonnie and the children were going to have at least this first-class experience after several years of substandard living.

We had left South America in summer and arrived twelve days later in New York to blowing snow and the sounds of Christmas carols, giving the children the best of both worlds. Tommy was then six, Julie five, Stephen four, and El Dorado-born Elizabeth, two.

For me and the family, the five years under deep cover had been a mixed affair. Professionally, I had learned and done some things that would be very helpful in later assignments. I had participated in some Operations that had succeeded and others that had failed. My confidence in the Agency, especially its ability to support its Operations Officers under Nonofficial Cover, suffered considerable erosion. At the time I saw this not as a systemic weakness but rather the shortcomings of individuals. As I was making the transformation back to the inside from deep cover, I severed all links that had been established with contacts and friends in El Dorado. This seemed to be required for cover reasons because I wanted to be assigned to some other part of Latin America fairly soon, this time inside a Station, and I did not want any of the barnacles from the NOC years to attach themselves to the new vessel. This amounted to cutting a large hole in our lives as we resumed life back in the Washington area. It was, in some respects, as though the previous five years under Nonofficial Cover had not taken place. Sort of like having been in Sing-Sing Prison.

7

Back Inside

FIVE YEARS after departing CIA Headquarters under deep cover from the old "Temporary Buildings" along the Tidal Basin in Washington, I reported to the new Agency Headquarters building in Langley, Virginia. Not only had the Agency moved most of its people several miles out into the Virginia countryside to a campus-like setting along the Potomac, but also by early 1967 CIA had undergone other observable changes. For one thing, I recognized very few faces as I reported back to the Latin America Division; practically everyone I had worked with before leaving Washington had retired or moved on to other assignments, most in the direction of overseas but a fair number went to other government agencies altogether. In a personal sense within the Agency itself, it was like beginning again.

I was working with people who had no idea why I had been sent under deep cover five years earlier to El Dorado; nor did they display any particular interest. I saw for the first time something one would not expect to find in an Intelligence organization: the tendency of people to ignore the past and to have no tradition or system to learn from our experiences, good or bad. This in part was a function of being under unrelenting pressure to deal with immediate problems and crises. Such pressure has the partial advantage of keeping one focused and practical and responsive, while it makes peering into the future seem a luxury and looking at the past downright frivolous. The nature of CIA as an active, thoroughly-American institution was beginning to unfold before me, but it would take the cumulative demonstration of such congenital shortsightedness to realize that, in the Intelligence race, the Agency is better compared to a 100-yard dash than to a marathon. As brief as this assignment was in my career overall, it represented a turning point in my own Agency education. Part of that education involved a South American nation which would profoundly affect our citizens' ethical view of CIA — the Republic of Chile.

Over at IO Division, where I had received Labor Operations training back in 1961, the roof came falling in within a few weeks of my return.

Their worldwide network was in the throes of death. In the wake of the *Ramparts* flap, a Commission headed by Undersecretary of State Nicholas Katzenbach directed that "no Federal agency shall provide any covert financial assistance or support, direct or indirect, to any of the nation's educational or private voluntary organizations." So-called "surge funding" was authorized to inject survival money intended to ease the transition for many organizations that had come to rely on Agency support but, on short notice, had to find new sources of funds or go out of business. Some managed to survive on their own, even with the public stigma of prior covert CIA association. Others, unfortunately, went belly up, like dead fish in the water. A few, notably *Radio Free Europe* (which beamed news into Eastern Europe) and *Radio Liberty* (which broadcast into Russia itself), made the transition with little difficulty; the U.S. Government began overtly and directly funding them like any other Federal Government program.

The treatment of Agency employees working in the IO Division network under deep cover varied considerably. Some were simply brought inside and resumed their careers without a great deal of pain or slippage. Many, however, were offered little or no opportunity to come back inside, especially those who were not full-fledged Staff Employees with the automatic right to resume their careers back inside. After years of operating footloose and fancy free, the CA officers found few doors open to them in the Area Divisions, which now more than ever were convinced that Covert Action was some form of virus. For many, the only viable option was an assignment to Vietnam; Saigon and the Vietnamese provinces suddenly got an infusion of CA officers whose other practical immediate choice was to resign.

I was in transition myself, getting used to being inside, being back in the States and working on a Headquarters country desk with no real Covert Action program beyond "media Operations" — feeding pro-democracy articles to foreign newspapers to counter the Communist-generated propaganda program in Latin America. So, I went about learning the names of the political parties and key politicians in the two South American countries covered by my desk. I also studied the operational program of each field Station including the assigned goals, clandestine agents, Intelligence production and any other financial or administrative matters of interest to that country's desk.

I had not been assigned to work on El Dorado Station matters. This was in keeping with the tendency of Operations Officers returning from the field to work on an entirely different country desk. Changing country assignments does spare the overseas field Station from having to deal with, or be second-guessed by, knowledgeable officers freshly back from their own Station. There are pluses and minuses in this matter, and under ordinary circumstances it really does not make a great deal of difference. CIA essentially places responsibility and authority in the hands of the overseas Station; the Headquarters desk role is primarily that of supporting the field, not *directing* it, even though every outgoing message is from the DCI — CIA's Director.

By contrast, the KGB does not call its Moscow Headquarters "The Center" without good reason; the KGB Center has historically called the shots on field Operations down to the minutest detail. The reason the CIA Headquarters guides its field Operations with lighter reins than does the KGB is because, unlike the Russians, the Agency trusts its people. As a result, CIA places enormous authority in the hands of the Chief of Station (COS).

The COS position might be the best job in government, as well as one of the most demanding. A COS has three key roles: Intelligence Chief to the American Ambassador, and thus a key player on the way we deal with the host government; representative of the DCI in his role as head of the U.S. Intelligence Community, thereby requiring that the COS coordinate all U.S. civilian and Military Intelligence activities being run in the country; and lastly, director of CIA's own extensive FI, CI and CA Operations in that country. This includes dealing with the host country's own internal security and Foreign Intelligence service, if there is one. This is by no means an iteration of some formal regulations or meaningless organization charts. The COS has, in the real world, the authority and resources to meet those responsibilities, and he generally has on hand the experienced people to do the job. When he does not, additional manpower can be on an airplane headed for his Station within hours of his sending a message for help.

This decentralization of CIA's Clandestine Service is the organization's second most vital strength, coming after the consistently high quality of its field personnel, something attested by outside and independent review including that of initially-wary, even hostile Congressional Staff members, who were favorably impressed in the 1970s when they got their first real look inside the Clandestine Service.

Soon after I got started on the country desk, we planned support for President Johnson's official trip to Punta del Este, Uruguay, where he would meet with the heads of state within the Organization of American States (OAS). CIA's responsibility focused heavily on security, as Headquarters and the Field Stations in Latin America worked in support of the U.S. Secret Service, checking out all kinds of individuals who might be intent upon harming our leader. Working with the Secret Service is always interesting, and for the Punta del Este visit the Service was especially goosey: the meeting would be taking place outside the turf they know best, the United States, and in Fidel Castro's part of the world where numerous Terrorist groups were operating. Terrorist groups exploited the benign security situations of such cities as Montevideo, Mexico City or Paris to support their insurgencies. There, they could make contact with the Soviet and Cuban Embassies, which orchestrated international covert assistance — arranging covert funding, guerrilla training, medical support, and weapons shipments — to an array of anti-American guerrillas throughout Latin America.

Three years later the Uruguayan Tupamaro Terrorists did in fact kidnap and then execute an American Public Safety officer in Montevideo. In 1967, CIA's job was to see that no harm came to President Johnson and, less than four years after the Kennedy assassination, the Secret Service was determined not to lose another President. They made their usually heavy requests for support, which were too much for a modestly-staffed CIA field Station.

Wanting to be certain that the Agency played its supporting role fully, we decided to augment the Station by setting up a temporary base at the beach resort where the conference would take place and where the President would be staying. One of the men we sent on this brief assignment was a young officer who had been two years ahead of me in the same Career Training Program. His name was Philip Agee. Within two years Agee would begin the decades-long personal vendetta against CIA, for which he has become well known. I met him at Headquarters where he read files and cable traffic off and on, playing the hotshot who was going to Punta del Este, Uruguay to make the whole thing work, or so he would have us believe.

I recall going home to my wife one evening and telling her that I had met a real lightweight that week who seemed an expert at playing up to senior managers. My gut reading of Agee was that he was lacking in character. History proved me right. Even back then, Agee was considered an opportunist by his peers. By contrast, he was liked by some superiors, those who received adoration gladly and could not read the troops as well as they could read each other.

Agee entered the Agency in 1957 after graduating from the University of Notre Dame, which had contributed many heroes to America's wars to defend freedom and whose motto is "For God, Country, and Notre

Dame." He resigned twelve years later while assigned to Mexico City as an Operations Officer and in 1971 went to Havana to write, with the assistance of the Castro government, an anti-CIA book he would publish in London four years later.

In the first two dozen pages of his book, Agee related how on three separate occasions he signed sworn Secrecy Agreements to protect, not reveal, CIA classified information learned during his employment. Then, in the course of over six hundred pages of *Inside the Company: CIA Diary*, he described in detail virtually everything he could remember about people, activities and events, with complete disregard for the damage he caused the United States, or the danger to which he exposed Americans and Latin Americans throughout the hemisphere.

He named classmates in the Career Training Program, peers for whom one might expect some degree of camaraderie. He named agents in the field to whom CIA had made assurances of secrecy and protection. He named foreign officials who cooperated with the United States against our worst and most dangerous adversaries, including Terrorists. He revealed very precise operational details, including pseudonyms and aliases used by sensitive personnel and secret sources. Agee described CIA operational projects and goals as well as its procedures for hiring and recruiting agents. He identified every operation he could recall from his field assignments in Ecuador, Uruguay and Mexico. He blew the cover and identities of deep cover agents and he compromised cover mechanisms. He destroyed valuable CIA information collection capabilities and Covert Action mechanisms for confronting the Soviet-supported Communist threat in the region. His damage to Counterintelligence was spectacular, opening the way for the KGB to take its own protective steps that severely damaged America's ability to collect Technical Intelligence on the USSR.

As damaging as Agee's book was, his other anti-CIA activities over the years that followed were in some ways worse. He was able to flaunt the Secrecy Agreements he had signed, to operate freely against the United States from European sanctuaries of our NATO allies, and to return to our country, whose policies he detests, and to collect speaking fees on the nation's campuses — with some funds coming from Public sources. His American passport was eventually canceled with U.S. Supreme Court approval, and he has utilized passports from the Communist Government of Grenada and the Nicaraguan Sandinista Marxists. Yet, no steps were taken toward his prosecution — at a minimum for failing to register as an agent of a foreign power.

In the words of Chapman Pincher, a professional observer and prolific writer on Intelligence, "Since defecting from the CIA in 1969, when he claimed to be disillusioned but was also in financial and woman trouble, [Agee] has become a full-time disseminator of information in the Soviet interest, being extremely adept at exploiting the Western freedom to express his views and the right of residence which would be barred to him under similar circumstances in the Soviet Union." Although Agee clearly is "a blatantly overt agent of influence," to quote Pincher again, the writer is obviously indulging in understatement when he speaks of Agee not being able to have done the same if he worked for the KGB, defected, and then returned to the USSR.

The jacket of Agee's first book sports an outrageous misstatement: "CIA is the most powerful secret police force in the world." With neither police powers nor an internal security responsibility, CIA could not be a Gestapo or a KGB even if it wanted to be, and it is an outright lie to make such a charge. His book sits, nonetheless, on the shelves of public and school libraries throughout the country, in many cases as the only first-hand account on CIA. Agee documents his own deceptions freely in both his first book and even his latest work, *On the Run*. The latter book implies that he was hunted down across Europe by the Agency and other Intelligence services. It is very difficult to know when he is sowing disinformation, but he does make the point that in his first Agency pre-employment polygraph he got away with several "half-truths" and was still hired. On resigning from CIA he made a special point of praising the organization in his letter of resignation when he was clearly disillusioned with it. In discussing the character defects that permit a person like Agee to betray his country, Pincher writes: "To perform his task and survive, the traitor has to be fundamentally dishonest. In addition to being a good actor he must be a consummate liar — a serious defect of character by any standard. Alger Hiss lied so brazenly about his Communist past and his relation with Soviet agents that he was jailed for perjury." And so it goes with Agee and those who ally themselves with the Russians, for whom truth has no moral dimension whatsoever.

Though the lengthy training period provides the Agency an opportunity to evaluate the character of new Operations Officers, unfortunately, the Agee-like chameleons with a natural talent for impressing those who can help them professionally can usually employ that skill with their first trainers and supervisors. They are less able to sustain fictions with their fellow Trainees, with whom they share car-pool, barracks life, three meals a day and hundreds of hours of unstructured free time.

Ironically, the people in CIA best able to spot future turncoats are the other Trainees, who are constrained by tradition and camaraderie from making their gut feelings known to the organization. The Agency itself, not wanting to degenerate into another KGB which spies on its own, also stays away from seeking peer evaluations. If it did not have such a policy, it certainly would have identified Agee (and later Ed Howard, another turncoat Operations Officer, who defected to Moscow in 1985).

There is some feeling even within the Agency that the organization is too restrictive in its selection of people and that we focus too much on the youthful excesses of drugs or sexual experimentation. In some respects that may be true; some of these mistakes reflect immaturity and foolishness, not some fundamental disorder of character. What cannot be dismissed, taken lightly, explained away or tolerated, however, are issues of integrity and honesty. Theft, date rape, academic dishonesty, drug trafficking on any scale, blackmail, a psychosexually-disordered life (whether homosexual or heterosexual) all reflect character defects too fundamental to be risked by an Intelligence service whose *principal vulnerability is not penetration from outside but defection from within* by those to whom sensitive secrets and lives have been entrusted. My brief encounter with Agee in 1967 would not be my last, but my street sense had told me to stay away from him (possibly a reason why I never showed up on his lists in which he tried to expose Agency officers for the purpose of having them, in Agee's own words, "neutralized." This is the same individual who later would erroneously try to blame CIA for the death of Allende in Chile, an effort on his part to "neutralize" the whole organization.

Although I worked days on Uruguayan-Paraguayan matters, I spent my nights in 1967 working on Chile, completing a thesis on Frei's economic stabilization program to meet a Master's Degree requirement at Cornell University. This was entirely my personal undertaking; Federal law, although it permits an employee after one year's service to take certain approved University courses, prohibits the government from sending an employee back to school specifically to obtain an advanced degree. I did the thesis on my own time and assumed the costs of its preparation and defense. I knew that an advanced degree would not alter my status within the Clandestine Service nor have much bearing twenty or more years later when I would retire. Nonetheless, I was determined not to leave it undone, simply because that kind of behavior can become habitual in life. Several of my colleagues got caught up with the work of CIA, especially those who served continually overseas for many years, and let Masters and even Doctorate programs go uncompleted over the thesis requirement.

As I examined the economic track record of the Christian Democrats during President Eduardo Frei's first two years of his six-year term, it was becoming clear that his "Revolution in Liberty" was flaming out on the economic front — bad news politically for him and his principal supporter, the United States. Everyone in Washington remotely sensitive to the pervasive poverty and social injustice in Latin America knew that some alternative to Castro Communism was needed. Christian Democracy had seemed, in the early 1960s at least, to offer such as alternative — even though that movement had within it elements that were inherently more anti-American than anti-Marxist. The lines between Christian activist and Communist guerrilla were becoming blurred with the rise of "Liberation Theology" as the new social gospel of fuzzy, well-intentioned non-Marxists who were overwhelmed by the region's injustices, frozen economic systems, and blatant public corruption.

The dilemma for the Americans was that, if Frei and the few decent, moderate leaders in the region did not succeed, we would find ourselves having to choose between Marxist guerrilla victories or total reliance on military solutions. The latter could surely guarantee the status quo, if that were the U.S. goal, and we could always count on the men in uniform to be nationalistic and basically immune to the blandishment of the Cubans and Soviets. We could, in fact, limit our involvement in the region to fighting insurgents by straightforward counter-insurgency programs, leaving aside the deeper social and economic problems. But America had already made a choice, one articulated by President Kennedy, to help transform the underdeveloped world: America stood for something better than corrupt Latin American oligarchies. Which is, again, why we favored supporting non-Marxist moderates who offered people a better life.

After examining in depth the Chilean economic situation, I ended my Cornell Graduate School Thesis as follows: "It should not be surprising that one is left fairly pessimistic about the political future of Chile upon reviewing the first two years of the Frei Administration. The chances are excellent that it will fail in agrarian reform, price stabilization, and in increasing national production. If that is true, it would be wishful thinking to suppose that the Chilean electorate will endorse the Christian Democrats for another term."

With my strong and growing interest in the Chilean situation, I was transferred in late 1967 to work on Chilean matters, specifically in Covert Action. As I got deeper into the political reporting and Intelligence coming out of Chile I saw that Eduardo Frei, the man who seemed to offer hope and had been so impressive in his Senatorial days, had real problems governing the country. It was equally clear that his own party seemed to be locked politically in the past, beating up on the weakened Chilean Right and displaying little stomach for getting down in the trenches to do battle with their more powerful foes, the Chilean Marxists, who united every six years behind the candidacy of the Socialist Party Senator, Salvador Allende. The next election, 1970, was three years away, but my economic and political reading of Chile suggested the democratic forces were in trouble.

8

CIA and Chile

EXCEPT FOR VIETNAM, few countries conjure up such disparate thoughts and emotions for Agency professionals as Chile, the ribbon of a nation tucked between Andean peaks and Pacific waters. For a time, it was the showcase for CIA's Clandestine Service, proof to Washington insiders that the Bay of Pigs disaster had been an unfortunate aberration and that Covert Action remained a viable option for American policymakers. Confidence in the vibrancy and vigor of Agency Cold Warriors was partially restored at a crucial historic moment, in fact only momentarily, on the eve of the escalation of U.S. involvement in Southeast Asia. Such was the situation in the fall of 1964 after the Agency helped pull off a major win by Eduardo Frei, the Christian Democrat who resoundingly whipped Marxist Salvador Allende in the Presidential election.

The rise of Christian Democracy was viewed in Washington as the needed center-left alternative to Castro-Communism and, after the Chilean election of 1964, CIA basked in the glory. The aura of Covert Action competence was restored and the mystique reborn. However, seventy-two months later, in September 1970, CIA would be viewed in the Nixon White House as inept when Socialist Salvador Allende won the Presidential election. Allende's victory demonstrated the impotence of Christian Democracy in Chile. Now, having placed its Latin America bet on the Chilean Christian Democrat horse, the U.S. Government had no broad political formula for the region.

While Chileans were sorting out their own affairs, they had the misfortune of having become a symbol in the East-West struggle at a time when Soviet international adventurism was prospering and America was beginning to display signs of running on empty. Three years later, in 1973, Allende was toppled in a coup that cost the Chilean President his life and the Chileans their normal democratic processes, not permanently as with Communism, but for the next sixteen years. As a result of the 1973 ouster of Allende, viewed against the backdrop of many years of Agency involvement, Chile would come in time to symbolize CIA Covert

Action at its worst and most unethical, at least among the American political, academic and media left. How was it that this nation of less than ten million people had been elevated to such significance during a time when more populous and more troubled countries might have come to occupy center stage? Why was Chile twice a showcase, first for America under Eduardo Frei and then for the Soviets and Cubans under Allende? Why, on a per capita basis, were Chileans the second highest recipients of U.S. AID funds in the 1960s, behind only the South Vietnamese? What made Chile so special?

A country of remarkable contrasts and extremes, Chile is a geographic wonder. World class concentrations of copper and nitrate in the north meet a rich fruit-producing central zone where Santiago, the capital, is located. Southward lie the farmlands, modest oil reserves and grazing sheep looking out on the Strait of Magellan, separating the mainland from Tierra del Fuego and then Antarctica. The driest spot on earth is the Atacama Desert where mummified remains have been found of Chilean soldiers who fought victoriously more than a century ago in the War of the Pacific against Peru and Bolivia. Geographic distinctiveness is matched ethnologically; alone among the Andean countries, Chile has a distinctly European flavor to its population, from founding father Bernardo O'Higgins to the descendants of Germany, England, Yugoslavia, and Spain. At the same time, the Chileans now boast of their Araucanian Indians, who greeted Spanish conquistador Pedro de Valdivia's quest for gold by making him drink a goblet of the boiling metal. The Araucanians were never subjugated successfully by the Spaniards, who eventually sued for peace with the hearty natives.

Modern Chilean political history dates from the first Administration of President Arturo Alessandri, who was elected after World War I, in 1920. He ran on a progressive platform directed against the landed oligarchy, which was generally blamed for post-War economic difficulties brought on by the rapid decline of nitrate exports that at the time accounted for a large part of the country's foreign trade revenues. President Alessandri — whose son Jorge would play a key role in the CIA-Chile drama a half-century later — tried to stabilize Chile's monetary situation, but the Chilean Congress blocked his efforts. In late 1924, he resigned the Presidency only to return to power the following February with the support of the Chilean Military. Arturo Alessandri dissolved the Congress entirely.

Quite unlike the military-supported leaders of contemporary Latin America, President Alessandri then embarked on a program of major social reform. He set up what were, at the time, advanced programs of social welfare, including a national Social Security system a full ten years before one would be instituted in the United States. He got tough, also, on the economic front. With the guidance of a North American financial advisory mission headed by Professor Edwin Kemmerer of Princeton University, Alessandri returned Chile to the discipline of the gold standard and set up a Central Bank, one not controlled by the government but by private banks and the business community. Chile was on its way to recovery when the 1929 stock market crash on Wall Street rapidly became the Great Depression, which wreaked havoc on Chile with its major dependence on international trade. The 1929 Crash hit Chile proportionately harder than it did other nations, in part because Chile clung so long to the Gold Standard — even after England itself had abandoned this costly policy.

Chile's subsequent economic disarray soon resulted in political turmoil. There were military coups and, in the early 1930s, the radicalism was reflected in the formation of a short-lived Marxist government that proclaimed itself "The People's Republic of Chile." After the intervention by the Chilean Military, Chile moved back to a government that pursued entirely orthodox economic and social policies along the unsuccessful lines of President Herbert Hoover in the United States. Chile stayed in a stagnant state but, in 1938, turned to a member of its Radical Party, Pedro Aguirre-Cerda, who was elected President behind a Popular Front coalition that included the Marxists. The Radical Party led Chile for the next fourteen years and set in place the underpinnings for big government — pursuing major development projects and worrying very little about monetary restraints or price stability. As a result, Chile in time became one of the inflation capitals of the Hemisphere, in 1946 reaching 30 percent annual inflation. The Administration that came to power right after the Radicals averaged 50 percent annual inflation in the years 1952 to 1958.

Chilean monetary difficulties were matched in those decades by other negative economic trends and problems. For one thing, Chile had allowed itself to become essentially a one-crop economy and, after the decline of nitrate in the 1920s, that "crop" was copper. As the world price of copper moved up or down, so did its foreign exchange earnings and balance of payments. By agricultural mismanagement, Chile had gone also from a net exporter of food to a significant importer, consuming in the process a large share of the copper revenues just to feed its own population. Population increases had also been clicking along at a net 2.5 percent, putting further strains on both agriculture and the social infrastructure of the country, particularly in education, housing, medicine and public assistance. Chile still retained the advanced social welfare system that had its beginning in the 1920s under President Arturo Alessandri, but Chile's capacity to deliver on its commitments declined steadily after World War II and the end of the boom created by the Allied need for copper and other Chilean metals. Having resorted to the government printing press to deal with the economic crisis, Chile became increasingly unstable politically.

Chilean Communists and Socialists were by no means primarily responsible for derailing the Chilean economy in the 1930s and 1940s, but they were certainly prepared to capitalize on the economic stagnation and political unrest. In 1948, they presented such a perceived threat to the country that President Gabriel Gonzalez-Videla declared the Chilean Communist Party (CPCh) illegal and shipped the CPCh ringleaders off to detention camps in the south. The "Law for the Permanent Defense of Democracy" was a product of the Red Scare of the late Forties and was withdrawn a decade later, in 1958, by outgoing President Jorge Ibanez, a former Army General who had played a key role in the coups of the early 1930s.

In the multi-candidate election of 1958, Socialist Senator Salvador Allende missed winning the Chilean Presidency by a mere thirty-five thousand votes behind a coalition that included the Socialists, the Radical Party, and the Communist Party of Chile. The latter Party was one of Moscow's jewels in the international struggle against Western democracy. The close Allende loss in 1958 may be attributable to the almost comedic candidacy of a wild-and-drunken defrocked Catholic priest known as the *Cura de Catapilco*, or Priest from Catapilco. Holding up a jug of wine and dressed in the garb of a Chilean cowboy, the Cura rode on horseback through the poorest slums of Chile shouting his Presidential cry, "This is Chile" — referring of course to the wine and costume. In a country with a habit of drinking much of its enormous wine production and an estimated million problem drinkers, a high percentage of them men, the former Chilean priest drew forty-one thousand votes, mostly from potential Allende male voters. This very likely made the difference in costing Allende the 1958 election and brought to power Jorge Alessandri-Rodriguez, whose father had ruled Chile in the 1920s. Had Allende been elected President in 1958, he would have taken office just fourteen months before another Marxist, Fidel Castro, marched triumphantly into Havana.

Inflation continued to plague the Chileans, and it went through two distinct phases during the Jorge Alessandri years (1958-1964). Price rises were held in the first year to 1 percent and seemed to be leveling out at 5 percent during his second year — virtual price stability for a country that had 2,080 percent cumulative inflation in the decade of the Fifties. In 1960, southern Chile was hit by a disastrous earthquake that prompted tremendous spending for reconstruction and returned Chile to its bad economic habits: spending more than it collected in taxes; maintaining artificially-high value for its currency, which subsidized imports and hurt the balance of payments; readjusting wages annually in accordance with prior-year consumer price increases; taking inordinately high-interest foreign loans; and failing to put together any kind of consistent economic plan. In sum, Chile did virtually everything possible to weaken its own economy and, in this regard unfortunately, it succeeded: inflation returned, increasing to 10 percent in 1961, 28 percent in 1962, and 45 percent in 1963.

The problem for the United States was that, just as the Marxists were becoming more confident and inspired by the Cuban Revolution, the Chilean government of Jorge Alessandri was losing direction and signs of vitality. Economic failure was causing political instability and improving the fortunes of those radical elements that thrive on adversity. As Alessandri's term drew to a close in 1964, Chile was failing economically: the economy was stagnant in terms of savings and new job creation, the external debt was enormous and escalating, and malnutrition was becoming widespread as Chilean per capita daily food consumption fell to 2,200 calories (little higher than India, with 1,900). This was not a rosy picture for democracy and a genuine challenge for the United States Government and, especially, for CIA which dealt with political subversion and instability.

For a CIA officer in 1964, Chile ranked as one of the most interesting places to serve in a region dominated by political chaos and economic turmoil. Castro-supported guerrilla activity ensured that virtually every Latin American nation mirrored to some extent the broad-scale competition that was taking place between East and West, between KGB and CIA. No one knew whether the eventual winner would be Kennedy's Alliance for Progress, which was trying to force unprecedented economic and social reform meant to protect democracy, or the Castro-Communism model, which the Russians were promoting in their program of subversion to sharpen class struggle within each country. The Soviets and Cubans shared one strategic goal: to split individual countries, and eventually the region, from political and economic linkage with the U.S. In this struggle, Chile became disproportionately important to both the Soviet program of subversion and the countervailing U.S. effort at nation building.

Why was Chile more strategically-important to the U.S. than other, even larger countries in Latin America? The answer to that question is a great deal more complex than extremists on all sides of the Chilean situation generally suggest. Was it the almost one billion dollars of direct American investment in Chile that motivated Washington? Not if you heard Kennedy's Ambassador there in 1964, Ralph Dungan, make it clear to American businessmen in Santiago that U.S. Government objectives did not coincide with the goals of American companies. A German, English or Japanese Ambassador with such a publicly-expressed position would have been fired and on his way home within twenty-four hours. American diplomatic efforts now have to take into account our own commercial trade situation, and no U.S. Ambassador is likely to exhibit public disdain toward overseas U.S. businesses. Back in the early 1960s, however, before America mortgaged its economic future beginning with the Johnson Administration's guns-and-butter spending binge, the U.S. economic position in the world was so strong that its overseas businesses could be basically left to fend for themselves. That was the way things were working in Chile at the time.

Was Chile's special significance derived from its strategic copper reserves? Only in part. Certainly, U.S. companies had major investments in Chilean copper mining but, in the 1960s, copper did not represent anything near the strategic or economic importance it enjoyed in World War II. For one thing, America is self-sufficient in copper, producing enough to meet its own domestic requirements. The Chilean copper was going to Europe or Asia. Copper itself had been losing strategic importance as substitute materials were replacing it in every industry, from high technology and communications to household and industrial plumbing. The Soviets, of course, are mineral-conscious due to their own significant foreign trade in strategic metals. This was reflected in their international program of subversion in southern Africa, which shares with the Soviet Union most of the concentrations of certain precious minerals of incalculable value in high technology and national defense. The KGB has been deeply involved in that region for decades, but not out of concern for the Africans; racism is so pervasive in Russia that most Africans who study there return to their countries with very little regard for the Russians or their system. Yet, copper alone would not explain the Soviet interest in Chile because whoever controlled that country, or Zaire with its rich copper deposits, would still have to sell that metal on world markets to survive economically.

Really at stake for East and West in the Chilean situation was the symbolic competition, an intangible gain or loss that could not be measured by counting the number of people, assessing the geography, or looking at the mineral deposits. The United States selected Chile as its "democracy showcase" because it looked like the right place to make that case. Chile had democratic roots and traditions, a highly literate populace, a homogeneous population, a broad middle class, a land with enormous agricultural potential, minerals to trade internationally, a technocrat class among the best in Latin America, negligible public corruption, and a military that had respected civilian political rule — for a few decades, at least. Chile was also the right size to serve as a model. If the United States could not make it happen there, what was the prospect for Central America, with so little infrastructure for development? Or in the rest of the Andes with their coca-chewing peasants? Or in enormous Brazil and Argentina with over a hundred million people and decades of governmental mismanagement and public corruption? Chile, then, took on significance because of its many potential strengths in a region dominated by weaknesses.

If Chile was inherently strong and could serve as the showcase for Latin American democracy, what was the specific American security concern in 1964? Why not just flood the country with economic aid and technicians, Peace Corps volunteers and missionaries, and let the *nice guys* get the job done? Why have CIA working covertly in a democracy that did not have an active guerrilla problem? The unique problem, and threat, presented in Chile had to do with an electoral weakness or vulnerability. Up to that point, and even today, Communists outside the Soviet Bloc had won no national elections anywhere in the world. In Chile, the Communists were in a position to take over the reins of government by exploiting a Constitutional weakness and a political alliance in which they would have the upper hand, the strongest grip. The United States, for its part, had no intention of watching a Soviet-supported Popular Action Front come to power in Chile, slipping into the Presidency with less than a majority of the vote. The psychological effect of such a breakthrough — coming soon after Castro's own rise to power in 1959 and the Bay of Pigs failure in 1961 — could be disastrous for democratic forces in the whole region. Letting the Communists have a continent-long land base for subversion into the rest of Latin America would be worse. So, the Kennedy White

House gave Chile an exceedingly high priority at the National Security Council level in Washington. It appointed as American Ambassador to Chile one of the "Irish Mafia" — Ralph Dungan — who had been serving on the President's staff. Attorney General Robert Kennedy, acting as point man on Latin America after the Bay of Pigs, let it be known at the Department of State, the Department of Defense, and especially out at CIA, that the White House would not tolerate "another Cuba."

In addition to its inherent democratic traditions, Marxist strengths and electoral peculiarities, Chile had a remarkable record in that period. In many ways, it dominated the region beyond its modest population. In the early 1960s, Chileans were winning almost half the grants and scholarships given to Latin Americans to study in other regions of the world. Chileans had so many options for studying in the United States that many would, for example, elect to take a Master's degree on the West Coast, at Stanford or Berkeley, and complete Ph.D. work in the East, at one of the Ivies. The U.S. AID Program was enormous. The Western Europeans, themselves now safely out of the Soviet reach in part thanks to CIA Covert Action in the 1950s, were active on every level — governmentally, commercially and through their own political parties and well-funded international foundations, including both the German Social Democrats and their rivals, the German Christian Democrats. U.S. foundations were by no means quiescent; Ford, Rockefeller and others poured money into everything from agricultural development to housing and cooperative programs. The Catholic Church expanded its missionary and social action programs in Chile, in part drawn by the allure of Chilean Christian democracy, which billed itself as a "Third Way" for Latin America — between the Scylla of Capitalism and the Charybdis of Communism. Everyone wanted to get in on the act.

Among the Marxists groups, however, there was less visible activity. The driving force behind the Popular Front alliance, the Communists, continued to grind along quietly, as they had been doing for decades. They had the prudence to permit their weaker partner, the Socialist Party, to take top electoral billing with candidate Allende, knowing that the Chilean citizenry was not ready for an out-and-out proclaimed Communist State or Communist President. Furtive, as always, the CPCh was discreet in its work and contacts with the Soviet Communist Party. Yet, high profile or low, they were unrelenting in their pursuit of victory in the 1964 election, confident that "history was on their side" — or so their Marxist-Leninist doctrine assured them.

This faith in the inevitability of their victory meant that, win or lose in 1964, they could look forward to another election in 1970. The Communist Party of Chile was headed at the time by the most effective Communist leadership in all of Latin America. Their solidarity with the Soviet Union was absolute, and they enjoyed special status in Moscow because they were unequivocally in the USSR camp on the ideological split with the Chinese Communists. The Chilean Communists enjoyed the international Marxist prestige of having endured successfully the government's persecution during the decade of 1948-1958, when they were declared illegal. In that period, they could not openly recruit members or hold party meetings, they could not hold union office and be recognized officially, they could not be elected to the Chamber of Deputies or the Senate, and the core leadership of the party was sent to penal camps — just the stuff of martyrdom. When the CPCh was permitted again to resume its full role in Chilean political life, it had leaders and members who, by virtue of the hardships of prison, were tough, resolute and more disciplined than their soft allies on the Left or their even-softer political opponents on the Right.

A friend of mine who served in Santiago in the early 1960s spoke with some admiration of individual Chilean Communists who turned their Senatorial pay over to the Party, who rode the overflowing public transportation with the people, and who continued to live and dress at the working class level when their positions would have allowed them to escape the poverty and leap to a higher level of Chilean society. In fact, this officer, who had worked in Political Operations, mused that, if stranded on an island, he would rather be there with members of the CPCh than any other single group of Chilean political activists. Their allegiance to Moscow notwithstanding, they were a force because of the quality of their people. They also had the perspicacity to know that letting Socialist Allende have top billing in effect allowed the Communist Party to play king-maker, rather than king — which was both their most practical and their most powerful strategy.

The quiet determination and confidence of the CPCh was more un-nerving than all of the public relations hoopla of their more expressive Socialist Party allies, who behaved more or less like other Chilean politicians, letting the world know just what they were thinking and doing. The Socialist Youth were becoming so radicalized that they sounded more inclined toward a Maoist or Chinese Revolution than the electoral path favored by the CPCh and Moscow. But the CPCh kept themselves and their Popular Front allies on the *via electoral*, the electoral path and slogan that promised eventual Marxist victory in Chile if they would all continue to work within the system and not polarize Chilean society by acts of Terrorism or guerrilla warfare. The Soviets were still training selected Chileans in such deadly arts, but that was an entirely clandestine and limited activity of Soviet Intelligence — just in case — and not the preferred way of gaining power. The CPCh strength came not merely because it had good leadership and loyal members but also because it had a game plan; it knew something very basic about Chile that worked in its favor. How could a group of Communists representing no more than 10 to 12 percent of the electorate, no matter how wise and disciplined, threaten democracy in Chile? Was this just American or CIA propaganda? Not at all.

The vulnerability of Chilean democracy arose from four separate realities, and these realities guided the Central Committee of the CPCh. First, most encouraging for the Chilean Communists was the fact that, under the Chilean Constitution of 1925, one could be elected President with less than half the vote. If no candidate received an absolute majority, the Congress would then select the President from the competing candidates. At that stage in the process, Chilean tradition virtually assured that the Congress would elect the top popular vote-getter to avoid the bloodshed, and probable civil war, that would ensue if Congress selected one of the other candidates with less votes.

Second, supporting Allende, the Communists were solidifying a Popular Front alliance that could win the three-way 1964 contest behind a coalition they would dominate in their disciplined, unflappable way.

Third, once in power, the possibilities for the Communists achieving their agenda were enormous because of both the inherent powers of the Chilean Presidency as well as their intimate knowledge of Allende's personal weaknesses, which meant that he could be "guided" by the CPCh along a proper revolutionary path. The Chilean Presidency is exceedingly powerful, more so than is common in other Western democracies. He appoints all Ministers of the national government and also appoints all of the provincial governors, who are dependent on the national government for all funding, increasing further the President's leverage. The President appoints the head of the powerful national police force, the disciplined and well-trained Carabineros who, because there are no local police forces, are responsible for all law enforcement in the country. He selects the head of each military service, a prerogative made more powerful by the fact that when he names, for example, the tenth general in line in terms of rank and seniority as head of the army, the nine generals senior to him must resign their positions and go into retirement. The President's choice as Minister of Interior also controls the Chilean internal security service, *Investigacciones*, which deals with subversives and other delicate internal security matters for the government. The administration controls its own media network, including public radio and television as well as a newspaper.

Earlier administrations, especially those led by the Radical Party, expanded and centralized the national government and much of the economic development infrastructure. As a result, crass political manipulation from the top was a real possibility. Even such noble social action programs as agrarian reform and slum-dweller assistance, urged on the Chileans by the U.S. Government, in fact were controlled from Santiago by the national government, giving the Chilean President tools to transform Chilean society in fundamental ways. The speed, direction and forcefulness of such basic societal change would depend, naturally, on who sat in the Moneda, Chile's White House, and how much public support he could generate for his social action program.

Fourth — and this was the final ace up the CPCh sleeve — the Communist Party knew that within a single six-year Presidential term, it could use the weak alcoholic Allende, the strong Chilean Presidency, and the Communist historic ability once in power to subvert a country from the top, to bring Chile into the Socialist camp; i.e., Moscow's orbit. Without a specific mandate to Communize Chile, and absent a majority vote in the Presidential election, the Communists would use a Popular Front victory behind Allende to alter Chile fundamentally during his term of office. In that period, as Communists had done successfully in Russia and China, Hungary and Romania, Poland and Czechoslovakia, Bulgaria and Latvia, Estonia and Lithuania, as well as Cuba and Vietnam, they could compromise, neutralize and eliminate all internal opposition by imprisoning and executing intractable elements, or driving them out of the country. With these four characteristics, the powerful Presidency government could be used to set in motion a Marxist program that would be irreversible, assuming the final obstacle could be overcome: the Chilean Military, which viewed themselves as *the last defenders of the Constitution*.

In both the 1920s and 1930s, the Chilean Military had stepped in to prevent political chaos by putting someone it considered responsible into the Presidency. Marxists, for their part, began penetrating the traditionally conservative and apolitical Military services and had more success in the newer branch, the Air Force, than in the Army or Navy. Adherents to the Allende program were primarily Military officers who had not reached senior levels. It would be necessary, therefore, for a Marxist President to neutralize the Military from the top, if it were to be done at all. The four realities, notwithstanding the serious obstacle of the Chilean Military, formed the external basis for CPCh confidence in eventual victory — reasons also why they worked to keep the hothead Socialists from pursuing the *via violenta*, the violent road and slogan being urged on the Socialist Youth by the Chinese (then entering their own *via violenta*, the Cultural Revolution that cost millions of innocent lives). The CPCh, and their Soviet backers, knew that the *via pacifica* would sooner or later pay dividends in Chile so, they reasoned, why screw things up with a few Molotov cocktails?

CIA, when at its best, also is seized by realities, collecting information on the world as it is, which is the primary step in the Intelligence process. In the case of Chile, the Agency was well aware of the Allende threat in the 1950s and the possibility of the Popular Front winning a three-way race in 1964. As the Area Division with the best overall record on penetrating Communist Party organizations, the Latin America Division had its pulse on what the CPCh was thinking and doing. Unlike 1958, there was no son of a popular ex-President around to rally public support in 1964; by law, Jorge Alessandri could not succeed himself. Nor, this time around, could anyone count on another Cura de Catapilco to ride into town on his horse to siphon off critical votes from Allende, avoiding a Marxist victory Chile once again by some *legerdemain*.

In addition, the most vehement political and ideological competition in Chile on an emotional level was not between the Marxist Left and the Conservative Right at this time; it was between the center-left Christian Democratic Party and the two shrinking parties on the Chilean Right whose weaknesses soon led to their merging into the National Party. As 1963 drew to a close, there was every sign that the Marxist dream was about to come true — there would be a close horse race between three candidates, and their man, Allende, would cross the finish line in first place with a vote in the high 30 percentile. The election losers in this scenario would be the Christian Democratic and the rightist candidates who would be splitting the remaining 62 to 65 percent of the vote.

Whether by a whisker or by a country mile, an Allende victory would set in motion the Marxist transformation of Chile. The CPCh would have unbridled Soviet and Cuban support. The practical, non-ideological aspect of the CPCh siding with Moscow was that the Soviets could be counted on to provide material support to their CPCh friends. The

Cubans were receiving an enormous annual subsidy. Marxists who had gone instead to the Red Chinese were given, by contrast, verbal support and a supply of Mao Tse Tung's "Little Red Books" on revolutionary thought and guerrilla warfare. For the ideologically purer (and poorer) Chinese, each nation had to sacrifice and make its revolution. The PRC would give guerrilla warfare training certainly, but little funding or tangible support would flow from China.

If realism is the goal and standard for CIA collection, it is also its guiding principle in Covert Action; it made little difference to a non-ideological Agency which non-Marxist individual or group emerged victorious in the 1964 election — so long as Allende and the Popular Front were defeated. This basic objectivity gave the same type of power to CIA as that enjoyed within the Chilean Popular Front by the Communists: The Agency was free of preconceived views and had freedom of action to move along whichever path would prove the most efficacious. In the Kennedy White House, there was a clear preference for Eduardo Frei, who was recognized as a kindred spirit among the liberal social activists of the New Frontier. Individual CIA officers certainly had views on who would be the strongest candidate and have the best chance of winning the race. But their personal preferences would be set aside once American policy had been set and the Agency ordered to get behind a particular candidate, if one emerged.

During the last five weeks of 1963, little attention was paid in Washington to Chile; America was in mourning over the death of President Kennedy. For the first few months of 1964, every effort was made in the Johnson White House to avoid any appearance of abrupt change. The policy toward Latin America remained the same. The wait-and-see policy in Chile shifted quickly as a result of another death, this time of a Marxist Congressman in a rural Chilean town called Curico.

A special election was held to replace a deceased member of the Chamber of Deputies, Chile's lower house of Congress, and it so happened that it shaped up as a three-man race similar to what was happening nationally with respect to the Presidential contest. In the Curico special election there were a Christian Democrat, a candidate of the Right, and a Popular Front Marxist candidate. The latter was a popular Socialist Party pediatrician, Oscar Naranjo, who, like the Cura de Catapilco, would be a bit player who made history. Naranjo won handily in the election, and the media immediately blew things out of proportion, transforming the lopsided victory into a supposed precursor for an Allende victory six months later in the Presidential election.

The Chilean Right got taken in by the press propaganda and became collectively apoplectic. The Marxists, by contrast, were exhilarated. A similar three-way race nationally would not be as one-sided as Naranjo's victory in Curico, but the Popular Front did appear to many to be on the verge of a national triumph. That was the case until cooler heads prevailed and a deal was struck between Chile's squabbling Hatfields and McCoys, the Christian Democrats and the Chilean Right.

Up to the time of Curico, the National Party had agreed to support Senator Julio Duran, a moderate Radical Party member, in an effort to forge a coalition of their own that might repeat what had been accomplished in 1958 when the center-right had elected Alessandri. The opposing candidates in that earlier election had been Salvador Allende and Eduardo Frei, the same individuals Senator Duran would be opposing in September 1964. The Curico Special Election results suggested to the uninformed that the Marxists had somehow surged ahead in strength, a conclusion not warranted by the facts. Curico was a tiny part of Chile and an agricultural zone at that. The election of Naranjo was a personal triumph due to his reputation as a doctor to the poor, not so much his political party affiliation.

Nonetheless, the Chilean Right has been spooked by Curico and agreed to get behind Frei, if not formally in an electoral alliance at least with discreet financing and, on Election Day, their votes. To keep the anti-Catholic Radical Party votes from going in its entirety to Allende, Duran agreed to remain in the race on a token basis. In that way, non-Marxist stalwarts of his party would not have to choose between voting either for Marxist Allende or "Papist" Frei; with such a limited choice, most Radical Party voters would vote for Allende. The result of the CIA-supported package deal was that the 1964 election turned into a virtual two-way race, one that the Popular Front and Allende could not and did not win. When the votes were counted in September 1964, Frei garnered more than half the votes and Allende fell just short of 40 percent. The remainder went to Julio Duran and splinter candidates.

The Presidential campaign itself had been a bare-knuckled affair. The Popular Front tried to portray Frei as a stooge of the Americans and of the Papacy; Allende in turn was attacked as an agent of Moscow as propaganda covered city walls with pictures of Soviet tanks going into Hungary in the 1956 uprising and of Cubans being executed in the wake of Castro's rise to power. Fidel Castro's sister was brought to Chile to appeal to Chilean women not to support the Marxists "or their children would suffer the same fate as the Cuban youngsters shipped off to Eastern Europe for Communist indoctrination." The Agency's role in Frei's victory has been widely publicized. David Phillips had that in mind six years later as he flew home to play a role in keeping Allende from taking power: "I knew that CIA had provided massive support to Allende's opponent, Eduardo Frei, in the 1964 Chilean elections."

In democratic societies, the people have to keep reaffirming their freedoms. The election in 1964 of moderate, progressive Eduardo Frei, was no guarantee of eternal Chilean bliss. His enormous electoral victory in September 1964, followed by a major Christian Democratic win in the early 1965 National Congressional elections, was not enough. Frei and his Party had been given clear mandates to govern, certainly. However, when I got into the Chilean Covert Action business in Washington halfway through Frei's term of office in 1967, the economic policy failures of the Frei Administration were clear. CIA, in terms of protecting democracy, was back to square one a mere thirty-six months after the Covert Action electoral success of 1964.

The advantage enjoyed by the KGB Covert Action (called "Active Measures") Officers was that, historically, when their Communist colleagues came to power, usually by violence, they stayed in power, again by Terror. They only had to assume control once because, once in power, the Marxist-Leninists were history's experts at disassembling and neutralizing political opposition. Dzerzhinsky's Red Terror campaign had been replayed around the globe time and again with an efficacy that would have made the cunning Polish Communist satisfied indeed. In fact, unlike the founding father of Soviet Red Terrorism, his successors in China, Cuba, Cambodia and elsewhere would not be in tears as they signed death warrants of enemies and potential enemies. The Chinese Red Guards, the Cambodian Khmer Rouge and the Castro Communists would carry out their carnage with glee, so hardened had they become in their half century of revolutionary development.

Was Chile in any such danger of slipping into the Soviet orbit in the late 1960s? At that time, halfway around the world in Southeast Asia, Communists insurgents were on the verge of victory in three countries simultaneously. In Africa, they had made such progress in Ethiopia and Angola that their pincer-like strategy threatened in time to cut Africa into more digestible halves. Not far from Chile, guerrilla bands roamed the Andes and, in 1967, counter-insurgency teams killed Ernesto "Che" Guevara in the mountains of Bolivia where he was trying to extend the Castro Revolution. CIA was concerned about the guerrilla threat and began training its own personnel, starting with the more vulnerable Chiefs of Station, in weapons and other counter-terrorist techniques.

CIA looks to its Field Stations for early warning on coups, wars, and major political developments that affect U.S. interests. The country desk at CIA Headquarters seldom has any real expertise or information not provided by the Station itself. By late 1967, every CIA Officer and State Department Political Officer who had served in Santiago during the political events of 1964 had gone on to some other assignment. Where the Soviets tend to leave KGB officers in key areas for extended tours that sometimes exceed a decade, the American way is to bounce people around every two to three years. The weakness in our approach has led some to conclude that the death knell for effective U. S. diplomacy can be linked directly to adoption of the two-year tour of duty as the basic State Department overseas assignment. This assignment pattern has taken its toll on U. S. Intelligence as well.

CIA's Santiago Station Chief in 1968 was a no-nonsense and remarkable individual, a man who was the Agency's Berlin Chief during the East German uprising back in 1953 — when I was still in high school. Having battled the Nazis, and then the Communists for two decades in the world's trouble spots, his aversion for Communism was total. He was wary of democratic leftists who, like Kerensky in Russia, facilitated the rise to power of Marxist-Leninists around the world.

The U.S. Ambassador was a mercurial Kennedy political appointee, a former European journalist and self-proclaimed Social Democrat. To the Ambassador, the devils were rightists who created the conditions of social injustice which made possible the Communist rise to power.

Clearly, the Ambassador and the CIA Station Chief viewed the Chilean beast from different perspectives and directions. Each view may have had its own justification and validity at different times and places in this century, but when they came together simultaneously in Chile in 1968, the stage was set for U.S. policy paralysis.

Part of the difficulty arose not only from philosophical differences, but also the fact that upon assuming their positions neither had any background whatsoever on Chile. In the whole U.S. Government, with literally dozens of Foreign Service and CIA Officers with previous service in Santiago, not one individual with prior Chilean experience was selected to serve either as Ambassador or CIA Station Chief.

Back in CIA Headquarters, meanwhile, I had been moved over to work on Chilean Covert Action because of my own deep interest in the area and the fact that I was writing some papers that suggested Chile was heading for real trouble politically. The economic bad news was already pretty clear but, as obvious as it might seem, little connection has generally been made between economics and politics when American policymakers deal with other nations, especially those in underdeveloped regions. The Foreign Service itself has two separate career tracks, one for Economic Officers and another, higher-ranking one for Political Officers — making one wish that *Political Economy* were taught still in the nation's universities. Very few CIA Officers have any background at all in Economics, either U.S. or International.

As I got into the job in late 1967, I began writing memoranda and messages to the Station that had the tone of early warning, a role reversal that made my Headquarters' branch managers nervous. In theory, the overseas field Station is supposed to tell Washington when trouble is brewing, not vice versa. So, besides doing some Covert Action work on the Chilean Congressional elections of 1968 — the last national election before the all-important September 1970 Presidential contest — I kept banging away at the theme that "Allende is coming."

It was not a matter of political genius that led me, almost three years before the event, to conclude correctly, that Allende would win. It was basically a matter of looking at the probable line-up of 1970 candidates and examining them in light of historic voting patterns. The conclusion was rather clear: Salvador Allende, who had been edged out in 1958 and beaten badly in 1964, would likely win the next time around.

The most logical place to look for an alternative to Allende was in the Christian Democratic Party, but President Eduardo Frei could not constitutionally run again. All indications coming out of that party suggested that his longtime rival, leftist Senator Radimiro Tomic, would get the Christian Democrat nomination. The Chilean Right, meanwhile, was talking about a return of former President Jorge Alessandri who, after four years of Frei Government economic mismanagement, was beginning to look in retrospect like a competent leader, despite his own Administration having sputtered to an inglorious end in 1964. Alessandri's advancing years, and lack of vitality or charisma, did not bode well for his electoral prospects. The animus towards him and the Chilean Right of the U.S. Ambassador meant that the U.S. Government would not approach the matter of helping find a democratic alternative to Allende with the detached objectivity that had succeeded in the two prior Chilean Presidential Elections.

Assuming the Americans, specifically the American Ambassador and the Chief of Station, did work out their differences, how might CIA help defeat Allende again and avoid a Communist-backed victory, one that would be celebrated from Havana to Moscow?

At Headquarters, we examined two possibilities in depth. The first, and most conventional, approach would require an accommodation between the Chilean Right and the Christian Democrats, the formula that worked in 1964 for Eduardo Frei. The democratic margin of victory in 1970 would not be as lopsided, but we knew there was no way the Marxists would win an essentially two-person race. Bringing about such a favorable arrangement hinged on the ability of the probable PDC candidate Tomic to move towards the center from his stridently-leftist position, becoming (for the election period at least) more vocally anti-Marxist and less anti-Rightist. Such an accommodation would have the virtue of being a "quick fix" — a simple solution appealing to a Washington bureaucracy buried at the time in things Vietnamese.

So we asked ourselves, "can Tomic move from his basic leftist Senatorial posture to appeal to a broader cross-section of the Chilean electorate?" We knew that what had worked for Tomic in his Senatorial mining district would not succeed in Santiago in a Presidential race, particularly among center-right voters who helped elect Frei in 1964.

The matter of Tomic's resilience was so crucial that we had our CIA Psychological Evaluation experts conduct an in-depth, remote evaluation of Tomic to answer the central question: could he move politically towards the center to become electable? We assembled data on Tomic going back to his earliest days politically, even to his youth. When it had all been digested, the conclusion was as direct as the question: Tomic could not do it! He was too wedded to his leftist ways to emulate Eduardo Frei, even to win the Presidency he wanted so much. It was then clear that Chile was in trouble for 1970. Unless, of course, an alternate approach — "Plan B" in Henry Kissinger parlance — could be taken. We then explored a second Covert Action path when the Tomic "shift-to-the-center" option was found to be unworkable.

In this regard, I wrote a think piece addressing the real, substantial Chilean electoral problem that had dogged the United States from the 1950s: *Chile was vulnerable to an undemocratic fate of having the Marxists assume power with less than half of the popular vote.* The paper suggested that CIA try to fix this real problem in the Chilean Constitution of 1925. Specifically, if the Constitution were amended to require a runoff between the top two vote-getters when no candidate had received a majority of the votes in the regular election, Chile would be spared of an Allende victory thereafter. In fact, no free people ever elected the Communists to run their country. Further, after messing up a country's economy and society — as they did so completely in the USSR, China, Eastern Europe, North Korea, Cuba, and Southeast Asia — the Communists would get even less votes in a free election once they ruled a country for any period of time.

Would a change in the Constitution's flaw, Chilean democracy's Achilles heel, be feasible, even assuming it was desirable? How would it be done? How would it be received by the Chileans themselves? The last question had indeed been answered for us in the affirmative through professional polls we conducted in Chile in 1964 and that showed three-quarters of the Chileans believed a runoff election to elect a majority President would be democratic and desirable. That question had been more or less a filler question to get to the real issue of voter preference in the 1964 election. Nonetheless, there was clearly no majority opposition to the idea of a runoff election even though the Marxists would not need ten seconds to understand the implications of such a Constitutional change — *they would not get to take power in Chile with little more than a third of the vote, ever!*

If a runoff election solution were desired, how could it be done? This would depend on the Chilean Congress and its political composition at the time a Constitutional change were proposed. As we scrutinized the Congress — assuming Christian Democratic and Rightist support for a Constitutional change, but total Marxist opposition — we found that CIA would need to encourage or persuade only a half-dozen Radical Party members in Congress to produce the needed votes to change the Constitution and require a run-off Presidential election.

Getting the additional votes would be an appropriate and manageable task for CIA, as would a covertly-supported press campaign to create the proper public atmosphere for its passage. The KGB, through its agent assets and the Chilean Communist Party, would be working just as assiduously against this change which would be the death knell for any minority path to power in Chile for the Communists. Moscow could be counted on to support the CPCh because of their backing of the Soviet 1968 invasion of Czechoslovakia and for siding with the USSR against the Chinese on who would lead the world's Communists.

In Headquarters, getting the authority to alert the Santiago Station to the Allende threat had earlier been a hand-wringing struggle. Now, getting out a Headquarters message discussing Constitutional change was almost impossible. Eventually, persistence, continual rewriting and cajoling paid off: a cable was finally sent to Santiago Station proposing the concept of a change in the Constitution to remove the potentially-undemocratic weakness. Our cable was greeted with silence on its substance, but the Station asked that I travel to Chile to review the proposal with them and the U.S. Ambassador. I made the trip, we held discussions but, in the end, nothing further happened.

At that stage, frankly, the U.S. Ambassador still held out hope that the Christian Democrats, even with Tomic, could pull off a victory in 1970. In any case, he was against any possible support for the Right. The CIA Station management believed that former President Jorge Alessandri — accurately as it would turn out — had the best chance against Allende. So, while the Ambassador chased a will o' the wisp, the Station trimmed its agent stable so that, in the end, it would not be in a position to support the Christian Democrats' hopeless cause if that were to be Washington's eventual orders. Officially and formally, the Embassy and Station, each with different views of the situation, denied in their official reporting that the upcoming 1970 election presented a problem. In the absence of a problem, they would not consider taking the unorthodox step of getting the Chileans to amend their Constitution.

I returned to Washington from my Santiago trip realizing that I had been unconvincing, even though the hard numbers showed Allende would likely win in 1970 against Tomic and Alessandri — especially if the Agency stood on the sidelines. I saw what was going to happen. Clinging to his view that the Chilean Right was finished, the Ambassador would block any support of Alessandri. The Station would place itself in a position where it could not credibly support Tomic, not only the weakest candidate but also a strong anti-American whose victory would do little for democracy or long term U.S. interests in the region. Allende would in all probability win the Presidency of Chile

With little doubt on where Chile was headed, I wrote a memorandum that DCI Helms presented in April 1969 to a National Security Council meeting chaired by Henry Kissinger. Helms made three key points:

- Chile was in trouble.
- No last-minute fix could replicate 1964 election operation success.
- An early start was recommended.

Institutionally, at least, CIA was covering its backside by warning the White House not to come over at the last minute and tell CIA to "save Chile." As it turned out, no real Covert Action operation in advance of the election was ever put together. Approached in early 1969, eighteen months before the Chilean Election of September 1970, I was asked if I would like an overseas assignment. A *change of venue* is a good way to get rid of a squeaky wheel, and by then I was not doing any real good. How many ways can one write "Allende is coming" without sounding a little close to the edge? So, I made plans to take the new assignment and put Chile behind me — except I bet another Agency officer that Allende would win, a bet I really hoped to lose.

A year later, on March 25, 1970, the National Security Council committee on Covert Action approved an amorphous program that supported neither Alessandri nor Tomic — the Ambassador and the Chief of Station were still neutralizing each other. The approval was for funding anti-Allende *spoiler Operations*, whatever that meant.

When the votes were counted in September 1970, Allende was first with 36 percent, Alessandri a close second with 35 percent, and Tomic a distant third with 28 percent. With the Constitution unchanged, Allende would become President in November 1970 assuming the Congress, in accordance with Chilean tradition, ratified him on October 24.

The Agency, having forewarned the White House back in April 1969, saved itself from being asked to do anything as dumb as trying a last-minute fix — correct? Not so. As David Phillips explained in his book *Night Watch*, "DCI Helms had been summoned to the White House on September 15. President Richard Nixon had instructed the CIA Chief to do whatever was necessary to keep Allende out of office. Helms's handwritten notes jotted down at the White House meeting:

> *One in 10 chance, but save Chile! Worth spending.*
> *Not concerned risks involved. No involvement of embassy.*
> *$10,000,000 available, more if necessary.*
> *Full-time job-best men. We have game plan.*
> *Make the economy scream. 48 hours for plan of action.*

This eleventh-hour reaction — the so-called "Track Two Program" that tried to keep Allende from power — failed miserably, discredited the CIA, and got DCI Helms eventually into legal difficulties and a misdemeanor guilty plea for lying to Congress. So much for doing our homework in advance! The quick-fix mentality had prevailed again and the results were appalling.

The events that directly preceded and followed Allende's victory are detailed in Congressional hearings and in *Night Watch* by David Phillips. Phillips — at the time serving as Chief of Station in Brazil when President Nixon and Henry Kissinger gave DCI Helms the word that Chile was not to be lost to the Marxists — gives an accurate sense of his frustration at being ordered to pursue a hopeless cause. "Should I allow myself to be involved? Should the CIA, even responding to a President's ukase, encourage a military coup in one of the few countries in Latin America with a solid, functioning democratic tradition?" So Phillips questioned himself in the fall of 1970 as he was ordered to put together an operation to keep Allende from coming to power.

My own problem with this last-minute White House intervention had more to do with feasibility than the *functioning democratic tradition* rhetoric. As anyone with any background knowledge was aware, a surgical coup would not work and would lead to a very bloody Chilean civil war, with the Communists and other Marxists gaining the moral upper hand this time. Knowing it would fail, why do it at all? If the Chileans chose to let the Marxists — with a mere 36 percent of the vote — take power, that was their choice to make. As the Afghans and the Poles were to show some years later, people who want freedom have to be prepared to make the necessary sacrifices. Allende's victory may have been the culmination of a two-decade subversive effort to bring Marxism to Chile but, until he took steps to weaken Chilean democratic institutions, a coup to keep him out of office was totally out of line.

As things developed, a group of Chileans acting independently of CIA, but which had prior Agency contact, tried to start a coup by kidnapping Allende's new Military Chief, General Rene Schneider, who was killed in the botched operation. This event brought an end to all Agency efforts to keep Allende from assuming the office of President. Three years later, Allende himself would die in a military coup that brought to power Army General Augusto Pinochet, who decided to suspend all normal political parties and activities for what would turn out to be sixteen years. In 1988, the Chileans voted in a national plebiscite to return to elected government, something no Marxist government has ever done since the Soviets came to power in 1917.

Hindsight tends to be 20/20, but I've always regretted not having done a better job in 1968 convincing CIA and the State Department that American interests — and Chilean democracy — would be better served by pushing constitutionally for majority rule. If that strikes people in today's climate as too deep a meddling in another nation's internal affairs, I would point to the Soviet dispatch of trained revolutionaries to Chile and other nations within five years of their own 1917 coup d'état in Russia, or even the tough taxation laws and agrarian reform programs the U.S. Government pushed overseas to shift wealth to an extent that would not be tolerated in the United States or England. In the 1950s and 1960s, the U.S., other nations, and a host of international foundations and religious groups were very meddlesome, if that is the correct term. In retrospect, the real Chilean tragedy was that the one critical change — one that could have prevented Allende (with 36% of the vote) from coming to power at all, and would have prevented the bloodshed around the Military coup — did not take place. The Constitutional flaw of 1925 had been left intact and exacted its high price. Ironically, Chile's laws now require a run-off election when no single Presidential candidate gets an absolute majority.

In July 1969, the Gilligans headed for what I will call Zaragossa. I would later be presented an Agency Award for the work I had done in Chile. I would have felt a great deal better if the Chileans had not had to go through the Allende three-year nightmare, the violent coup, and the permanent polarization of that otherwise placid society. The Agency meanwhile was about to enter its own dark decade, one in which it would take hits for perceived excesses in fighting and winning the first two decades of the Cold War. It was a time in which the U.S., reeling from failures in Southeast Asia principally, turned on its institutions, especially CIA, despite the Agency's demonstrable record of having called the shots accurately on the quagmire in Southeast Asia and in Chile too. As I had learned in my Chile days, it is not enough to be correct; CIA has to persuade the White House on such matters. Being right is 49 percent of the job; convincing the President is 51 percent.

9

Assignment to Zaragossa

As I got ready in Headquarters for my next tour of duty, I had mixed feelings; letting go of Chile was not that easy. I knew that the correct thing to do professionally, according to the Clandestine Service unwritten code, was to let go without emotion and get on with the next task. Agency people, on many occasions, had to put unfortunate or even disastrous situations behind them — Bay of Pigs, Albanian invasion, Hungary, Czechoslovakia, and Tibet. Like good soldiers, CIA people had learned to swallow hard, wipe away a tear on occasion, and stuff the pain down inside where it would not interfere with the next job. Although Chile had not yet come apart at the seams, I knew as I got ready for the trip to Zaragossa that, within fifteen months, Salvador Allende would be elected. Bonnie knew how badly I felt, and more than once we discussed getting out of the Agency altogether, going back to New England, and starting over. But it was not easy to let go after nine years. Still, if we did go abroad we would be passing the point of no return. What really made the difference was that Zaragossa sounded like a great place to serve, and this time we would be on the inside. The new Chief of Station had also been the Santiago Station key player in the successful Chilean election operation of 1964, so we had that in common and could commiserate on Chile as it tilted towards Allende in the months ahead.

Once fully committed to Zaragossa and before leaving Washington, I became so busy that I had no time to dwell on the past. I had to take some advanced technical training that would permit me to run Operations that made use of spy gear I had never used in my years in Covert Action. For several weeks I learned about and played with technical devices, not so that I would become a Technical Operations Officer myself — three lifetimes would not be enough to convert me into an expert in the silent drilling of holes for listening "bugs" — but so that I could manage a large program that had several Technical Operations going on simultaneously.

Like the salesman of scientific gear, I did not need to be a scientist, but I sure had to know what the gear could and could not do in support of our clandestine Operations. This was not an assignment that would place a premium on analysis, political or otherwise. It was a nuts-and-bolts tour of duty where I would be working against Foreign Intelligence and diplomatic targets in what was essentially a Counterintelligence role not unlike what an FBI officer might be doing in the United States against hostile government installations.

The new job also had considerable supervisory responsibility for a middle-grade officer. I had four Operations Officers reporting to me. Among the several Operations I managed, another twenty locally- recruited agent assets worked in the Counterintelligence network I would be running. The budget amounted to a few hundred thousand dollars, not astronomical by Covert Action standards, but a pretty large percentage of the Station's overall Operations budget. The most agreeable part of the job was that it would allow me to work with some deep cover officers who were, happily, among the most valuable in Latin America. Not surprisingly, after my own outside experience in El Dorado, I found that they had been rather casually appreciated and supported overall, a function again of the inside officers' tendency to look after their own careers and let the deep cover NOCs fend for themselves.

We left the United States in July, arriving in Zaragossa feeling wonderful to be Americans; Neil Armstrong had just landed on the moon, and for the first time in several years the country had something to feel good about. Being away from home again brought back that mixture of adventure and culture shock that invariably vie for dominance in the emotional life of an Operations Officer. I had to recondition my thinking along clandestine lines; no longer could I treat casually telephones, strangers on the street or even my ride to and from the Station each day. The Soviets and Cubans and the rest of their gang were in Zaragossa going about the business of subversion, and our mission was to keep them from succeeding. In turn, they were targeting on America and Americans when they were not devoting their energies to supporting Latin American Communist Parties and guerrilla groups from the favorable position they all enjoyed in Zaragossa. It was easy indeed for me to get into the work; there was much to do.

The family transition was also relatively painless compared to the deep cover years. For one thing, having an official American passport meant that we faced none of the red tape and delays associated with bringing personal household effects into the country. The kids could have their own beds and toys, and we would be living abroad with our own furniture for a change. Bonnie would have the family car to use as she drove the four children to and from school and ran errands around town. I had full-time use of an Agency car. Station support was available for house-hunting and getting the personal vehicle registered, and there was official temporary housing to use until we found a permanent place to live. There was a medical staff for official Americans, including an American nurse, shots and medicine from the States and cleared local physicians who were trained in the U.S. in all of the major specialties. "Care packages" sent from home could be received through the official mail, and American food could be ordered within certain reasonable limits. Serving inside was going to be easier than being under deep cover for which CIA pays a ten percent premium pay that does not begin to compensate for the enormous differences.

More than the lifestyle benefits (if I had placed the highest premium on comfort, I would simply have remained in the States) this tour was my chance to be a member of the Station team in a way not possible for me in El Dorado on the outside. I would know more quickly and completely what the Station as a whole was doing. Rather than have to rely on someone else keeping me informed, I would be attending the Station meetings in the sound-proof room (or "bubble") where the most sensitive matters were discussed and the COS set the direction of major Operations. I could read the incoming and outgoing messages between Zaragossa Station and Headquarters, except for messages dealing with personal matters of Station personnel and the exceptionally sensitive operational cables for the COS only. Because I managed the stable of Operations and assets that worked across all of the Station targets, I would see virtually all messages sooner or later. As a day-to-day inside member of the Station, I would have the opportunity to present my own ideas and operational suggestions directly to the COS. There would be fewer cover problems as an officially-covered Operations Officer. I could take care of my own administrative affairs. I would have a safe place to store everything from my disguise kit and operational funds to the reports on agent meetings and technical spy gear that I would be using in abundance. I would have a chance to be the inside conduit to the deep cover NOC officers and could even bring to bear some of my own experience as the guy at the end of the line. I would have regular contact with a range of Station personnel, including the hard-working Agency secretaries and communicators who are the unsung heroes of the Agency. In sum, I was beginning an altogether different kind of assignment and probably the type of tour I should have undertaken my first time abroad. I had not really been prepared for deep cover isolation and, during the Sixties, CIA was ill-equipped to support deep cover officers, as I had learned the hard way.

Covert Action in Zaragossa had a relatively low priority and principally involved placing anti-Communist theme articles in local newspapers, not so much to influence Zaragossan attitudes or policies but for replay in other parts of the world. The Agency could take a situation, locating a cache of Castro-provided weapons in country X for example, and replay it in countries Y and Z. Then the local reactions to the story in Y and Z could be retold in other countries, with the result that the story's effect was multiplied. Its real impact would be determined ultimately by its truth. Fabricated propaganda articles ordinarily have limited impact and a very short life.

In the early years of the Cold War, the Agency's psychological and propaganda activities were massive and covered the globe. The Red Scare was at its peak and the Communists pulled out all the stops in their ideological battle with the West. By the 1960s, much of the propaganda capability of the Agency had lost its raison d'etre; the Soviets had completely lost the battle for hearts and minds of the majority throughout the world and, after Stalin, there was no chance that they would again have the broad ideological appeal they enjoyed in the Thirties. The Clandestine Service kept its propaganda capability nonetheless, partly for selective use when there was a clear Covert Action goal — for example, publicizing in country A that a government leader in country B was in cahoots with the KGB or drug traffickers. There was also a purely self-serving and bureaucratic reason why we kept pumping out propaganda of a very generalized and amorphous variety, with no specific goal in mind. It had to do with a pernicious trend that would haunt America in Vietnam: we were falling into the *numbers trap.*

Propaganda Operations often proved useful substitutions for genuine Covert Action, the kind that really made things happen. As CIA lost its real CA power in the late Sixties, it used press placement of articles to keep itself at least partially in business and to make it appear as if it still had some clout. For example, when President Johnson became exasperated over Vietnam and the Soviets, he ordered the Agency to "do something" to inflict some pain on Moscow. Not having a solid way to carry out that order, the Agency launched a worldwide press campaign that may have had some nuisance value but was unlikely to make the Soviets change course or suffer greatly.

By contrast, when Soviet interests were directly threatened, as in Czechoslovakia in 1968, their tanks rolled in and they straightened things out, irrespective of the weight of world public opinion. Unlike Americans, they had no abiding need to be loved — just respected, or feared, or both. They knew that the world, soon enough, forgets. CIA's Psychological Operations kept Soviet actions before the world a while longer, but mainly they chalked up some numbers that could be used to show that CIA was doing something, at least. So many hundreds of propaganda articles placed in X number of countries totaling Y column inches of materials — of such was the stuff that bureaucratic survival was made. This did not disguise the fact that paralleling America's international decline under Johnson was the dissipation of Agency Covert Action. I was happy not to be working CA Operations in Zaragossa; playing the numbers game was not why I came CIA.

There were some partially-offsetting benefits for the lowering of CA from its prior position of dominance. We were seeing more and better FI Collection Operations and recruitment of what are known in the business as *hard targets*, specifically Russians, Cubans and other officials of hostile nations. More than any prior Director, DCI Helms had pushed for Operations Officers to get out and go after these very difficult targets, and the new emphasis was paying handsome dividends around the world. The new COS in Zaragossa, himself a superb recruiter, brought to the new emphasis on FI his own impressive style and leadership. The third leg of the stool, Counterintelligence, had previously occupied center stage in Zaragossa but was slipping in priority as the Clandestine Service, after years of unsuccessfully hitting its head against boorish old-line Stalinists, found that the new generation of Soviet officials was quite recruitable. So, my stable of agents was increasingly directed in support of FI recruitment Operations and, therefore, less emphasis was placed on CI in Zaragossa.

Was this a reflection of a studied, well-considered Agency decision? Not really. It so happened that the new way to make career headway was to go out and recruit a "hard target" agent, and it was not very long before everyone was doing, or trying to do, just that.

For the previous decade or so, CA Operations had made careers; now it was FI that did so. Unfortunately for the Agency and the country, CI never enjoyed that privileged position. It was too painstaking a discipline and devoid of the instant successes of CA Operations or FI Operations. Consequently, Counterintelligence Operations historically floated along between third-class and no-class status. Careerism was obviously having its impact on the direction of Agency Operations and this reality had its impact from Headquarters to the CIA Field Stations.

The FI role resumed its primary place partly as a result of the widespread assault on Covert Action, which no longer represented the fast career track for fast-rising whiz kids. An added boost in FI Operations arose from the fact that they were better suited to the new and growing emphasis on numbers to identify which Area Divisions, Stations, and Operations Officers were "doing the best job."

Two distinct aspects of FI Operations lend themselves nicely to quantification: Agent recruitments and Intelligence reporting. The former can be reflected in the number of "scalps" collected in any specific reporting period. It also is relatively simple to count the number of Intelligence reports produced by a Station each month and use that as the basis for rewarding one unit or motivating another.

In Southeast Asia, the saying went, the peasants would soon begin throwing rocks in with the rice if all one did was weigh them and not examine contents. The body count trap that Bob McNamara's band fell into, as they led America down the Vietnam drain, illustrates the futility of letting the quantifiers serve as sole arbiters of performance. Peter Drucker, the wizard of management, cautions against the use of a single, one-dimensional yardstick to measure organizational effectiveness and with good reason: it drives the people in the organization to take steps that undermine the institution itself.

CIA was not immune from this numbers game malady. One Agency bureaucrat, a real pro at the numbers game, called a first-tour officer into his office one morning when the junior officer had submitted for transmission to Washington a comprehensive Intelligence report on the country's political developments. The old master bean-counter showed how the one good report could be turned into three separate reports — the result: a definite loss in quality and coherence but an increase in the number of reports being recorded in Washington. More rocks in the rice bags! This type of thinking affected FI recruitment Operations and, in time, resulted in the firing of Operations Officers who created nonexistent or phony recruitments to make themselves competitive for promotion.

Some of the Operations I ran were handled directly by me and they required a lot of agent meetings in and around the Zaragossan capital. These agents did some bread-and-butter work that enabled the Station to track the movements of the *black hats*, as we called the Russians and their Bloc partners. In our minds, CIA and the KGB were as different as night and day — we stood for freedom and they stood for bondage. It wasn't merely a game played between representatives of two similar superpowers;

we were the good guys and they were not. So, operating against them was a reward in itself, and I had no difficulty working night and day against the black hats — Russians, Cubans, Czechs, Poles, Chinese, or Central American Marxist revolutionaries.

I generally left the house each weekday between 6:30 and 7:30 AM for early morning rounds that produced "the take" from the previous day's Operations. I would get home in the middle to late evening, in time usually to see the kids off to bed, but seldom much earlier. I also was busy almost every Saturday and sometimes Sunday as well. Holding the reins to the Station's operational support infrastructure meant that every time one of the several Operations Officers had an idea, I was called upon to pitch in. If I had felt like a long lost stranger under deep cover in El Dorado, I did not feel left out in Zaragossa. As little time as it gave me for my family, I preferred my new role.

Adding special significance to the assignment was my job as inside contact for three NOC officers, including two veterans of Zaragossa who worked on Technical Operations for which I was managerially responsible. I was their supervisor in a formal sense, giving them direction and writing their performance evaluations. They were all experienced in their specialties, dedicated and selfless in their work, and patient with the Agency system that chose often to ignore their personal needs. As a result, I soon developed enormous respect for them.

I made up my mind that if there was one thing I would absolutely assure during my years in Zaragossa, it was going to be proper use and support for these deep cover officers. My own workaholic ways and commitment to fight our adversaries ensured that I work the hell out of these deep cover officers. But I also saw to it that they got proper handling and recognition. Each of the three had been frozen in pay grade for several years; all three were promoted during my second year. One of them, so convinced he would never see the senior Operations Officer GS-14 level, was in tears the evening we held a car meeting in the outskirts of the capital and he learned directly from the COS that he had been promoted. I made sure that the Chief of Station personally went out to give the promotion news. Was it the enhanced rank — and the six percent increase in pay — that emotionally affected this very courageous Intelligence pro? No, it was the fact that, by promoting him, CIA was saying thank you and was acknowledging countless sacrifices as well as thousands of unpaid night and weekend hours of work.

Here we had an American staff Intelligence Officer who had served out in the cold for two decades. There were only a handful of NOC officers in the whole world who had survived outside that long. When I met him, his pay grade level was the same or lower than thousands of government workers back in Washington whose greatest risk was that they might choke to death on lobster at the annual Christmas party.

On one Operation, this fellow performed a task that should have been handled by at least two officers. He was wiring up some telephones in a major Zaragossan hotel where some foreign Communist diplomats were staying. It was important that we know whom they were contacting, and because there were dozens of lines going out of the hotel through a major switchboard, it was impossible to tap the right phones without doing an inside job. An outside phone tap would have inundated us with thousands of unwanted hotel calls. To install the phone tap wires, our NOC had to enter a ventilation shaft that ran from the top of the hotel more than a dozen floors to the basement. There was no light, so he had to hold a small flashlight between his teeth while he held onto the ladder with one hand to keep from plunging to his death. He used the other hand to run the wires. All the while he had to keep from gagging because that shaft happened to run past the hotel bathrooms. Also, hotel employees with an urge for the perverse used to enter the shaft to watch people through the bathroom vents, using the occasion to relieve themselves against the walls of the air shaft. For this mission alone, our NOC deserved a medal.

On another occasion, he was on the roof cutting wires to one of our telephone-tap listening posts as Telephone Company inspectors were climbing ladders to that roof trying to figure out where CIA's pirate wiring was headed. This NOC carried out his work without benefit of diplomatic immunity or the camaraderie enjoyed by those on the inside.

Even though we insiders worked long hours, there was at least the benefit of a certain normal rhythm to our lives. Most of what we did was accomplished between 7:30 in the morning and 9:30 in the evening, six days a week. The NOCs often had no clock saying when they were on duty or off duty. They possessed compromising CIA materials. American holidays meant little in their lives. One of the NOCs, someone I had brought to Zaragossa for special work, had to put in a very long day in his cover job and do all of his CIA work in the evenings and on weekends. The cover income went back to the Agency in an offset, of course. In some instances around the world, NOC officers turned in to Uncle Sam more cover income than they were actually paid by CIA — two jobs and two lives, but one modest Agency salary.

Only special people make this kind of sacrifice and each of these three NOCs was special indeed.

I worked very hard to see that the NOCs were well recognized, and eventually my advocacy on their behalf stimulated the ire of one of the inside senior managers. When he wrote his performance evaluation of my work, he commented favorably on my operational work but gratuitously added in the narrative portion that I was "too sympathetic" to the deep cover officers. He had never served on the outside, obviously. Like most of the Clandestine Service, he had come to think of the NOC officers as local contract hires and not as fellow Agency officers deserving of our wholehearted support.

The inability of Agency personnel, in general, to empathize with the NOCs, the defectors, and the field agents has caused more CIA failures than the active efforts of our hostile adversaries. I had seen it in El Dorado from one angle. I saw it again in Zaragossa from another. And, people being people, I would see it again in the years ahead as the Agency aged, became increasingly bureaucratized, and got away from its original ethic.

Not all of my time in Zaragossa was serious. There were lighter times as well. Four of us officers were of similar age and arrived more or less concurrently to begin our tours of duty. We each had different responsibilities operationally, but there was sufficient overlap that we worked together some of the time. We all hit it off personally, as did our wives. Soon a strong bond existed between the four families. This was a real treat for Bonnie and me after the deep cover experience in El Dorado. It was great to be able to socialize outside work with people who shared the same professional goals. We could relax together and not have to be on guard all of the time.

Unfortunately, the only marriage of the four to survive was Bonnie's and mine — such can be the long-term stress of this demanding, mobile career. I long believed that this high rate of divorce was an Agency phenomenon. Years later, when I got back to New England, I was having dinner one evening with a childhood friend and our wives. One of the first things he said that evening was that he and his wife were the last married couple among the group that they had formed after college. Obviously, it is not only in CIA or the Foreign Service where such casualties occur.

On arriving in Zaragossa, I had inherited some very fine agents who, in combination with the NOC officers, gave Zaragossa Station some capabilities that were among the best in the Agency. Being an old Labor

Operations guy, I had also strengthened the economic situation for the locally-hired agents, making certain that their pay did not suffer due to inflation. I brought their real earnings up to appropriate levels. While I was adjusting their pay, I also formalized the Agency's responsibility to make a severance payment (the traditional Latin America formula of a month's pay for each year of service) in the event they were ever let go without cause. Certainly, a CIA field agent would have a difficult time seeking contract enforcement in a court of law. Nonetheless, the written provision formalized the Agency's moral obligation in this regard, especially since this internal document was approved in writing by the COS. In time — due to Philip Agee's defection — the new contract provisions would become very important.

The local Zaragossan agents were excellent assets. The core group had been recruited many years earlier and their loyalty to the Agency was known to all who worked with them over the years. One key agent had more street time in support of Agency Operations than almost all officers in the Clandestine Service. In the three years we worked together, there was never an instance in which he did not respond well to our requests, even to harebrained schemes the Station occasionally directed. For several days, he and his surveillance team members watched a highway leading out of the capital because we had information that a Soviet agent would be traveling to the area. We were determined to identify this individual at all costs. As was often the case when such an operation was concocted, it was the field agent who paid the price, not the inside Station manager who thought it up.

I remember a very cold and rainy night when the team leader spent nine hours lying prone in a flooded gutter beside his car; it was the only way he could keep his eyes on the doors of a Communist embassy from which we were expecting a defector to make the break for freedom. Most officers and agents would have remained in their car at the risk of being spotted, but not this pro. He knew that someone else's safety was at stake and he made sure that he could not be seen by the Communist diplomats or local police driving past in their patrol cars. He could easily have come back to me and reported that the area did not lend itself to surveillance. But in this and numerous other ways he showed his willingness to pay a personal price to protect Agency equities. A man like this made the Zaragossa experience a good one for me.

As I got ready to depart Zaragossa, I knew I would not be seeing any of these agents again, even though we had spent three years of very intensive work together. I might have an opportunity to meet again with the NOC officers when they came to Washington, but not the local agents. Just as I was about to depart, word was received that former Agency officer Philip Agee had been in Havana and was considered by the Agency to be a probable defector. His primary vehicle for revenge would be a book he was writing. Agee obviously knew some of the CIA agents around Latin America. Corrective measures had to be taken to protect people. I was sure the Agree exposure would affect part of every Station's stable of agents and NOC officers, including Zaragossa's. As I headed back to the States in 1972, I had no idea how broad the damage would be.

Just before I left, a very private message came in from Headquarters for the COS, explaining that steps should be taken to dismantle each and every operation Agee could possibly have known about — i.e., virtually every agent in Zaragossa who had been around for any length of time would be fired. Similar messages had been sent to other Stations in Latin America. They were all sent at the direction of the Latin America Division Chief, a man with a reputation for being absolutely decisive. He had made a name for himself out in Southeast Asia, in good part because he could play the body count and numbers games to the satisfaction of the American Military. Most who had worked with him said he was mean and emotionless, a man who drove himself and others unceasingly. "Mr. Decisive's" first reaction was to ascribe omniscience to Agee and terminate every Latin American operation in existence back in 1969, when Agee had left the Agency.

I spoke with the COS and made a strong plea to oppose the decision, reminding him that Agee had not been a serious Operations Officer when it came to digging in and doing his homework. In his last assignment, in Mexico City, he had been substantially on the outside, serving in a so-called Olympic Attaché role that kept him away from most Station files and activities. Before Mexico, he had flitted around Headquarters kissing up to anyone who could help his career, spending little or no time even on the Mexico desk in advance of his own assignment. Could he hurt the Agency? He certainly could. But should we be so foolish as to dismantle everything, pretending that Agee had been a thorough professional when he was not? The COS was in agreement intellectually and, as I left for home, I assumed that he would put up a good fight to protect the Operations, the NOCs, the agents and, ultimately, the Agency itself.

We left Zaragossa and, rather than go right back to Washington, landed in Texas for the beginning of an incredible journey through the

American West. The children were then twelve, eleven, ten and eight, and for the previous three years we had done very little together as a family except for trips around the Zaragossan capital on Sundays after church. I had had three years of very hard work, with too little time with Bonnie and the children. I had used so little of my vacation time that we decided to go all out and take the children on what would be a 9,500-mile trip. It would last fifty-two days and hit all the great national parks, the Grand Canyon, Disneyland, and Salt Lake City. When one of the kids' cousins joined us in Texas, we had five children between eight and twelve years in the back of a Station wagon for close to two months. There was no way that I was going to dwell too much on Zaragossa and Agee. I was too busy chauffeuring and keeping track of five excited youngsters whose energy levels never seemed to lessen.

As we stopped near the Grand Tetons on our way up to Yellowstone, Bonnie got very sick. We scooted quickly past Old Faithful and went on to Billings, Montana, in search of a doctor. What we feared, some kind of flu, turned out to be no malady at all; Bonnie and I were expecting our fifth child, who had decided to let us know he was along for the ride. We got back to Headquarters in late summer, in time for the children to enroll in school. We spent several days cleaning up the house; our last tenants had been two weird women with several dogs who had chewed up the drapes and urinated on all the rugs. We had initially rented it out to a Marine Corps Officer and family, who had left the house in immaculate condition. We had no such luck with the second tenants, and before moving back in I had to do the house over, top to bottom, as Bonnie wrestled with morning sickness and managing four children facing reentry into U.S. grade schools and a disintegrating 1970s America.

By the time I got back to LA Division two months had passed and the Agee train had picked up a full head of steam. The COS in Zaragossa may have made an appeal of sorts, but in the end it had been to no avail. Every operation I had worked on was being terminated, every agent I had inherited upon arrival in Zaragossa fired, including new agents who had been added to the support structure. Two of the three NOCs were forced into early retirement. They knew that they had never come into contact with Agee, and this made the whole business very disagreeable because it did not make any sense. Dave Phillips, who would take charge of LA Division the following year, wrote that the Agee defection meant that a "program of cauterization was already underway: agents known to Agee were being terminated, and some relocated for their safety; and every operation which Agee might have been privy to was being terminated."

I was no sooner back in the Division than someone came over from the Zaragossa desk and said that the Station had asked that I take a brief trip back to the Station to help in firing all the CIA agents with whom I had just completed three years of very close association. It was not that anyone was suddenly getting sentimental. The Station and Headquarters were concerned that the firings would not go smoothly, that there might be further defections or trouble because the agents knew a great deal about Agency officers and past Operations. Any one of them would have been valuable to the Soviets or Cubans who, after they milked the former CIA agents for information, could then have used them to publicize the extent of Agency activity in Zaragossa. This would have embarrassed the local government, provided the local Communists with some grist for their propaganda mill, and forced further retrenchment by CIA. The Station was very capable of handling the firings, in which it had acquiesced, without outside help. But they knew that I had excellent personal relationships with the agents as well as the NOCs and could do the dirty work with less pain — for the Station at least.

I accepted the request to go back to Zaragossa primarily to make a final appeal to the COS to fight this mindless decision. Having met Mr. Decisive in Headquarters, I knew that getting him to change course had little chance of success. But if anyone could influence him to be reasonable it would be this senior COS, who could always appeal to the DCI, whom he personally represented in Zaragossa. The die had been cast, however, and the firings went forward.

I met with the team leader and tried, as best I could, to soften the blow. Here was a Zaragossan being fired with all his fellow surveillants because of betrayal by an American CIA Operations Officer, Agee. The only solace I got was that the Agency was going to have to make a hefty payout for the defection of Agee and for the stupidity of its Division Chief; the Contract Amendments I had included years before suddenly had real teeth and meaning. The pay-out to the Zaragossan agents was so large that Latin America Division had to get a special release from the Agency Reserve Fund.

The management types at Headquarters were livid, but it was all written down in black-and-white so there was no way of squirming out of the payments. Did the agents get rich by this? Hardly. The more senior ones got the equivalent of twelve to fifteen months pay, and they would need every peso to make the transition to the real world. They had come to work for CIA in their late twenties and were now in their mid-forties, with no transferable commercial skills and no way to get a letter of reference from their long-time employer, CIA. Some found that when they could not provide such a reference, prospective employers were convinced that they had been in prison. So, while I was glad that I had written the month-per-year formula into their contracts, I wished I had somehow fattened it up even more. We were firing individuals Agee could not have identified and when he got around to publishing his book three years later — with Cuban Intelligence support — none of the Zaragossan assets or NOCs was named publicly. Mr. Decisive had gone overboard and damaged U.S. national security enormously.

The national damage from Agee's defection eventually went far beyond the immediate Agency losses in Zaragossa. In just one Station where Agee had served, Mexico City, the complete dismantling of the Counterintelligence network opened a wide breach in America's defenses, one which served the Soviet KGB just thirty months later.

"One night in April 1975, following an extended session with cocaine, Boyce suddenly confided in Lee that he had access to certain material that could be worth a lot of money to a foreign country. Lee was interested and they made a plan. A week later, Lee flew to Mexico City, went directly to the Soviet embassy, and announced that he had information of interest to the Soviets. Within minutes, Lee and Boyce were on their way to becoming two more self-selected Soviet sources." So write Corson and Crowley about the so-called "Falcon and the Snowman" — Christopher John Boyce and Andrew Daulton Lee — who did great damage to U.S. Technical Collection against the Soviets.

Agee's books on CIA, his violations of his Secrecy Agreement, and his betrayal of Agency sources, methods and even Operations Officers' identities attacked CIA's very fiber, resulting in a Counterintelligence debacle for the Agency both in Headquarters as well as overseas.

10

Deep Cover Doldrums

IF I HAD MANAGED to bring something good to Zaragossa from my own prior deep cover experience, my next assignment increased that opportunity enormously. I was offered the task of running a new program managing all of the deep cover Operations Officers serving in Latin America. The challenge was enticing; I did not have to rely on the high resignation rate of Nonofficial Cover Officers to know what a poor job CIA was doing with our deep cover cadre. I had seen it all first hand in the field, and here was a chance to help the Agency and its outside officers. Also, the job's complexity would ensure I did not sit around moping about Zaragossa and my three years of operational work suddenly going up in smoke, due to Agee.

Hard work was precisely what I needed and hard work was guaranteed by an edict that ordered me to expand significantly the number of deep cover officers in Latin America. We weren't managing, supporting or using the NOCs already serving in the region; to think we could do so suddenly on an expanded basis was extremely optimistic. But that was the directive from the LA Division Chief, Mr. Decisive, whose excessive zeal with the Phil Agee defection-cauterization had inadvertently put CIA out of the Counterintelligence business in his region of responsibility. As a result, America had no effective protection from Soviet Intelligence along its own southern border and would eventually pay a high price for this vulnerability.

CIA deep cover Operations were in a sorry state. NOC officers were quitting the Agency at an alarming rate and, as a result, we were losing officers after three to five years of training, often before they had even had an opportunity to contribute operationally. The Agency was wasting its own resources — financial, training and cover — and getting very little back. More importantly, the situation was crushing the morale of many of its most motivated personnel, many of whom quietly resigned, not to be heard from again by CIA. Because most deep cover Officers resigned without fanfare, the full extent of our deep cover failures was masked almost entirely. Only those working specifically on deep cover management could appreciate how poorly we were doing. The most knowledgeable on this subject were administrative types whose clout within the Directorate of Operations was extremely limited through the Sixties and the Agency's first twenty-five years.

The Operations Officers of CIA historically represented the Agency's elite career service, and it was from their ranks that the first-generation CIA leaders emerged. Dulles and Helms came from the Clandestine Service. Chiefs of Station exercised power in the field. Operations Officers were seen as the organization's cutting edge. Very few of them, however, had any patience for the administrative or bureaucratic side of the organization. In fact, some of the highest ranking Operations types were notoriously lax attending to their own expense reporting.

Due to this DDO aversion for things administrative, a number of critical tasks within the scope of clandestine Operations were relegated to non-operational status. Handling of defectors was one such responsibility and, as a result, the Agency's track record in defector resettlement was poor long before anyone had ever heard of KGB officer Vitali Yurchenko (whose ostensible 1985 defection-redefection made a mockery of CIA). Another responsibility shifted to administrators was the business of deep cover management — from the selection of an appropriate cover vehicle to the handling of the NOC officer's career. Both of these vital operational elements had been turned over to administrative types because the tasks were deemed too mundane to be handled by hotshot Operations Officers.

We should bear in mind that the collapse of the worldwide Covert Action infrastructure back in 1967 was a seismic result of this trend. No Operations Officer with even an elementary understanding of security and compartmentation would have linked so many incompatible funding channels, or Covert Action activities, in the first place. Yet, that is precisely what those responsible for the covert funding had done. And, when the whole funding network for Covert Action Operations worldwide exploded like a series of claymore mines, the internal Agency response was to fault the media for exposing the weak foundation cover arrangements. No one asked the Operations pros what they were doing when the house of cards was being built by administrators who were untrained in operational security or just too lax to do the job correctly.

I had witnessed the casual attitude toward cover twice in my El Dorado experience. Partway through my assignment, I was in need of a new cover backstopping and went back to the States for that purpose. The Station attitude was clear: go back and get something, anything, and get back as quickly as possible because we have a Covert Action election program to run. This was a far cry, certainly, from what we know of the "sleeper" Operations run by the British, who take the craft of spying very seriously. They had, for example, the patience to place what appeared to be an elderly retired couple in a key foreign port area many years in advance of war. When hostilities did break out, the sleepers awoke and Her Majesty's Secret Service had superbly-placed agents who reported on enemy shipping movements effectively, because they were above suspicion. Why? Because they seemed so harmless and natural. The work that went into Richard Sorge's cover planning illustrates the seriousness with which the Soviets take espionage and one of its essential elements, the development of suitable, durable deep cover mechanisms and agents.

By contrast, I had been sent back from El Dorado to Washington to pick up a new cover as though I were fetching a pen or typewriter ribbon from the stock shelf. The cover selected by the cover administrators made no sense whatsoever for El Dorado — not as bad as trying to market refrigerators to Eskimos, but a close second. I would now be representing a firm that had no interest, real or potential, in El Dorado that would warrant their having a full-time American on the payroll. I knew the cover stunk; I told the Station how inappropriate it was, and they told me to take it anyway and get back to the Station as quickly as possible. Two years later, after departing El Dorado permanently, the *Ramparts* foundation flap broke and I saw how faulty the underpinnings of my earlier academic cover had been as well.

In looking at the Agency cover history, it is important to keep in mind our own nature as Americans and how that affects our work. Unlike the British or Russians, we do not have the patience to do top-quality work in all areas of Intelligence. Though the Operations people are capable of excellence in the glamorous high-profile activities, they generally cannot be bothered with the equally-important, though mundane, matters of cover development, funding channels, defector handling, and the Agency stepchild, Counterintelligence.

The career management of deep cover officers has been another weak link in the NOC chain, again because it has been treated traditionally as an administrative function. In the early 1960s, a deep cover program was put together to develop a long-term career cadre. It made enormous improvements in the bureaucratic management of NOC officers; they got paid on time and were given the feeling that someone back in Headquarters was thinking about them and supporting them on a continual basis. A great improvement over the earlier administrative chaos, it looked as though centralized deep cover management was there to stay. Quite against Clandestine Service style, the deep cover officers were able to communicate directly with their mentors in Headquarters on career and administrative matters. For a while, it seemed as though a workable solution had been found, one that would give the Agency the necessary deep cover capability and at the same time assure that it was not done at the expense of the NOC officers themselves. American Intelligence seemed to have learned something from our own British mentors and our principal adversary, the Soviets. As with many thoughtful, long-range initiatives in American Intelligence, however, American impatience for results brought the deep cover enterprise to an unceremonious ending.

One of the casualties of the experiment was a young officer who had entered the Agency after military service and graduation with honors from the Naval Academy. He did very well in CIA Operations Training and was selected for the new, hush-hush deep cover program — CIA was going to develop its own Richard Sorge-like cadre of deep cover illegals — or so the young man thought. He ostensibly resigned from the Agency and went up to New York for what appeared to be the beginning of a career in business. In fact, he was embarking on a program of cover development. He was going to be both a legitimate businessman and an undercover operative. Two years later, after total immersion in his new commercial profession, he was dispatched to a major underdeveloped country for a cover-building tour — no clandestine activity, except for his own personal development in foreign language and cover. When that tour was completed, he was transferred to another country where he continued to develop his cover credentials. This time, he was carrying out clandestine tasks directly for the Chief of Station, who was reminded by Headquarters that this was one of the special group of long-term deep cover operatives who should be utilized very judiciously and with great care to protect the CIA investment.

At the end of that tour, having done all that CIA had directed him to do, he visited Headquarters and had a chance to meet face to face with his deep cover superiors. The meeting took place in a downtown Washington safehouse; he was not authorized to enter the Headquarters building itself as that could have compromised his well-developed cover. Even his trip to D.C. had been circuitous to make sure that no airline passenger list showed him as having been in the nation's capital. Nine years into his career he was expecting a "well done" for the way he had developed into a pro in international business. He was expecting also that the Agency, after a decade of preparation, was now ready to dispatch him to an assignment of paramount importance, one that would make use of his impeccable cover, his military experience, and his Agency Intelligence training.

When the head of CIA deep cover came out to see him, the first thing he told the NOC officer was that he was in trouble: in comparison with his original Career Training Program peer group, he was now ranked forty-sixth out of forty-eight! He had not been sufficiently productive in Intelligence to compete for promotion with peers whose cover preparation had not been so elaborate or demanding. (Nor could Rembrandt compete with a Kodak Brownie camera, if quantity is the way one measures results!) The Agency had crafted a deep cover masterpiece that it did not even recognize when it was completed.

I first met this young man shortly after I took charge of the deep cover program in Latin America where he was now serving again. He had been reassigned to the country he had been first sent to several years earlier to begin his cover-building odyssey. This was a country where the Intelligence Operations climate was so benign that one could operate there without much cover at all. Ten years of hush-hush for this! To make things worse, he was still competing promotionally on an uneven playing field, carrying the ball uphill while the rest of the deep cover officers were able to coast. He was still carrying a heavy cover load and working two jobs. The other NOC officers at his Station had little or no cover burden, so they could do their CIA work full time. Again, the CIA version of Richard Sorge was in career difficulty, and I was directed to do something to get his career back on track.

I had read his complete file in Washington and was eager to match the man with the relatively sterile paperwork. His personnel file reflected only the official version of events — that, for some unexplained reason, this deep cover officer had failed to sparkle after many years of Agency investment. In fact, the file would suggest, he had even been sent back to a country he knew well and still had not set the turf on fire with activity.

We shook hands and sat down in one of those Agency safehouse apartments that gives itself away by the pile of unopened mail, the six-month-old magazines, the instant coffee on the counter, and the half eaten box of crackers. We chatted a bit about his trip to Washington and I thanked him for a chance to get together. I downplayed the fact that I had been placed in charge of a new deep cover program. This poor guy had been assaulted enough over the years by self-important bureaucrats promising him they were finally going to fix the NOC program. Instead, I simply mentioned that I had spent five years under deep cover in Latin America. That was all that was needed. He knew that I knew.

By this time, I also knew enough about the way the Clandestine Service really worked to avoid falling into the trap of seeking an ideal solution to this fellow's career difficulties. It was much too late for that. Two years had passed since the deep cover Chief had gone out to tell him how badly he had been doing. Like the zoo elephant whose spirit is broken by axe-handle whacks across the forehead, this NOC officer had also been broken of any self-respect as an Operations Officer. It was now merely a survival case, trying to find some way that he could salvage his career in accordance with the way the Agency really is, not as it ought to be. In the realm of the ought-to-be, one could make a case that an officer in his mid-thirties, with impeccable cover and a technical/military background, could fill a void in American Intelligence that the Soviets had been successfully closing: there were hardly any CIA Operations Officers with any substantive familiarity with Science and Technology. We were in an S&T age and we had less than a half-dozen officers who could be considered reasonably comfortable with scientific disciplines.

If the Agency had known what it had in this NOC a few years earlier, before telling him he was not cutting it, it might have turned this into a splendid career and a productive deep cover operation. As we sat in the safehouse, however, I knew that heroics were out of the question. This fellow, who had obviously been sufficiently impressive to get through the screening for one of the service academies and later for CIA's own Career Training Program, showed none of the verve that must have been there on the two occasions he had stepped forward to serve his country. After the meeting, I returned to Headquarters and scurried around until I found a new assignment in another part of the world, in a field Station with the best reputation for using its deep cover officers. Some months later, he landed in the new job and, as far as I could tell, was put to work on some good cases. But it turned out to be too late. Shortly thereafter he got caught in one of the reduction-in-force exercises of the Seventies and placed on the list for separation from the Agency. His military and Agency years just barely qualified him for a modest early retirement annuity, so he was not officially fired. Like too many other deep cover officers, his career was either misdirected or mismanaged by uncaring misfits who, in fact, ought to have been the ones who were fired.

I did not need a shot of adrenaline to get up for this work. Officers out in the cold needed both intelligent and compassionate support, more likely to come from someone who had himself experienced deep cover. I got lucky relatively early in my assignment when I went into work one Monday and learned that Mr. Decisive was moving on; his replacement would be Dave Phillips, then serving as Chief of Station in Caracas. Phillips had served under deep cover in the field — in Chile, Cuba, and Lebanon — and knew about NOC life as well as any Officer in the Clandestine Service.

Phillips's most perilous moment under deep cover had come in 1960 in Havana, where he was getting a bird's eye view of Fidel Castro's betrayal of the Cuban Revolution, which had ousted the corrupt Fulgencio Batista. Executions of democratic leaders had begun on a scale reminiscent of the rise to power of Communists in other countries — the *paredon*, or firing squad wall, had become the most vivid symbol of the new regime. One fine day Phillips went over to the Havana post office to pick up a package and, on opening it, found that CIA had mailed him his Central Intelligence Agency Intelligence Medal for the work he had done six years earlier in the ouster of Arbenz in Guatemala! Someone in Headquarters obviously thought he really had resigned from CIA and had moved to beautiful Cuba, then in utter turmoil, to begin a new life. That Phillips was not discovered and executed by the Cubans was due only to his own survival instincts, cool head and ingenuity, which had aided his successful escape from a German prisoner-of-war camp back in WW II. He rewrapped the CIA "gift package" and mailed it from the Cuban Post Office to his Havana address, later making arrangements for its safe disposal.

As an Operations Officer inside Field Stations, and later as Chief of Station, Dave Phillips had come to know a number of the deep cover officers personally. Unlike Mr. Decisive and most of the Division hierarchy, the new Division Chief saw the NOC officers as special people worthy of special support. With his arrival, my job was made easier as I worked to make the system itself more rational and humane.

To do this, I had to deal with the Agency trend toward becoming a more bureaucratic, legalistic institution. Administrators and lawyers were moving into positions of increased responsibility. They were also contributing to the writing and massaging of new regulations, rules made necessary partly because the operators in the Clandestine Service had tended to run footloose for most of the Agency's first twenty years. Now, the career bureaucrats had their chance to call the shots, and they began a process of empire-building that would convert the Directorate of Administration (DDA) into the largest of the four Agency Directorates. As the number of administrators grew arithmetically, rules and regulations grew exponentially.

Within the DDA there was another development which made the conduct of clandestine Operations more difficult: most of the newer administrative types in Headquarters did not have overseas experience themselves, and so they had little understanding of field Operations and the flexibility needed for this business. By contrast, the first generation of support officers had as much overseas service as the clandestine operators, and both understood and identified with the covert work being done in Field Stations. For someone trying to set up a new deep cover program, the trend in bureaucratization was not at all helpful.

Deep cover at its best is inherently unorthodox and should manifest none of the features of government service. Administrators and government lawyers, who worship at the altar of orthodoxy, want deep cover officers to fly on American air carriers even though no genuine American businessman would fly on Pan Am if he could get a seat on Swissair. Nonofficial Cover, by its very name, demands that the approach not mirror government service; the bureaucracy was treating the deep cover officers on the same terms as inside, officially-covered officers in an effort to make things conform to the government system — the closer to the procedures of the Poughkeepsie Post Office the better as far as the admin types were concerned. In sum, admin types wrote rules, loved those rules and avoided any risk-taking themselves. The clandestine operators, by contrast, were stifled when the rules noose was pulled too tightly, especially when deep cover officers operated outside the government cocoon.

The only way I could get my job done and place dozens of NOC officers in Latin America in a two-year period was to push the administrative structure and its people very hard. Fortunately, in addition to Division Chief Phillips, I also had the backing of a very supportive direct boss. I had reached the point also where I did not care whether people liked what we were doing, so long as they either helped or got out of the way. This push against the support people was partly out of my frustration with the collapse of the CI network in Latin America. Some of them were extremely supportive and did everything in their power to help get deep cover officers to the field. The obstructionists, however, were what psychologists might term "passive-aggressive" individuals who wore you down with bureaucratic obstacles, requiring still another piece of paper or memorandum — *just for the record.*

I used to muse that, if I were a KGB Chief able to place only one mole in CIA, I would make him an administrator. I would then direct this mole to simply follow the rules, all of the rules, all of the time. Eventually, he would rise in the hierarchy and, in the course of that ascension, he would wear down the Operations people and demoralize them more than a dozen KGB officers attacking from outside could achieve.

Besides pushing deep cover matters in Headquarters, I also traveled Latin America, helping Stations with their NOC problems and NOCs with their Station problems. Most of the time the problem was one of poor communication, not unusual given the tremendous gulf between the inside and outside world of Operations. Once, I traveled to the southern cone of the continent to rescue a very gifted senior NOC officer from the mismanagement of that same senior officer who, back in Zaragossa, had felt I was too nice to the deep cover officers. The quick transfer of this very talented NOC to another Station resolved the difficulty, but it supported my growing theory that people stay the same and are inherently unchangeable after a certain age. Operations Officers who display good judgment early in their careers tend to grow into wise Chiefs of Station. Officers who have little regard for the well-being of agents or NOCs in one time and place do not become compassionate senior managers.

In the course of a trip to meet NOCs in the region, I got to know one of the Agency's great officers, Dick Welch, then COS in Latin America. Welch was a Greek classicist from Harvard, a dynamic leader who was one of a half dozen officers worldwide destined to head all clandestine Operations. His work was excellent, his Station effective, and his leadership abilities hands-on. Around the time I met Welch, I was dealing in his Station with a young, locally-recruited deep cover officer who was close to broke and lacked any of the benefits and protection of regular deep cover personnel. His wife was expecting a child in a matter of days and he had no medical insurance, a potentially disastrous situation anywhere. Welch was out of town when I arrived at his Station for what I expected to be a fairly routine meeting with his deep cover officers. When I met the young NOC and his wife, it was clear that they had reached a high level of desperation. He had not wanted to push the Station for help for fear of appearing inept or venal; she was scared that she was going to end up in some public assistance hospital. I had no authority to act in someone's field Station, but I advised the distraught wife not to worry, that CIA was going to pick up the delivery costs.

This had the immediate effect of lowering her anxiety level — and put my neck in the noose administratively. Under such circumstances, the COS upon returning to the Station could have pulled the lever and let me twist in the wind. I had no authority to offer what I had offered. But, Dick Welch was too big a person to quibble about where his line of authority began or ended. He had close to absolute authority within his Station area, and on bureaucratic grounds, I was dead wrong. He could have made an example of me, but he appreciated the intervention, thanked me personally, and paid for the delivery out of Station funds.

Dick Welch was next sent to Athens, Greece as Chief of Station. John Ranelagh, in *The Agency: The Rise and Decline of CIA*, describes his fate: "The name and home address of Richard Welch, who in 1975 was Chief of Station in Athens, where he was serving under State Department cover as a first secretary of the embassy, were published in the English-language *Athens News* on November 25. On December 23, 1975, Welch was shot dead on his own doorstep. In the edition of *Counterspy* that had earlier identified Welch, Agee had written: The most effective and important systematic efforts to combat the CIA that can be taken right now are, I think, the identification, exposure, and neutralization of its people working abroad…The people themselves will have to decide what they must do to rid themselves of CIA'."

Anyone who knew Dick Welch cannot help but feel rage that Agee — who betrayed his country, his former employer, his coworkers, the West, his wife and democracy — has the gall to write and say what he does. And to think that the ACLU and the Justice Department lawyers think he should not be prosecuted! It is ironic that my most vivid memory from three years of deep cover management was not of deep cover officers, but of two insiders, Dick Welch and Philip Agee, who represented the Agency at its finest and its worst, respectively.

I stayed with the NOC management job for three years, longer than I had originally planned but what was needed more or less to deal with the challenge. Partway through this period, the Clandestine Service undertook yet another Directorate-wide initiative on deep cover, partly in response to the inordinate number of NOC resignations occurring in Asia. Some of those working on the problem in Headquarters were deep cover officers who had been compromised by Phil Agee and been forced to come back inside for the remainder of their careers.

Within a few years, the lot of deep cover officers seemed to improve in the other Area Divisions. Most telling was the fact that promotions increased dramatically for the NOCs, in part because they were being used more effectively and also because they now had solid support in Headquarters from those of us who had served on the outside. NOCs were now selected specifically for deep cover service; we were no longer sending inside officers outside as though the two career tracks were interchangeable. A centrally-administered support structure was created again, and the training of deep cover officers was placed on a par with that given inside officers. This was especially important as it placed the NOCs in a position to come back inside later when, for many of them, the inevitable occurred — either they got blown out of the water or they tired of the lonely life outside. We seemed to have learned from our mistakes and taken corrective action. On a personal level, I had the satisfaction of knowing that some of my family's sacrifices in El Dorado and my own NOC management experience in Zaragossa contributed to the new approach.

Meanwhile, I had reached the fifteen-year point in my own career and needed to do some assessment of my own. My mid-career personal review could not have occurred under more difficult circumstances, notwithstanding my promotion a year earlier to GS-14 and my NOC successes. One of the wheels, deep cover, was temporarily in better shape, but other wheels were falling off the Agency wagon faster than they could be repaired.

11
Turbulent Times for CIA

THE SEA has always conjured up frightening images for me. The struggle of Odysseus and the story of the Ancient Mariner fascinated me and, as a child watching movies at the local "flea house" where I could see two features and an adventure serial for twelve cents, the raging storms on the water scared me more than any horror film. The business of secret Intelligence has its share of risks — part of its appeal. But the sea, with its force approaching infinity, is where man's finitude is vividly manifested. And it is the sea that comes to mind as I recall the Agency in the mid-1970s.

Back in my earliest days in CIA I knew, on an intellectual level at least, that harmonizing an Intelligence career with family life was not going to be easy. The Agency was only a dozen years old when I had joined, so there was not an extended history from which to learn how a marriage would hold up under the strain of a secret life and career. Nor was there a good way of knowing what effect, if any, it would all have on the development of our children. Yet, although conclusive evidence was lacking, there were signs that clandestine operators were faring no better, and probably worse, than the Foreign Service on the matter of family life. Contributing factors were similar in both professions and shared by certain fast-track occupations at home — too much booze, endless parties, frequent unaccompanied travel to exotic places, unbridled career ambition, long work days, a widening psychological gulf between men and women, and the emerging sexual revolution with its low-risk infidelity. The Intelligence operator and his family had additional forces against them and, as early as 1960, we witnessed family troubles plaguing a surprising percentage of the Operations Officer corps.

First, there was the whole aura of secrecy. Operations Officers did much of their wining and dining of developmental contacts at night, in bars and restaurants, where the atmosphere and alcohol broke down the inhibitions of otherwise stalwart family men. They also did, as a matter of course, secret things all the time. They met agents, sometimes of the opposite sex, in safehouses, car meetings, and out-of-the-way places. When other men were home for the evening, Operations Officers were slipping out into the night when the local internal security service or KGB security officer had presumably called it quits for the day. They arrived home in the wee hours of the morning and, because there was a cover life to maintain, they would leave the house the next morning as though they had been home all evening. The CIA wives, especially in the earliest years when they knew no better, were not inclined to probe deeply into the night work, which was, after all, wrapped very nicely under the cloak of "national security." The conditions were perilous for the well-intentioned, but absolutely perfect for the promiscuous.

Secondly, Intelligence work itself had become a "mistress" for many, directly competing with family for attention and fidelity. The mission of the Agency involved matters of national consequence for both the United States and the country in which or against which CIA was operating. Collecting secret Intelligence, penetrating a foreign government (especially a hostile one), trying to overthrow a Marxist regime, protecting a democracy from Communist subversion — these were stimulating activities to which an Operations Officer had little difficulty devoting his whole being. Too many Intelligence operators succumbed to the calls of the Intelligence sirens. Meanwhile, their wives and children were paying the price.

Early in my career, a fellow Trainee and I sat over at the bar at the Farm and talked about career and family. Most of us in the Career Training Program, I said to my colleague, would go on to successful careers as Operations Officers and finish respectably in the GS-14 to GS-15 range (CIA equivalent of Lt. Colonel or full Colonel). Some would soar to the highest levels, and a few would fall short. The important thing, I said, would be to complete our career with the same spouse and with a family as proud of us as we would be of them. The best way to accomplish these very tough goals would be to establish the right priority in life, making our spouse first, our children second, and our career third. If we do that, I said, we could have it all — a good career, a very good marriage, and a great life.

My talk was Trainee talk, of course, and reflected thinking that was consistent with the thrust of my Boston College education. There, the Jesuits had anticipated Vatican II changes a decade in advance but had also maintained the tradition of a value-laden education and an emphasis on clarity in thought. As an Officer brand new to Intelligence, I had little difficulty articulating a view that was balanced, wholesome and simple. Living that formula was going to be more difficult and complex than I had appreciated.

Clearly, when I undertook the long-term deep cover assignment to El Dorado, I was acting much like every other Trainee, placing career considerations at the forefront and letting my wife and children come along for the ride, like it or not. The children were too young to be affected in their schoolwork. My wife was acting like virtually all the other wives, content to go where asked in support of my career. There was also an illusion, which I helped foster, that living in Latin America was going to be just dandy. I had no idea what deep cover was going to be like. In my orientation into CIA, senior managers had spoken about the marvelous support we give our people overseas. One of the most articulate speakers in this regard, I would recall years later, never left Washington once in his career, and he rose to its highest level.

Upon leaving El Dorado and getting ready to come back inside, I was thinking about volunteering for Vietnam; rumor suggested that, sooner or later, we would all end up assigned to Southeast Asia. Upon arrival back to the States, I threw my hat into the ring for possible assignment, with family, to a Caribbean country that was in turmoil. The Agency was gearing up for an election operation to keep a proclaimed Marxist and friend of Castro from taking over the government. I knew that this would be a great career opportunity. I gave little thought to the difficulties of bringing Bonnie and four children ages three to seven into a country where the basic health and sanitation facilities were terrible. My earlier thinking about the right priorities in work and life notwithstanding, seven years into my career I was still very close to being a 100-percent company man, at least in the matter of assignments. I wanted to be at the center of things. Why come into the Intelligence business if you're not going to grab every chance to be where the action is? The Caribbean assignment went to someone else; and the Vietnam affair had still another few years to play itself out. But Vietnam, the nightmare that undermined America's self-confidence as leader of the free world, was the issue over which my wife and I had our most difficult career disagreement.

Operations Officers were being sent to that area in droves, both recent Career Trainee classes in their entirety and middle-grade officers from all Divisions of the Clandestine Service. The normal tour of duty was eighteen months — unaccompanied; the family could either remain in the States or go to an Asian safe haven where they could be visited periodically. Financial incentives were impressive, including sufficient premium pay and allowances to enable someone to get out of debt or establish a healthy nest egg. The opposition that was developing within the U.S. against the war in Southeast Asia had the effect of strengthening the resolve of many officers within the Clandestine Service. Going to Vietnam to help win the war and prevent the further spread of Communism seemed the right thing to do. I told Bonnie around the time of our return to the States that I was thinking of volunteering for a tour in Vietnam. After deep cover, frankly, anything looked good. Also, some remnant of the boy in me wanted to play John Wayne and fight Communists on unconventional battlefields in Southeast Asia.

Bonnie was taking care of four children, one of whom not long before had surgery to correct a diarrhea-induced hernia in El Dorado. She had her hands full. As I blithely floated my Vietnam tour of duty idea in front of her, mentioning the financial incentives that would help us recover from the deep cover financial stagnation, all hell broke loose. Bonnie reminded me of my first obligation to her and the children, telling me that my priorities had gotten all screwed up. She was right, of course; most of the real sacrifice of serving in Vietnam would have been theirs, not mine. I also learned in time that not everyone was going to be obliged to serve there, as I had initially believed. Almost everyone who went to the war zone, except for brand new officers, did so by personal choice. Some wanted the excitement and responsibility CIA had in the Vietnamese provinces, where Agency Operations Officers who once had been Army Lieutenants were now instantly the equals of Vietnamese Generals and U.S. Military field grade officers. Some wanted to make money for their children's education. Others wanted to get away from home. But, good Operations Officers were simply not forced to go out to Southeast Asia, and those who refused even a so-called "directed assignment" suffered no lasting career damage.

The Vietnam tête-à-tête between Bonnie and me was a watershed because it refocused my priorities, bringing them back to where they were when I entered this profession with its peculiar stresses and demands. Rather than looking at future assignments with a ratio of career, 100 percent, family, zero, I started trying to find a path that would give equal emphasis to both. There were some more volatile and more career-enhancing prospects than Zaragossa, but I had taken that tour because it was a place where I could be challenged and the family had a shot at decent schooling and living standards. Taking that assignment in 1969 had brought me past the point of no return; I was really committed to a full CA career now because, when this tour ended, I was already thirty-five.

After Zaragossa I had to decide how I would spend the remainder of my time in the Agency, and the choices were pretty impressive by most standards. Would I remain in the Latin America Division where I could have a normal Operations career, alternating in assignments between Headquarters and overseas? In terms of promotion and probable career progression, this certainly would be the course of action I would counsel someone in my shoes at that time — the more overseas time and the more traditional assignments, the better. Promotion panels tended to advance officers whose career paths resembled their own.

I had already spent several years in Covert Action, which was in decline, and under deep cover, clearly the poor cousin within the ranks of the Clandestine Service. My acceptance of the task of working with the Latin America Division NOCs, potentially beneficial as it may have been for the organization and my vulnerable deep cover colleagues, further kept me out of the mainstream. But in the course of that work, two very good job prospects sought me out, so to speak, and I had a decision to make. I still had an urge to get back out to the field even though the children were entering the middle-school years and Latin America was becoming less attractive from the standpoint of their education. The smaller Stations with the most activity were in the poorest countries with the worst schools. The larger Stations usually had better schools to offer, but the cost of living was high for a government employee with five kids, no other income and a single, very modest salary.

If I did return to Latin America as a field Operations Officer and advancing middle manager, I could breathe the air of freedom that Intelligence professionals breathe. I could be part of a Station team running secret collection Operations, ranging from penetrating the local government and foreign embassies to running Technical Operations aimed at a code room, nuclear weapons facility, or international narcotics ring. Each day would bring new situations and new challenges. I would learn about another society with a depth rivaled only by an anthropologist or historian.

Shortly after I returned from Zaragossa, I was offered a very attractive assignment in Europe, where I would travel the continent overseeing international labor matters. Although the constant travel was not appealing, the job had its good points and it would get me away from Latin America and a decade of professional disappointments — Allende was in power in Chile although 64 percent of the Chileans had voted non-Marxist and the Latin America CI network was now wiped out, with no sign of near-term recovery. Why not get away permanently from that snake-bitten region and try somewhere else?

Unfortunately, Watergate occurred, Nixon tried to get CIA to wrap this very dumb hooliganism under the cloak of national security, and DCI Helms, who would not go along with the cover-up, was fired. Before resigning, Nixon elected to punish CIA by appointing a DCI who would mete out some vengeance on the Agency. CIA was in trouble, and its Covert Action capabilities were going to be kept on hold, if not gutted altogether, once Congress got through with the Agency. Europe would have been sweet, and I would have had a free pass to tour the Continent for a couple of years, but it clearly would have been a professional charade, a non-job. There was no sense dragging my family out of the U.S. for something that had lost any substantive operational merit. So, I decided to forget Europe and turned down an assignment that would have placed me in its choicest location.

The conclusion that Covert Action was dead, at least for the time, was not mine alone. Soon the senior Officers responsible for worldwide Covert Action were out seeking new assignments, a sure indication that CA was in for hard times. The seas were starting to churn.

Some months later, in early 1974, I was offered the job of heading our Cuban Operations program in a Station run by an old colleague from the Covert Action labor days. Ironically, although it would mean an assignment away from Latin America Division, it involved work against the hemisphere's biggest troublemaker, Fidel Castro. We would be transferring to a civilized place with very good schools. On the surface it looked ideal, and I took a short trip to discuss the assignment with the Chief of Station. I had already made up my mind that this was a good opportunity. So, I sat down and did some calculations that yielded some stunning results which meant the Gilligans would be living at two levels — I would be out on the town eating filet mignon and drinking fine wine; my family would be home eating peanut butter sandwiches and counting pennies. So much for fancy spots.

Even though I weighed these two field assignments within eighteen months of my return from Zaragossa, I was really in no great hurry to go anywhere. There was some pressure to get overseas since the Directorate of Operations is primarily a field service. But I had just been promoted and, shortly after arriving back in Headquarters, I was presented an Agency Award for the work I had done on Chile.

It was a Certificate of Distinction for the early warning on the 1970 election, an alert that had not been heeded beyond allowing DCI Helms to warn the White House to get started early because Chile was in trouble. I had no great pride in the matter, in part because I always felt that I ought to have done a better job in ringing the gong. But, the award at least gave me a chance to bring Bonnie into Headquarters for the award ceremony, her first visit to the Agency's inner sanctum. It was presented by Clandestine Service Chief Tom Karamessines, who had the class to recognize my wife's contribution, something too often overlooked when organizations pass out accolades. Bonnie had spent many hundreds of evening hours alone with the children when I was working the Chile election problems. She deserved credit for her silent sacrifices and "Tom K" — as he was affectionately known — made sure that she got it. The award was given, the photographer took his shots, and because I was still under cover the award was immediately taken back to be placed in an Agency vault until my retirement.

In other respects, my career was doing fine. I attended the Agency Mid-career Course, no big deal in itself, but a rare opportunity for Clandestine Service officers who usually shied away from training of any kind. For me it provided a senior, Agency-wide look at Intelligence, world affairs, and the Washington scene at a time when things were beginning to go very badly for CIA and the country as a whole. I also was appointed to the Operations Directorate's (DDO) first Management Advisory Group (MAG), which was created supposedly to bring the ideas of promising middle-grade officers to the attention of the senior managers. It provided another perch to observe and assess what was going on around CIA. The view, unfortunately, was not reassuring. A crisis of leadership was hitting the Agency and I had a front-row seat.

Historian James McGregor Burns writes of the "sunburst of leadership" that blessed America in its Revolutionary days. Washington, Jefferson, Madison, Monroe, Hamilton, the Adamses, Franklin and Jay were a few of the many who combined wisdom and courage to make freedom possible for their time and future generations. To extend Burns's metaphor, the country's leadership in the 1970s was suffering a solar eclipse. Out at CIA things were not any brighter.

As I went about my deep cover management job, I weighed what I would look for in my next assignment but could not escape what was going on internationally, domestically, and at the top of CIA itself. The Seventies were proving to be terrible years for the Agency. Returning to the sea analogy, the ship was taking on water and crewmen were being thrown overboard in 1973 as a result of Watergate; in 1974 and in 1975, the engine room was flooded and power was lost; finally, in 1976, the stage was set for a Captain Queeg to take command and head the rudderless ship straight for the rocks. Hyperbole? Probably an understatement.

The fall of Southeast Asia to the North Vietnamese occurred in two distinct stages: first in 1973, when the U.S. troop withdrawal was negotiated in Paris; and then in April 1975, when South Vietnam collapsed in one rapid implosion. As a result, the Soviets stood to pick up a new strategic base in Asia. In Africa, the Soviets and Cuban proxies were making steady gains. In Latin America, Castro was still in power although the Allende Marxist regime in Chile was now gone — the latter a development for which the Agency would eventually pay a huge price for a coup it neither conceived nor supported.

On the national scene we watched Watergate unfold, bringing down Nixon and strengthening the hand of Congress. With no real power to do, but a great deal of skill at undoing, Congress's gain had the net effect of weakening the American Government internationally just when it was suffering major losses both in power and prestige. In 1974, Congress added the Hughes-Ryan Amendment to the Arms Export Control Act, forcing CIA to report to eight separate committees. In all, 163 elected Senators and Representatives, and half again as many unelected staff members, became privy to Intelligence activities that included such sensitive areas as Covert Action. Later that year, Congress cut the ammunition flow to South Vietnam so drastically that it set the stage for the fall of Vietnam. In 1976, it created foreign policy, using the Tunney-Clark Amendment to cut off the covert aid to anti-Communist fighting forces in Angola — another victory for Moscow achieved, not on the battlefield, but in the halls of Congress. Drunk with power, Congress was using that power in ways that would harm U.S. strategic interests and our ability to deal effectively in the international arena with Soviet-supported groups, from Terrorists to political extremists of every conceivable stripe. When it came to sowing the seeds of instability throughout the underdeveloped world, Moscow was remarkably flexible and non-doctrinaire. Meanwhile, two Congressional committees went after CIA, one headed by Senator Frank Church of Idaho, who made no bones about wanting to propel himself to the Presidency; CIA bashing was to be his propellant. Over at the House, Representative Otis Pike of New York led an unruly committee through a highly politicized attack on the Republicans, again using CIA as the whipping boy even though the Agency had been the servant of three Democrat and three Republican Presidents since its founding in 1947.

As the Congress did its level best to weaken the President and the Presidency, Nixon had his own score to settle with CIA. John Ranelagh, author of the most penetrating examination of the Agency ever done by an outsider, points out that Nixon appointed "James Schlesinger... probably the most unpopular DCI the Agency had experienced in its first twenty-five years." In his five-month tenure as CIA Director, Schlesinger conducted a politically-based purge that was as harsh as it was rapid. Called at the time "Nixon's revenge," the new DCI had a particular dislike for the Clandestine Service and made certain that the majority of the forced retirements, resignations and outright firings were concentrated on that Directorate. He made the mistake of believing that technically-collected Intelligence was so exacting, predictable and cost effective that the age of the human spy had passed. He was also ambitious to an extreme and saw the Agency as a stepping stone to bigger things for himself. Before leaving CIA in mid-1973 to take over as Secretary of Defense, he set in motion a review of the organization's twenty-six years of covert activities to see what wrongdoing may have been done. And then he left, but not before showing loyal CIA employees a cruelty that, Nixon aside, was generally uncharacteristic of Washington players.

After the DDO completed its painful and painstaking review to decide whom to fire or force to retire, it found that there were about two dozen officers who would suffer enormous personal hardship if let go. Some were just a few months shy of qualifying for retirement after a generation of service. Some had paid a terrible personal price for their service overseas (such as the death of a family member). Some were currently going through hardships, such as cancer, that did not surface until the pink slips were issued. A notebook with the personal profiles and mitigating circumstances was assembled for the DCI. The senior DDO career management officer carried it to the seventh floor to discuss these cases, already marked for separation, with the DCI himself. Schlesinger's stock in the organization he came to purge was so low that he had armed guards posted outside his office. The career Clandestine Service officer explained that, of the hundreds of people who were being forced out, there were less than thirty Operations Officers for whom reconsideration was requested because of catastrophic circumstances that came to light only after they had been placed on the hit list. The notebook was handed to Schlesinger who reportedly pushed it back across his desk with three words that tell it all: "Fire the bastards!"

With a fortitude that escapes most administrators, the senior DDO Officer carried the notebook back to the Clandestine Service and shredded it, lest the DCI or one of his staff decide to ask for the names. The Operations Officers in jeopardy were then hidden around the Agency in a series of moves that protected them until Schlesinger headed off to the Pentagon as Secretary of Defense. The harm he had done to many individuals and their families was monumental because many of those who were fired simply had the misfortune of being away from their regular home Division when the axes were sharpened. But this DCI's most profound effect went beyond the personal wrongs; he also broke a covenant that had existed for CIA's first quarter-century — that loyalty to the Agency would be reciprocated.

If the Agency was unfortunate in being on the receiving end of the Nixon and Schlesinger punishment, it fared no better when the new DCI was selected. William Colby had been Schlesinger's Executive Director and as a career Clandestine Service officer had made a name for himself in Vietnam. Colby had the thankless task in his two and a half years as DCI of dealing with two witch-hunting Congressional Committees whose appetites were fed in part by Colby's own hand. His "Family Jewels" report had been pulled together on Schlesinger's orders two days before he went over to Defense, and Colby elected to take this 693-page compilation of every reported Agency transgression and reveal it to Congress. It described various activities that were not within CIA's charter, some things that plainly violated U.S. law, and a host of activities that looked bad through the 20/20 lens of hindsight but were not illegal (and even seemed appropriate) when conducted during the tougher years of the early Cold War. All Agency employees had been directed, under penalty of legal action, to report *anything CIA had ever done that may have violated U.S. law.*

The problem with this thinking that went into the "Family Jewels" process was that it had people in the Seventies judging the actions of two decades earlier — when we had been fighting regional wars, when the Soviets and Chinese had been successfully subverting whole regions, when North Koreans with Soviet support had been brainwashing American POWs, when Intelligence reports suggested that the whole Scandinavian production of a new psychedelic drug, LSD, had been purchased by the Soviet Intelligence services, and when we had not been certain that global war could be avoided.

The Family Jewels Report had a profound effect on the image of CIA, both inside and outside the organization. It was not just the matter of having colleagues blowing whistles on each other. It was what would happen to any institution made to hemorrhage in this fashion. No major hospital or medical center dealing with life and death issues continually could remain viable if the screw up of every doctor, nurse, radiologist, surgeon, anesthesiologist and pharmacologist over a twenty-five year period were suddenly revealed to the world. What confidence would remain? What would happen to morale? Would it have to shut down for reasons of reputation alone, not to speak of the legal difficulties?

Colby claimed that he had no other choice, that the best way to protect America's Intelligence capability was to clear the decks and create an *American Intelligence Service* that may violate other nations' laws but never our own — a fitting subject for a symposium on ethics or international law, to be sure, but little comfort to those caught in the vice of the new *ex post facto* morality. The material Colby sent over to the hungry Congressional wolves was red meat indeed, and it placed some Latin America Division and senior Agency officers in legal jeopardy over Chile. One was former DCI Helms whose subsequent *nolo contendere* plea to two misdemeanor charges directly traced back to Colby's decisions to come clean — with other people's lives no less!

This negative view of Colby's handling of his responsibilities was shared by President Ford, among the cleanest politicians to come out of Congress, and Nelson Rockefeller, who as Vice President had headed an inquiry into the charges of CIA involvement in assassination attempts against foreign leaders, specifically Fidel Castro, Patrice Lumumba and Rafael Trujillo. Both were chagrined that Colby was not protecting even legitimate secrets as the National Security Act of 1947, and common sense, bound the DCI to protect. Colby was ousted in January 1976. The following month President Ford put an end to the public hemorrhaging of CIA secrets and added an epitaph to Colby's Directorship:

> It is essential that the irresponsible and dangerous exposure of our nation's Intelligence secrets be stopped. Openness is a hallmark of our democratic society, but the American people have never believed that it was necessary to reveal secret war plans of the Department of Defense, and I do not think they wish to have true Intelligence secrets revealed either.

After three years on the Schlesinger-Colby bobsled, and a plummeting slide from the pinnacle of the Washington hierarchy to the bottom, the

Agency course was temporarily corrected by George H.W. Bush, who took over as DCI for the last twelve months of the Ford Administration. Bush restored a degree of normalcy at CIA and with Congress, which he understood well from his own prior service in the House. It was too late for some, however, and many fine CIA Officers went into early retirement during this stormy period, some to go fishing, some to start a business career, and one to help defend the Agency from those bent on its destruction. In mid-1975, Dave Phillips retired and took up the battle against the disinformation campaign being waged against CIA by Agee, whose book had come out in England and who was being interviewed on American television at the time.

The month following Phillips's retirement, I permanently left the Latin America Division. I had been offered a Branch Chief position in a Division that concentrated on the recruitment of spies. My own spirits were so low that I too would have retired if I had met the minimum qualifying requirements. The man who came in to replace the remarkable Phillips was another beancounting numbers guy, the same man who a decade earlier had shown the young officer how to split one good Intelligence Report into three acceptable ones to get more credit. He was also the COS in Latin America who had given Joseph Smith a cold, unceremonial retirement farewell in the Embassy waiting room, in my opinion inspiring Smith to pen *Portrait of a Cold Warrior*, a book that compromised a number of Agency CA Operations and agents.

As a member of the DDO MAG advisory group, I had seen that, internally, we were too paralyzed to do very much to place our own house in order. Our first reports had ended up in the bottom of the DCI's or DDO's safes with no action taken.

One MAG report made the case that the Agency could not credibly conduct Covert Action under the existing groundrules of reporting to Congress. The report recommended that the Agency seek to take itself out of Covert Action until such time as secrecy could be assured and agents be protected. We had no ethical problem with CA, but we were convinced that, no longer feasible, CA was doing genuine harm to the organization, its Officers, and its agents in the field.

The second DDO MAG report described the extremely sorry state of the Clandestine Service Career System and career track, which had slipped to last place in comparison with the other three CIA Directorates, the Foreign Service, or the FBI. In this report, we recommended that the DDO conduct a survey of its employees to measure the state of morale and identify ways to restore confidence in the organization and its leadership. No action was ever seriously considered. DCI Colby carried the DDO MAG Career Service paper around in his briefcase for several weeks, but he was barely staying afloat himself and missed an opportunity to display some leadership and show DDO personnel that he cared about them, their morale, and their career opportunities.

For the government as a whole, and for CIA in a special way, 1976 was a time for marking time. Gerald Ford was an interim President; George H.W. Bush was an interim DCI. Tall ships sailed majestically into East Coast harbors in early July to celebrate the American Bicentennial, but the national government's Intelligence vessel was stalled in the doldrums. The American people wanted a change and we were to be reminded fairly soon that not all change is for the better.

12

Headhunting and Beancounting

IN MID-1976, after serving for a year as Chief of a Headquarters Branch responsible for three Field Stations engaged exclusively in recruiting spies, I took a field assignment in the same Division. As Chief of a field office, I was now back in the mainstream to the extent that Foreign Intelligence Collection was pretty much all that remained of the Clandestine Service's three traditional missions — FI, CI, and CA. FI was the business of recruiting and running spies, and the Headhunting Division (HHD) was solely concerned with recruiting them. Covert Action was now on hold, and no new initiatives were likely in this election year, especially now that the details of CA Operations were being reported broadly and directly to elected Congressional opponents of Ford Administration foreign policy. Counterintelligence was in limbo, substantively and bureaucratically, since DCI Colby forced CI Chief James Jesus Angleton into retirement the previous year. Overall, Agency leadership was in crisis — CIA was estranged from its traditional mentor, the President, and had become an easy target of the Congress. Morale out at Langley was very low, but was CIA dead?

Within the beltway that surrounds Washington, things did look rather grim. Dave Phillips had gone out on the writing and lecture circuit, specifically with the survival of the CIA as his personal goal.

Two positive developments suggested, however, that all was not lost. In fact, with the Vietnam tragedy now history, the U.S. was not about to put an isolationist head back in the sand or put CIA out of business.

To begin with, the American people had not jumped on the U.S. Congress-induced anti-CIA bandwagon. Had the public taken the bait, the Agency could well have been reduced in responsibility, possibly even dismantled, and its functions transferred to other parts of the Federal bureaucracy. Technical Collection of the Directorate of Science and Technology (DS&T) could have been vested in the Department of Defense. Much of the satellite collection program pioneered by CIA under Richard Bissel — fired over the Bay of Pigs failure — could have been shifted to the Air Force, which already had achieved a position of primacy in this field. The analytical function of the Directorate of Intelligence (DI) could have been assumed by other think tanks, both public and private. The Clandestine Service's collection of political, financial and economic Intelligence could have been assigned to the State, Treasury and Commerce Departments, respectively, all three of which did those categories of reporting without the benefits, or risks, of recruited spies. Taking CIA apart was not beyond the realm of possibility, or so it seemed in the mid-1970s. But the American people were not clamoring for CIA's destruction. The country was not buying into Senator Frank Church's "rogue elephant" charges, and he was finding that he could not capture the Presidency over CIA's dead body. Opinion polls taken at the height of the Congressional and media hysteria showed that the American public still believed we needed a CIA to deal with this uncertain world.

In addition, during even the darkest days of the Congressional investigations, CIA overseas Field Stations continued to perform because the morale slippage in the field never dropped to the extent experienced in Headquarters. Operations Officers serving overseas were confused by media accounts of the "Family Jewels" report, certainly, and by the Schlesinger purge of the Agency. They were bewildered also by the behavior of CIA's seventh floor senior managers on occasion. Basically, however, they had been sheltered by those same individuals from direct Congressional meddling in field Operations. The decentralized functioning of the Clandestine Service assured field autonomy and operational continuity. This, in turn, kept CIA viable under conditions that would have immobilized most organizations. In sum, the common sense of the American people and the ability of the Operations Directorate to perform under pressure helped the country and the Agency get through this very difficult decade.

My decision to go to the field was not without considerable misgivings. More so than colleagues who were overseas during the period of decline, I had been seeing things in Washington that were disturbing for the long-term viability of the Clandestine Service.

One problem was that managers were displacing leaders at critical points in the organization. They spoke new languages, such as MBO (Management by Objectives), and introduced other tools suitable for factory production but less than adequate for a service organization.

Also, the support side of CIA was growing into the Agency's largest and potentially most powerful Directorate. One of its Chiefs brought in by DCI Schlesinger, in fact, tried to place himself over the other three substantive Deputy Directors: Operations, Intelligence Analysis, and Scientific & Technical Collection. His attempted power grab involved converting the support component into the Directorate of Management and Services (DM&S) and taking hold of the whole Agency's budget process, using the control of the purse to maximize his own power at the expense of the others. The Office of Management and Budget (OMB) — James Schlesinger's own springboard from academia to the top of the Federal bureaucracy — had grown in power relative to other agencies and departments precisely because of its control of the Government-wide purse.

Congress, for its part, was increasingly using its own budget and appropriation authorities to micromanage the Executive Branch to an extent it would not have tolerated for itself. Bear in mind, that the hypocrites in Congress passed a Freedom of Information Act in this period to open up Government information to the general public on a scale never practiced before — *and then Congress exempted itself from the provisions of that same act!*

The DM&S attempted coup was not formally successful; the other Deputy Directors drew together and the upstart component was downgraded to the Directorate of Administration, ruling out its pretended role as general manager of the Agency. Nonetheless, the language and psychology of quantification, MBO, had taken hold, and the power of the bean counters increased.

This was no more vividly demonstrated than in the Headhunter Division, where the effectiveness of Field Stations and field Chiefs was now directly and exclusively related to the number of "scalps" put into the bag each year, or quarter. As Branch Chief, I was very much aware that numbers were all important, not only driving the process but pushing otherwise solid professionals into unprofessional behavior on occasion. The Headhunter Division had a reputation for playing the numbers games and flimflamming well before I had taken the Branch Chief job. Operations Officers in the line Divisions used to react with frustration, and sometimes amusement, over HHD recruitment cases and claims. I knew this before departing the Latin America Division but, at the time, was making an assignment decision based entirely on family considerations. I knew about the numbers pressure, about the supposed bogus recruitments, and about the games that were being played. But, I also figured that, regardless of the overall pressures and tendencies to cut corners in order to chalk up the numbers, I could do it right, be professional and, by sheer hard work and determination, avoid falling into the numbers trap. To an extent I was successful; to some extent I was not.

The numbers game pressures, especially in this period when the Clandestine Service was under constant attack, bent this service Division out of shape in the same way they had bent the U.S. Military in Vietnam with the body count, kill-ratio and other self-deceiving tools of that war's quantifiers. *Facts and figures are useful, but you can't judge a war by them. You have to have an instinct, a feel*, DDO Desmond FitzGerald told Defense Secretary McNamara back in the 1960s — unfortunately, to no good effect. McNamara was number trapped.

In HHD, the distortions brought on by the numbers game were serious: agents were being recruited who were not really needed, exposing them and the Agency to risk; CIA focus was shifted from the difficult, important targets to easier, non-vital ones — to Third World individuals and away from Russians; the same access individuals were being used time and again to get to Soviet targets, making the Counterintelligence job easier for the KGB and increasing the long-term risk to all recruited Russian agents; and Agency Counterintelligence standards were lowered or overlooked to increase the prospects of landing recruitments. The business of spying is obviously one where risk plays a continual role and the Intelligence professional's job is to reduce that risk as close to zero as possible In HHD, the opposite was taking place.

At the same time, HHD was recruiting some agents of national Intelligence potential, spies who were materially contributing to our knowledge of the secret plans, intentions and activities of hostile foreign governments. But the emphasis on numbers was substantially decreasing the Priority Target effort and, as I went out to the field, I was determined to go after the more important, difficult recruitments. I was particularly seized by two scientific and technical problem areas: first, the proliferation of nuclear technology and its possible use in weapons systems; and second, the technology theft and transfer being carried out by the Soviet Union. My field assignment area had good potential on both targets, so long as we avoided joining the African-a-Month club or Latin American-a-Month club; i.e., going after the easier-softer recruitment targets from the Third World.

The nuclear proliferation problem is fundamentally of the West's own making because no one has been more circumspect in sharing that technology with other nations than the Soviet Union. Most of the underdeveloped world's nuclear engineers and scientists working on power generation and secret weapons programs have been trained in Europe or North America. By 1976, when I went to the field, there was a broad understanding within the Federal Government and the general population that the spread of nuclear weapons to other nations, especially in the volatile Third World, spelled eventual disaster for all nations. My efforts against the problem of nuclear proliferation, specifically recruiting foreign scientists who were returning to their country's nuclear program, were in keeping with Clandestine Service Operations throughout the world. The best information on this problem was being produced by CIA and its recruited spies.

The Soviet technology theft problem was an entirely different matter and on this, unfortunately, I was out ahead of the Agency and the Government. It was still too early for Washington to recognize that *détente* meant entirely different things to America than to the Soviet Union. In an educational exchange program which I call "spies for schoolteachers," the Soviets displayed a focus, cunning, and seriousness that contrasted dramatically with the scatterbrained, naive and whimsical approach of the Americans. God forbid that we should be as careless and deceived in the future as we were under détente when, from the standpoint of national survival, we might as well have been collectively smoking opium. The following is from a CIA unclassified document:

"During the late 1970s, the Soviets got about 30,000 samples of Western production equipment, weapons and military components, and over 400,000 technical documents, both classified and unclassified. We estimate that, during this period, the KGB and its military equivalent, the GRU, and their surrogates among the East European Intelligence services stole about 70 percent of the technology most significant to Soviet military equipment and weapons programs. These acquisitions have saved the Soviets hundreds of millions of dollars in research and development costs and have accelerated the development of some programs by as much as five years. For example, the Soviets' new space shuttle is based on U.S. designs; and the plans were available over the counter in U.S. government and contractor documents.

There are many other examples:

- The Soviet trucks that rolled into Afghanistan came from a plant outfitted with $1.5 billion worth of modern American and European machinery;
- The precise gyros and bearings in heavy missiles were designed in the U.S.;
- The radar in their AWACS is ours;

- Many of the latest Soviet advances in avionics, fire control and navigation systems, cruise missiles, and aircraft power plants are based on U.S. technology.

We expect that U.S. technology is going to contribute to some other Soviet aerospace projects during the next decade. These include:

- Two new bombers, and six new series of advanced fighter aircraft. One, the Mig-29/Fulcrum, compares favorably to our F-16 and F-18;
- Ten new ballistic missile systems, and six new surface-to-air missile systems;
- A program designed to achieve military superiority in space. Today, military systems account for more than 70 percent of Soviet space launches; only 10 percent are purely scientific projects;
- Microelectronics technology is an area where the Soviets have relied heavily on the West. The Zelenograd Science Center, the Soviet equivalent of Silicon Valley, has been equipped from scratch with Western technology."

How were the Soviets able to make such enormous, tangible progress at our expense? They did all this by taking advantage of every conceivable opportunity and playing to win while we hardly played at all. They stole wherever possible, they recruited Western industrialists to sell items prohibited for export to the USSR, they bought important items ostensibly for civilian purposes and later converted them to military uses, they used the Polish, Czech and East German services to steal technology (while they used the Bulgarians for assassinations and the Cubans to fight their Africa wars), and they used so-called scholars to collect Intelligence within the United States. They did all this while CIA chased less-essential Intelligence targets, in full pursuit of our numbers games.

Each year, the Soviets would send a group of "scholars" to this country, accomplished research scientists, KGB and GRU Intelligence Officers, and select relatives of elite Soviet leaders. Each had been carefully selected to go after some specific U.S. strategic military, industrial, or scientific information. The Soviets chose the academic institutions and sponsoring American professors with care, and they altered each Soviet scholar's ostensible background and research history to make him more likely to qualify for approval by the U.S. Committee on Exchanges, chaired by the State Department. They disguised the classified nature of prior work in the USSR and their collection requirements here in the States, working their way into academic institutions where the most advanced scientific work was under way.

The Soviets gave their "scholars" unlimited Xerox expenses to copy every relevant American doctoral thesis in their field (ceramics, optics, lasers, computer time sharing and so on) bringing them back to the USSR for translation. In some cases, they sent their scientists back a second time to study under American professors who had become involved in classified research on the Trident submarine and other advanced military systems. Learning which academic and industrial laboratories were the most lax in controlling their movements, they placed their spies in those facilities that gave them the most direct access to key people and programs. They spotted Americans for invitation to the USSR where Soviet Intelligence could work its own recruitment schemes.

The Soviets gave away next to nothing in the so-called exchange. Many American academics were surprised at the end of a Soviet's nine-month stay in their university to hear the Soviet give a talk on developments in his field back in the USSR. The impression after the talk was always the same: "The poor Russians are ten years behind in everything and poor Yuri is so far behind too." The Soviets managed with great success to bait their hooks with boloney and still catch their American fish! Of course Yuri, if that was his real name at all, was going to reveal nothing sensitive about Soviet advances in his field. If he did, he would lose his head.

On the American side of the exchange program, two incredible weaknesses had their roots in the State Department acceptance of the "spirit of détente" while the Soviets continued to play tough. In the first place, even when serious members of the Intelligence Community opposed a Soviet scientist's acknowledged research plan as "likely to represent an unacceptable technology loss in a critical military-related field," the State Department was just as likely to approve the exchange and merely send a form-letter caution to the American academic sponsor. The second weakness was American willingness to participate in an exchange program where the U.S. received Soviet spies and sent to the USSR some Russian-language teachers from America's junior or senior high schools.

The Intelligence Community was not entirely of one mind on this program, of course. Some agencies saw it as a way to recruit Soviets who would remain here and tell what they knew of Soviet classified programs or, preferably, return to the USSR as spies in place. At the same time, the American exchange students we were sending to the USSR were also KGB recruitment targets for Moscow. The KGB was not interested in recruiting career schoolteachers, but it did try to compromise and recruit young Russian-language scholars who might be induced to get jobs in Washington, especially in Foreign Service, Defense or the Intelligence Community.

With the proliferation of secrets being passed around Capitol Hill, the Soviets were also interested in gaining indirect access through the Congressional staffs. Former CIA officer David H. Barnett, who offered his services to the KGB six years after resigning from the Agency, had been targeted by the Soviets to go against the Senate Select Committee on Intelligence, where he could be a valuable source of sensitive Intelligence information. Barnett had refused to seek reemployment at the Agency specifically for fear of the polygraph, a deterrent that is easily eluded on Capitol Hill.

As field Chief, I sent letters periodically to the DCI, a practice instituted by President Carter's appointee, Admiral Stansfield Turner. Within weeks of his appointment Turner was at war with the Clandestine Service, and the letters were his way of getting around the DDO management and developing direct, personal access to Chiefs of Station. In one letter, I addressed only the U.S.-Soviet exchange program, advising the DCI that we were being badly hurt by adhering to the spirit of the program while the Soviets used it as a weapon against us. At no time during the Carter Administration years was there any sense of reality on technology transfer and theft. The technology losses in the late 1970s were unparalleled. It would take the Soviet invasion of Afghanistan to awaken Carter to reality.

My job, of course, was not to make or influence national policy. Except for reflecting occasionally on the big picture and fighting the administrative battles, I concentrated on recruiting Foreign Intelligence sources of every variety during my first year back in the field. Gradually, I intended to shift to the scientific and technical targets against which my region offered special potential. The recruitment of spies is a very serious, step-by-step process with high stakes on all sides. How does it work? Does it generally take place on a quiet country road or in a cozy restaurant? The setting can vary quite considerably, but there are some basics on recruitment that usually apply.

"Getting to know you, getting to know all about you." This line from *The King and I* captures the essence of Intelligence recruitment more accurately than does the image set by James Bond. Recruiting a spy in the real world hinges on the tedious collection of information and insights about the target for recruitment. The formal recruitment "pitch" is but a natural extension of the development process. In the first stage of recruiting, the headhunter is like a cat in the corner of the room, looking all about to see if there are any mice around. He tries not to draw undue attention to himself, and he uses cover that suggests to the casual observer that he is harmless and uninteresting. The backslapping, gregarious individual who may make it in the sales fields tends to have too high a profile for Intelligence; everyone in town soon knows just what he is up to.

Another reason for using cover and discretion at this early, observational phase is to get to know the target as he really is, especially when he does not think he is under scrutiny. A young job applicant being interviewed formally for a job has polished his resume as much as possible. He has shaved and showered, dressed his very best. He watches everything he says and may have rehearsed his answers. But suppose a company recruiter casually meets the same young man while vacationing at the beach, or at a cookout, when the fellow is having a beer, mixing it up with his friends, and making no effort to polish his image. The second, unvarnished exposure is what we seek in Intelligence because it is more likely to show the person as he really is, when the facade has been stripped away.

These groundrules are especially important when recruiting a Russian. Why so, more than any other nationality? Because their seven-decade system made paranoia essential for survival. They present a special challenge in the first, getting-to-know-you stage. Sometimes no single source or observer is up to the task, and multiple sources of information and insight are necessary. What emerges under those conditions is more a mosaic than an integrated, coherent and complete sketch of the Soviet person. It is often quite contradictory as well because it is in the nature of totalitarian systems that its members display different faces to different audiences.

Before deciding to pursue any recruitment target beyond the stage of observation, the Intelligence professional tries to answer three questions to his satisfaction: First, does the individual being assessed have Intelligence potential? In other words, does he have access to information of national consequence to the U.S. which is not obtainable by open sources or by low-risk technical means?

Second, if he does have such access, is he the kind of individual CIA could and would want to work with? A deranged person may be alienated from his system but offers nothing in the way of agent material. A would-be agent must be able to function not only under normal circumstances but also under the stressful and demanding conditions of the clandestine life.

Third, the final question in the Intelligence recruitment process is whether the individual with access and with the talent to perform as a spy is, in fact, recruitable by CIA. The sequence in the process is important; in far too many cases one has bumped into a recruitable person and then ends up contriving the first two elements, to no avail — that is, finding that the recruitable agent really can do nothing of value or, worse, may be an accident waiting to happen in terms of potential performance as a spy.

In the real world, the process comes down to this: First, can Yuri get his hands on Soviet state secrets; second, is he our kind of guy; and third, can we recruit and prepare him to survive as an American spy back in Moscow?

One difference between Hollywood and the real world is that there tends to be more sex and violence portrayed in a single film than most CIA Officers see in a lifetime of clandestine Operations. An Agency officer who moves into the gutter to do his recruiting and other Intelligence work usually gets fouled up in his own marriage and in other parts of his life. Agee's alienation from America and CIA was preceded by his own moral disintegration and excesses, which he hid behind his CIA cloak. Essentially, his bosses looked the other way.

Are there any groundrules for this business, or is the recruitment of spies guided by the law of the jungle? An appropriate principle is spelled out in *Man and the State*, where Jacques Maritain outlines a very direct and clear-cut standard: *people in Intelligence and police work may have to work with the corrupt, but they have no right to corrupt*. In that spirit, if the recruitment target, Yuri, is a skirtchaser, we might use a female agent to get his attention. On the other hand, we could not ethically try to screw up happily-married Vladimir by employing a hooker to get his attention. Hold your nose, if need be, and work with imperfect individuals, but never defile another human being. That is the basic way CIA — at its best — operates in the real world, where there are limits to behavior.

Does having some principles, even scruples, place CIA at a disadvantage when going head to head with the KGB? In a given situation it may, but in terms of the whole fabric of the organization and its people, it does not. The Agency does not, for example, have its male or female officers jumping in and out of beds to recruit spies. Does it ever happen?

Of course, but very likely relatively less than what occurs in the world of business or in journalism, for example. The reason ultimately is as much practical as it is philosophical: spying is too serious and risky to enter into for a little sex. The appeal must be a lot deeper and more substantial if Yuri, or Vladimir, is going to jeopardize all to provide secrets to the United States — alone, back in Russia, with a KGB bullet in the head if caught or exposed by someone in CIA who knows of him and defects to the Russians. Soviets assigned abroad know what happened to Colonel Popov of the GRU when he was caught: he was thrown alive into a furnace in Moscow, a reminder to others of the Soviet price for betrayal.

The recruitment pitch or act has to build upon and flow from the foundation established in the first two stages of the process. The pitch remains a serious and delicate step regardless of the good work that may have been done up front. Crossing the line to become a reporting source, colleague, collaborator, spy, quisling, traitor, patriot, agent, asset — whatever term happens to apply — is one of the biggest steps an individual can take in his life. Agreeing to work for a Foreign Intelligence service, even one like CIA that lets you quit, is a decision that touches the center of one's being. It profoundly affects all aspects of loyalty and life thereafter — whom to report on, confide in, or get drunk with, who can be trusted and who can be seen as a threat, who loses if you are caught, who will respect you for your courage, and who will hate you for your treachery.

Unlike the resort community salesman, who tries to get the purchase agreement signed immediately, my personal style was to build into the actual recruitment scenario some reflection time, so the individual being asked to spy could think over what he was being asked to do, only saying yes after he had mulled over its implications. Such an approach may reduce the number of instant acceptances, but it was my conviction that it resulted in recruitments that stuck and avoided those that evaporated with time. This matter of personal style, by the way, is important to understand because CIA has no handbooks or regulations outlining how to go about the business of recruiting new sources or handling old ones. One myth perpetrated during initial training by those who had not worked agent Operations, was that we had to be careful not to reveal our modus operandi, or M.O., to the opposition. This lingo must have been picked up from the old gangster movies because CIA has no M.O. when conducting its Operations work. Certainly, there are basics on recruiting or selection of a good dead drop site for hiding secret messages. But overall, this is a highly individualistic business, and no two Operations Officers function alike, push buttons in the same way, or go after sources or information in the same manner. This is an American trait, and when the security or Counterintelligence standards are observed, it is a U.S. Intelligence strength.

In the final analysis, the recruitment pitch must be explicit so that the individual understands what he is being asked to do, what will be done in return (including any payments, relocation in the event of exposure, death benefits to survivors in high risk Operations), and what the risks are as well as how they will be reduced by using, for example, secret writing, dead drops, safehouses or couriers. When Intelligence Officers gloss over the details at pitch time, a "recruited agent" walks away not knowing what our officer has been getting at, especially when the recruiter has weak foreign language skills or is oblique in his pitch. Some "agents" have gone right home, told their spouse, and been told in Chinese or Russian, "My ass, you will." One went all the way through training in the use of a clandestine radio and threw it in the nearest trash can, never to be heard from again. Some new agents have flipped out, suddenly seeing spooks everywhere and thinking they are on someone's hit list. One new agent left the training and took off all his clothes in a public library, the pressure of it all obviously more than he could bear. However, some CIA field agents have gone on for decades of useful service; in fact, Soviet agents of CIA have actually retired in the Soviet Union after long, faithful service. That may be the ultimate achievement — getting the Soviet system to pay retirement to one of our spies in their midst. It certainly has worked the other way around often enough.

In the early days of the Cold War, the Russian who was pitched by CIA usually felt obliged to throw his drink in our guy's face and storm away, so that any nearby KGB colleague or informer would know that he had not agreed to spy against the homeland. As the Soviet officials abroad have become more relaxed and sophisticated, the *nyet* comes more politely. CIA may even float the proposal gently enough so that Yuri can deflect it if he does not want to get involved. He may be asked to think it over and give his answer the next time he is in the West — "just don't report the pitch and subject yourself to any special KGB scrutiny." The key point is that CIA will respect Yuri's freedom to say yes, no, or maybe. No harm is threatened and every effort is made to assure that the recruitment act poses no harm to him either. The Agency is trying to penetrate a closed and historically dangerous society; it is not in the business of intentionally trying to mess up lives. Neither theirs nor our own.

Not long after I had taken charge of the field Office, one of the Operations Officers said he wanted me to meet someone, an agent we were using to meet and assess Soviet scientists and Intelligence operatives. My middle-aged colleague was titillated as he described our agent who was, supposedly, an absolutely gorgeous woman in her early thirties. He suggested that I might want to handle this case personally. I read the file, which showed that she was good at cultivating Soviets and very good at masking an abiding disdain for their system, and I agreed to go out and meet this special source. My colleague introduced us and we chatted about her operational work. She was everything he said she was: strikingly attractive, intelligent, and clever. I had seen enough. I went back to the office and assigned our *femme fatale* to the personal care and operational handling of another Station officer, an accomplished female Operations Officer who, I knew, would have none of the problems we males would have dealing secretly with such an attractive woman. Obviously, I failed the James Bond test on this one, but I had seen too many Operations Officers, especially as they approached their forties and fifties, fall into this trap and lose what was really of value in their lives.

My responsibility as field Chief was to chalk up recruitments, and the program I developed worked on two levels. First, we had to keep doing the bread-and-butter recruitment Operations with a reasonably good shot at success. In this regard, we went after a variety of targets and recruited a few new sources, enough to keep the counters in Headquarters satisfied during my first year.

The second approach was against the hard targets, Soviets and nuclear types. To get to these we needed brand new operational bridges, which we built during my first year in the field. We made use of alias identities in all instances, but some were overused and none of them had any genuine backstopping when I arrived in the field. My background had taught me the value of good cover. So, I saw to it that the newly-arrived younger officers had an opportunity to build and develop new identities from the ground up. Only then would they have the requisite tools to go after the most difficult targets on a sustained basis without compromising themselves or the target in the process. Operationally, things were heading in a positive direction. Unfortunately, trouble came from an entirely unexpected direction. Headquarters was in the midst of turmoil under DCI Turner and CIA's administrative side shut down.

In addition to running and directing recruitment Operations, as Chief I also dealt with Washington to see that the troops were taken care of. I expended a lot of energy on painfully-mundane matters during the first year. We were operating in an inordinately-expensive area. Before leaving Headquarters to take over my new office, I was told by the administrators that, as soon as the lawyers ruled on its legality, a special addition to compensation would be forthcoming to meet the area's high cost of living. Fair enough — they even took out the calculator and ran off the numbers, so I was able to tell Bonnie that this time we would not be taking another financial beating. I also could inform my field personnel that the added funds would be in their next paycheck. This was the summer of 1976, election year, but for several weeks we heard nothing and hoped things were still on track.

As summer passed and autumn progressed, the temperatures dropped and gradually we all started feeling the financial pinch. I sent cables asking how long it would take to get the approval. The response kept coming: "The lawyers are working on it." By Christmas I was signing off on messages every few days, asking for quick credit-union loans for others and myself; still the same response came, asking us to be patient. By then, I was kicking myself for having departed Washington in the first place; if only I had just planted my backside on some bench in Headquarters until approval was given!

The final straw came when I learned that our secretary, a young woman raising a two-year-old on her own in the dead of winter, was keeping the heat in her apartment at fifty-five degrees to cut costs; still she was sinking deeper in debt. I sent an angry cable to Headquarters. This occurred eight months after arriving in the field and eleven months after the addition-to-compensation memo had been sent to the CIA lawyers for their opinion on its legality. In my cable I asked to travel to Washington. I wanted to see the Inspector General and the DDO himself so I could tell them personally why I had to return to Headquarters short of tour.

Approval was granted for the trip and I headed for Washington and most probably a career setback. I explained the economic plight of the office and eleven-month delay on "legality" when an Agency office only two hundred miles away had been getting the necessary survival pay all along. That very night the same Agency lawyer who had sat on the matter for almost a year wrote his opinion that CIA indeed had authority to pay us. I was asked and agreed to remain as field Chief for the remainder of the tour, shortly afterwards being approved for a third-year extension. I felt relieved and was happy to get back to the Operations and away from things administrative. The third-year extension would allow us to get out of the debt we had accumulated since arriving in the field. I assumed that the matter was behind me. But I had broken the unwritten Agency "law of hierarchy" by going to the Agency's Inspector General.

Well into my second year, after being approved by the Division management for a third year, I was due for my annual performance evaluation from my boss in Headquarters. The reports overall thrust was very positive, and I received high marks for the operational recruitment program, at least for that which satisfied the numbers game. Nothing was said or acknowledged about the Science and Technology targeting, but that was par for the course. If it worked out, fine; if it did not, Headquarters would have no responsibility. No-fault management, I called it. Anyway, in the performance evaluation, as an almost casual afterthought, the Headquarters' evaluator wrote that "even though every employee has a right to avail himself of the various avenues of communication to the very top, this officer should keep in mind that discipline is the *sine qua non* of a professional Intelligence Officer."

Benign enough on the surface, the comment had the immediate effect, despite the continued good marks for my Operations work as field Chief, of plunging me from the upper third in 1977 (of GS-14 officers being considered for promotion to GS-15) to the lowest quarter in 1978.

Over the years, I found that Agency Operations Officers seldom suffered permanent career damage for very poor performance or incompetence, even when agents were killed or compromised due to faulty tradecraft or other professional mistakes. However, those who violated the CIA law of hierarchy were banished to some faraway post or, as in my case, had their career torpedoed. This incident suggested to me that Inspector Generals in CIA really ought to come from outside the organization altogether, even though some fine Agency men and women have served in that difficult office. Employees in sensitive organizations ought to be able to make a just appeal over the heads of lethargic administrators without having the appeal itself become the basis for career destruction.

When I learned about my slippage in the ranking, I considered resigning. Eventually, I worked out a transfer from headhunting. Why had it come to this? Why was Headquarters unable to deal routinely with a relatively routine matter? What was behind the administrative paralysis?

Unfortunately, CIA had entered another era of uncertainty and everyone in Headquarters was keeping his head down. When Jimmy Carter of Plains, Georgia, was elected President in 1976, it was crystal clear that CIA would be getting a new DCI. George Bush, appointed by Ford, had been a Republican Congressman and head of the Republican National Committee, probably the most political job in a political town. Carter's first choice as Director was rumored to be Theodore "Ted" Sorenson, a brilliant liberal from the Kennedy Administration and, like Bush, a thoroughly political person. The Sorenson trial balloon, greeted with skepticism at CIA and around Washington generally, never materialized.

To head CIA and the American Intelligence Community, Carter finally had turned to a classmate from the Naval Academy, Admiral Stansfield Turner, a scholar-athlete at the Naval Academy and now serving as Commander-in-Chief of Allied Forces in Southern Europe. In early March 1977, when Turner took over as DCI, the Agency and most of the government had been on hold since the previous summer.

Outside Navy circles, Admiral Turner was a virtual unknown when he got the nod from President-elect Carter, but that soon changed. He took command of an organization that had severe morale problems at every level but especially back in Headquarters where Turner got his first glimpse of the organization. A Bible-school teacher on Sundays, like Jimmy Carter, Turner brought to this new assignment a moralistic view of life. He had headed the previously-tranquil Naval War College in 1972 and shook that institution to its foundation. Now, Turner was determined to make his mark out at CIA. The new DCI was aware also of the legal difficulties of one predecessor; Richard Helms had just come back from Iran and had Justice Department prosecution hanging over his head, not for things CIA *did* under his Directorship but what he *testified* to Congress in public hearings about CIA activities in Chile. The Agency and its Director were in the middle of a legal minefield.

Turner-the-Moralist decided early to root sin out of CIA, and he brought into the Agency another fundamentalist Sunday-school teacher who was given carte blanche to find the sinners operating in this spy outfit. Operations Officers found to have been engaging in sexual activities in Agency safehouses were subjected to severe career-damaging administrative sanctions on narrow, legalistic grounds: they had misused government property.

In time, even Turner would find how responsible and disciplined the Operations Officer corps of CIA really is, but his initial instincts told him that he had just entered a den of thieves and murderers. His initial instincts on a host of issues were off the mark. For example, he could not believe that we should pitch a foreign naval officer because, in

Turner's mind, "no naval officer would report on his own service." We made the pitch and the man accepted and reported, but such was the narrow thinking that Turner brought to his post as head of the West's premier spy agency.

Like other self-righteous preachers, Turner had a way of setting rigid standards of behavior for others which, when it suited him, he could dispense with rather easily. He railed initially against what he derisively called "double dippers" — retired U.S. Military personnel now working in civilian jobs within CIA. Yet, at the end of 1978, Admiral Turner abruptly retired from the Navy and *became the highest-paid double dipper in the history of CIA.*

Turner-the-Shaker soon ordered a cutback in personnel, principally within the Clandestine Service where 820 Operations Officer positions were abolished in two years. This came only four years after the Schlesinger purge of 1973 and the Turner cuts had another devastating impact on DDO employee morale. The cuts themselves were aggravated further by public statements that Turner made which disparaged those being forced out. Schlesinger had broken the covenant between the Agency and its personnel. Turner was now effectively saying that there never was such a covenant. Nothing he could do, or say, thereafter would change things, and he was unable to command the respect or loyalty of the Clandestine Service from that point until he departed.

Yet, Turner's decision to make the Operations Directorate cuts evenly from top to bottom may have made more sense than a plan proposed by DDO management. They had suggested we stop hiring new personnel altogether until, by attrition, the full cuts in positions had been absorbed. Their proposed figure was 1,100 cuts, which seemed modest enough; a previous Clandestine Service Chief, upon retiring a year earlier, had written and left a letter on the post-Vietnam morale problem, attributing it to the size of the Clandestine Service. With Southeast Asian Operations down the drain, he had suggested a much trimmer DDO. That letter sat in the DCI's office for the next year, during which yet another DDO would be appointed and soon retire.

Then along came Turner, who decided to cut a lesser absolute number, do it faster, and make the cuts at all levels, so that hiring of new officers could continue. His decision, given the options he was presented, was the least bad choice. Unfortunately, besides handling the public and human relations aspects poorly, Turner was cutting into a service that had already lost considerable talent in the previous three years. The organization, in fact, was not in need of repackaging or more management; it needed leadership. The senior DDO officers were taking cover, trying to stay off a hit list that would force them out the door early. Part of their concern was their own personal dignity; who wants to complete a successful three-decade career, including a real war and a Cold War, with a pink slip? There was also a very practical concern: economics.

Congress had passed a whopping pay raise, for itself of course, and for senior government officials. Because their retirement income is based on their *pay level in the last three years of service*, those who could survive the Turner cuts would increase their lifetime annuity by two-thirds or more! The difference was staggering — hang on for three years and get a fat retirement that would enable the CIA manager to retire in Hilton Head for good golf and fine living; get a DCI Turner pink slip and your tight pension check would have you heading into retirement in Biloxi for catfish fishing and fast food joints.

The Agency institutional paralysis extended into its sixth year. No wonder we could not get any action on our problems in the field; the senior officers back in Headquarters were too worried about themselves. They had a reason to be. Reduction-in-force panels were put together to decide who would be forced into retirement or fired outright. Being on a panel deciding which lower-ranked officers were to get pink slips was no protection in itself; a more senior panel reviewing that person's grade level might decide that his days were numbered. Well, one might suppose, at least the members of the most senior panel that reviewed the highest level — GS-18 at the time — were safe from the purge. Not at all. When one of the three members of that senior panel departed Headquarters and returned to his Station, this Station Chief found a cable waiting for him when he arrived — the other two panel members had placed that Chief's name on the hit list, even before he had gotten to National Airport to take his flight. One might envision the three shaking hands as they completed their difficult work, the field Chief thinking that surely he was safe; he would not get a pink slip and have to go home amid the public firings and face his family. One overseas Station that day got a cable telling the COS to advise three Officers, on an operational visit to his Station, that they were goners. Ironically, the fellow in the Clandestine Service, who ran around the building to synchronize the many firing announcements, found a pink slip on his own desk when he got back from his rounds.

My deep cover colleague — the one the Agency had taken a decade to develop into the *perfect NOC Officer* — got forced out as well. Serving out in Asia on assignment under deep cover, he was one of many Operations

Officers fired that day by telegram. What a way to end a twenty-five year career in service to your nation!

Turner-the-Wary decided that on his watch there would be no illegalities. He wanted to avoid *improprieties* also, a reasonable goal for the DCI, but quite a challenge for a moralistic Naval officer now overseeing a secret spy outfit that had to deal with a KGB and Terrorists that did not attend Carter's or Turner's Sunday school. To police the propriety campaign he called on the Agency lawyers who had increased in numbers from three to several dozen in recent years.

There were several problems with the ascendancy of lawyers in the world of Operations besides the pervasive dampening effect it had on people who must show initiative and take risks. First, propriety for Turner did not mean solely that the Clandestine Service actions should conform to acceptable social behavior, as required at the Navy Officers' Club. He was really aiming much more deeply into the world of ethics and, frankly, well beyond the training or competence of most attorneys. Certainly, lawyers are equipped to advise on what can be deduced from statutes or understood inductively from case law. But, even Chief Justice Warren Burger expressed continued concern over the ethical vacuum in which attorneys are trained and practice their craft. A further problem was that CIA lawyers did not know clandestine Operations. They were being asked to make legality and propriety decisions by Agency managers who referred all matters large and small for review — effectively covering their backsides because the Operations Directorate had been intimidated by DCI Turner, by Congressional witch hunts, by Justice Department prosecutors, and by the "Family Jewels" campaign.

During that Schlesinger-Colby campaign, Agency lawyers issued an Employee Notice warning that any admitted unlawful activities would be referable by them to the Department of Justice for possible prosecution. So, concerned employees were advised to seek private legal counsel. In effect, CIA Operations Officers were on their own.

The Office of General Counsel (OGC) also had become limited to protecting the DCI personally, not the whole organization — and certainly not the Operations Officers at the end of the line. At about this time, I bumped into a senior Operations Officer, who retired a couple of years earlier after a Covert Action career that had begun against Hitler and lasted through the Cold War years. After an exchange of pleasantries, he told me in a paternal, concerned way, "Tommy, do not stick your neck out. No one out there will protect you." This was a man who had taken risks for freedom all his life. Yet, seeing what he did from the outside, his view was that the Agency could not be trusted. No wonder the Headquarters management had slipped into neutral and we could not get any support! The Operations side was under the moralistic guns of a judgmental Director as well as the legal guns of our own attorneys. For the first time in Agency history, the head of the Clandestine Service was not selected from the Operations Officer ranks.

The issue for me at this point was not whether I would go do something bold and daring, as my retired friend feared, but whether I was going to travel any further with the Agency. The thought of moving my family for the ninth time in eighteen years was awful. Our four oldest children were in the eighth through twelfth grades and had changed schools too often already. Bonnie was tired and I was discouraged — and not solely by the administrative problems, as bad as they had been. Due to my recent tour of duty in Washington, I understood better than most the survival game being played by the senior officers in Headquarters. More discouraging was that I had been shafted within the system for using the very system. Senior secretaries had told me over the years that no sooner had an employee left the Inspector General's supposed sanctuary after reporting a sensitive matter than the phone would ring in the Division Chief's office — the IG was privately letting the line manager know that one of his people had been in for what was supposedly a confidential matter. I had gone to the IG on the cost-of-living matter and was paying a career price for having done so.

13
The Farm Revisited

BEFORE ACCEPTING my next assignment, I went to Washington to meet with the new DDO, John McMahon. Already that summer I had sent in a resignation cable, only to withdraw it later. My spirits were low, because of my own career but also for the state of things in CIA overall. If career alone had been important to me, I would have done things differently during the headhunting period.

For one thing, I might have winked and taken an under-the-table twenty percent allowance offered by the Division to me alone during the cost-of-living turmoil. This would have been fine for my family, but it would have killed any such prospects for the other nine people at my Station. It would have gotten the senior Division management off the hook because, as field Chief, I alone was in a position to send cables and put Headquarters on the spot. But, again, I hadn't bought into any of the deals a career-wise officer probably would have made.

I also had no idea what would happen next. Vietnam was long gone. I no longer belonged to the Latin America Division, where I had spent fifteen years. In all likelihood, if the DDO did not fire me for being such a pain in the neck, I would probably go back to Headquarters and a quiet job moving paper from the left to the right side of the desk.

I took the elevator to the seventh floor and walked down the pristine corridor in an otherwise worn building — past the Director's office, past his Registry through which flows the most sensitive information in the world, and into the outer office of the DDO. I introduced myself to his secretary; I was a few minutes early and took a seat. The door of his office opened and, for the first time, I got to meet a man about whom I had heard a great deal, so far all of it good. His name had first come up when my former Chief of Station in Zaragossa was being transferred back to Washington. Word had it that he would be going over to head an Office that handled the CIA Technical Operations and whose Deputy Chief at the time was John McMahon. The way people spoke of McMahon indicated that he had a very special way of taking care of those working under him. The Technical Operations people had genuine need for a friend upstairs; except for Agency communicators and Clandestine Service secretaries, they were the most forgotten group in CIA. For years they had labored as a subordinate office within the DDO. Now that they had been moved into the Science and Technology Directorate (DS&T), their promotions, pay, and career management were much improved across the board.

The new DDO had come into CIA in 1951 fresh out of the College of the Holy Cross, a small liberal arts school of less than 1,800 students that was known in those days for fielding national-caliber basketball teams. His career began on the support side of CIA and an overseas assignment to Germany, where he performed some administrative functions in a Station that numbered in the hundreds. Good fortune sometimes has a way of finding good people and, by the latter part of the 1950s, McMahon was assigned to work on the super-secret U-2 reconnaissance program still being run at that point under the Clandestine Service. McMahon did one good job after another, and when the DS&T was established in 1962 by DCI John McCone, McMahon was well on his way up the ladder of what very quickly became the best-run part of CIA. To compete for talent in the private sector, they established significant salary incentives to attract and retain scientists and engineers. The regular DDO clandestine pay structure resembles that of old-line government departments, insufficient to convince excellent people to leave private industry for careers in government.

The burgeoning world of S&T collection had been doing marvelous things and, with the exception of the Gary Powers flight, causing few of the flaps and headaches of the Operations Directorate. Satellites could go into orbit and collect almost anything without provoking the retaliation that greeted a manned aircraft. Remote sensors could pick up particles in the air and tell a great deal about nuclear weapons tests. McMahon knew next to nothing about things technological when he began at CIA, but in time he headed offices that collected electronic Intelligence and ran Technical Operations around the globe using the latest eavesdropping gear. He may have known nothing about widgets, but he knew people.

After a brief exchange of pleasantries, the DDO got to the point. I was one of his field Chiefs, but I could obviously not stay in the field with the headhunters — nor did I want to. We spoke briefly about my career and prior assignments in deep cover. Then he made an offer that at first touched a funny nerve, though there was nothing funny about my situation or how I felt overall. He asked if I would consider going to the

Farm as an instructor. The first thing that flashed across my mind was college rivalry: the Holy Cross guy sitting in the driver's seat was sending the Boston College guy, me, back to the minor leagues. At other times and with other DDOs, that may well have been the case. But as we sat there in his office I began to see a difference. He explained that he was personally approving all assignments to Training. Other Clandestine Service Chiefs may have said that before, either to get someone to take such an assignment to fill a quota or to get an officer to take a needed rest from Operations. McMahon then mentioned the clincher, words that showed he was serious about Training; he said that he was also personally approving all onward assignments after the Farm to make certain that good officers got very good field assignments.

I accepted and headed down to the Farm for a brief visit, my first since leaving there seventeen years earlier as a spanking new Operations Officer with nothing but confidence for the future. I was not feeling very good about my own situation. The Agency was still reeling from the DCIs Schlesinger-Colby-Turner turmoil. America was approaching the halfway point in Carter's term. There was very little to feel good about as the twin-engine aircraft pulled low over the trees and onto the strip that served the Farm where so many had come and gone over the last three decades — Operations Officers who gave their lives in service to their country, foreign agents who were trained "black" at the Farm and sent to fight for their homelands in guerrilla wars, even some villains who would betray all that was decent in modern society.

McMahon had spoken of the high caliber of the new Officers in Training, but I still had doubts. My skepticism was quickly dispelled as I was introduced to some people known throughout the DDO as excellent Operations Officers. A fair number had worked mainly against the Soviet target and, therefore, had gone up against our strongest adversary. And these men had prevailed; they had gotten the "Yuris" and the "Vladimirs" to work in place for CIA. They had handled professionally the top Soviet defectors. "Peter" was the escort officer for Lt. Viktor Ivanovich Belenko, who had flown to freedom in September 1976 and brought along a Soviet Mig-23. In his book, *Mig Pilot*, Belenko expressed his deep respect for Peter, whose compassionate handling and support brought Belenko through the profoundly troubling depression and confusion that invariably follows defection from the Soviet system. Peter was a military veteran, a Russian speaker and a graduate also of Boston College. He succumbed within two years to a lung disease contracted overseas, one of the true silent heroes of the Agency and his country. As people gathered for Peter's funeral Mass, they could not miss the photographers across the street taking pictures of all Agency personnel in attendance. These were the anti-CIA group from *Counterspy,* Agee's cohorts.

Another new arrival to the staff was the officer who had escorted Josef Stalin's own daughter to defection during a visit to India. Over the years this officer, on his own time and personal expense, had tried to keep her on an even keel. This was not an easy task given the enormity of her father's murders (including that of her own mother), which outdid Adolph Hitler's in absolute number. As with most defector cases, the Agency lost interest when the Intelligence Reporting and Covert Action potential of Svetlana Stalin had been fully exploited. She eventually re-defected and then finally "re-re-defected," a certain sign of the psychological turmoil associated with breaking with tyranny.

The excellent quality of personnel was matched by an improvement in training content. The arcane world of clandestine arts, the Tradecraft Branch, was headed by another Soviet Operations Officer and was about to undergo a transformation. The Clandestine Service was about to move from an organization that had two Tradecrafts — one for the "denied areas" and a poorer version for places outside the Soviet Union, Cuba and Eastern Europe — to a spy organization with one excellent level of techniques for the whole globe.

Historically, the basic Operations Training given to all Operations Officers had been sufficient to operate in those countries where there was no hostile internal security service. When an officer was being assigned to operate in the Soviet Union, however, he or she received advanced training to permit the successful handling of penetrations of the Soviet Government under the very noses of the KGB. A CIA officer was typically trailed during the whole tour of duty by four KGB vehicles, with four surveillants in each car and a number of traps set throughout Moscow to catch a CIA Intelligence Officer who erroneously felt he had eluded his pursuers. Subtlety by the CIA Officer was always crucial because losing the KGB chase cars in a blatant manner really angered them and turned them mean; détente or not, they might engage in direct harassment, including false arrest or anything else that would neutralize the effectiveness of the CIA officer. If they tried all their tricks and still felt they were being shafted by our officer, the Soviets might declare him or her *persona non grata* and order the officer out of the Soviet Union within twenty-four or forty-eight hours. A pal who served two years in Moscow with considerable success said it really felt like ten years, given the pressures and stress to keep agents from being caught and executed.

Having a Soviet Operations pro heading the Tradecraft Branch turned out to be a godsend. Despite all the negative things happening to the Agency in Washington, the organization was about to change for the better in a vital way. This change came not from any considered plan put together at the top — except for DDO McMahon's key decision to place good officers in Training — but evolved over the course of many months as instructors met, talked and argued about the tradecraft needs for the future generation of Operations Officers we were then developing. This was a watershed time for the Clandestine Service.

Toward the end of the Sixties, the training at the Farm had been increasingly geared toward paramilitary Operations because graduates were generally on their way out to Southeast Asia for their first tours. In the first half of the Seventies, new hiring of Operations Officers slowed to a trickle as the Agency had to absorb many hundreds of personnel from the Vietnam, Laos and Cambodia Stations that were being shut down. The 1970 firings also had diminished the hiring of new Career Trainees because one experienced person had to be let go for each new recruit brought in — or at least that was the way recruiting was perceived in an organization under attack. By the time I arrived at the Farm in 1978, the Clandestine Service was in very serious trouble.

The cumulative effect of the Schlesinger-Turner firings, early retirements and slow recruiting for several consecutive years left the DDO short of personnel on many fronts. We were an army without lieutenants, and most of the captains and majors had been trained for a specialized part of the business — paramilitary and counter-insurgency Operations. Almost none of the officers had been prepared to handle agents under difficult operating conditions. Yet, the world was becoming more difficult for CIA because of the changing targets (more Terrorists), better informed opposition (thanks to Agee and the like) and the fact that America's place in the world had slipped from the days when we were broadly viewed as the vigorous defenders of freedom.

The new instructors that arrived in Training in 1978 and 1979 joined the Soviet Operations pros already in place, and the transformation got underway in earnest as the Tradecraft Branch Chief moved up to be Course Chairman of the Operations Course, CIA's primary spy training for all new recruits. Those officers coming in from Asia and Europe who had been trained in and used the specialized techniques got immediately behind the program; those of us who had served many years in the field without the benefit of the full array of spy tricks were even more enthusiastic. After all, we had been required to muddle through for many years without all the arrows in our quiver; it took only a little reflection and humility to acknowledge that we would have been better Operations Officers if we had been better trained ourselves. The assignment that had initially seemed like a jerrybuilt affair, after running a headhunting office, soon took on almost a missionary quality. I had a chance to help mend a battered Clandestine Service, and we worked ourselves hard at a time and place that lent itself to cookouts, tennis and golf. Instead, we worked on casing, dead drops and surveillance detection.

Dramatic things happened within two years of the new approach to training. First, overseas Station Chiefs began singing the praises of the new Operations Officers, requesting more as they became available and specifically complimenting the training, which up to then had been held in relatively low regard. The general disdain for Training and Trainers was part of the Clandestine Service posturing and lore; at least one senior DDO manager never missed a chance to express his contempt for training, and he used to tell one and all that he had never had a single day of it since entering CIA. Yet, during the OSS years, records showed, there was a direct correlation between the success of OSS missions and the quality of training that preceded the operations — when corners were cut in the preparation of field-bound OSS operatives, casualty rates soared. The anti-training senior officer changed his own tune in time, after his own son went through Agency courses and told his dad what he was learning. Fortunately for the Agency and its agents in the field, we had not waited until the DDO senior officers saw the light.

Secondly, as the new, better-trained officers began arriving in the field, a generation gap arose as they were better equipped and more professional than their own field supervisors, who had not been given the skills and techniques to run their Operations under harsh operational conditions. For a time, the ill-equipped, first-line field supervisors resisted the new clandestine techniques, forcing their charges to operate the old, less secure way. The numbers trap had forced them to emphasize high productivity — large numbers of agents handled, large numbers of recruitments made, and large numbers of Intelligence reports collected and disseminated. In time, the new tradecraft message got through and smarter managers were clamoring for the same training for themselves. They stopped trying to supervise young officers who could fly Tomcats with the tactics that had been adequate for propeller-driven aircraft.

As an instructor during my first year on the Farm, I learned a lot more than I taught the Trainees, except when it came to the matters of deep cover Operations and NOC management. I might have taught some valuable lessons on Covert Action Operations but, until the Soviets went into Afghanistan in December 1979, the Agency's CA program was in an advanced state of dismemberment and heading for extinction. Almost no officers had been hired for Covert Action in fifteen years, and most of the veteran Cold Warriors had retired or been forced out. As much as we were strengthening the training of the new Career Trainees, we were turning out FI Collection Operations Officers only; we taught virtually nothing on Covert Action or Counterintelligence. The CIA stool now had one leg, but at least it was becoming a good one, thanks to the hard work and innovation of some very fine officers.

For my second year, along with my duties of teaching and counseling new Trainees, I had responsibility for introductory Operations training. Operations-Familiarization, as it was called, had traditionally been given in a single six-week course to a limited number of Intelligence support personnel assisting overseas Operations, either at Headquarters or in the Field Stations. Not ranked high on anyone's list of training priorities, it was seen almost as a nuisance course for non-Operations Career Trainees who did not need the whole clandestine Operations Course. On the surface, it did not seem like a very stimulating opportunity, but it at least gave me something to work on outside the structure of the regular Operations training.

As I looked over the course, it struck me that it had two essential purposes, each with a different significance for the Agency. Both purposes had been blurred by packaging them into one catchall program. First, there was the basic matter of orienting other Agency personnel in the essentials of secret Operations. Second, there was the more intense and demanding matter of giving some clandestine skills to technical officers and others who would be going overseas and working on the streets in direct support of the Operations Officers. I decided to split this twenty-year-old course, creating two new courses addressing the different needs for training. And because no one either had a vested stake in the little Ops. Fam. Course, or cared very much what I did with it, I used my freedom to make necessary changes.

We were soon training hundreds of professional and secretarial personnel in a seven-day orientation course that outlined the clandestine mission of an overseas field Station. For the first time in Agency history, field-bound secretaries going anywhere in the world — not just the Soviet Bloc — were told how and why a Station does what it does. We opened the course to people supporting Field Stations from Headquarters, whose understanding and motivation were essential if the overseas operators were to get their job done effectively. This included the CIA lawyers and administrators, whose action or inaction often made a difference in field performance. We opened it to the spouses of Operations Officers, some of whom had served more than a decade overseas but had never been given a single systematic briefing on what her husband or his wife had been doing. Most such spouses came away with a new respect for their mate's profession having learned for the first time the difficulty and importance of Clandestine Service. The course had the advantage of being given at the Farm, free from the interruptions and distractions that undercut Washington-area training. It was given by the same staff that conducted the real spy training.

The second course I created was a four-week session in Clandestine Operations street skills needed by those who would be going to the field in support of Operations. This course, much more instructor-intensive than Ops. Fam., was reserved for the limited number of Agency professionals who really needed the specialized training. Both of these courses were successful because they addressed very real needs in the organization, one for general knowledge and the other for tradecraft skills in clandestine photography, dead drops and other techniques.

The training assignment was turning out to be beneficial for me as well; it provided a positive way to work myself out of the disappointment of the prior two years in headhunting. It also turned out to be beneficial for the DDO as I was able to direct my energies along lines that helped the Clandestine Service at a difficult time. Clearly, there is a therapeutic benefit in taking disappointment, anger and self pity, and directing them toward helping others. I knew the organization, its strengths, and its weaknesses about as well as any Operations Officer my age — not because I was so smart, but because I had experienced more of the Clandestine Service than peers who had stayed in a single Area Division or career track.

I would have left the Farm after two years, but I was offered the position of Chairman of the main Operations Course. This position was made especially challenging because DDO McMahon directed a 50-percent increase in officer training for my third year. We had already made the training itself very instructor-intensive by the modifications in course content — it was a lot harder teaching casing and dead drops out on the street than lecturing to Trainees in an auditorium or classroom. As Course Chairman, I had to figure out how to meet the DDO's wild order that we push through half again as many Trainees.

.

My initial impulse was to increase the number of students in each course session, a move that would have changed the instructor-student ratio enough to force the training back into the classroom and away from the hands-on instruction that had so enhanced its quality. There was no point in doing that; it would have undone all the good that had been done the previous two years. The Clandestine Service would have been very seriously damaged for years to come if we had accepted again the idea of two tradecrafts. Nor could we go back and tell the DDO that he had to modify his numbers; from Iran, where hostages were being held, to Afghanistan, where Soviet troops were committing genocide, the Agency was under enormous pressure, and we did not have enough Operations Officers to meet the expanding demands of the White House or Congress, which was now clamoring for action on several fronts.

Having done some course repackaging on the Familiarization level, I recommended that the course be run three times a year, not twice, an adjustment that maintained the integrity of the clandestine training itself. It also was a tremendous challenge for the instructor staff as we trained more Operations Officers that year in the full array of tradecraft skills than had ever been done before. We continued that year to run the two mini-courses I had created as well. Needless to say, by year's end the instructor staff was worn out. Since then, the Agency has not tried to push through so many Trainees in one year. We had been asked to do so because the damage done by the Schlesinger-Turner purges of the Clandestine Service had left CIA, by 1980, in a desperate situation.

One of the most vivid changes in the Operations Training Course during those years was the dramatic increase in female Career Trainees. The jump from a very modest number in my class in 1960 to a significant share in 1978 reflected the changing role of women in American society and, more specifically, the enhanced role of female Operations Officers in CIA and around the world. The Agency had found that the low status of females in other societies, especially in the Third World, gave us operational advantages — female officers were collecting secrets that had once been the preserve of their male counterparts. We found in the Operations training that they did better than men in the people side of the business; they had learned to assess and develop people better, probably in self-defense in a still male-dominated American society. As the training shifted to clandestine street skills, the men tended to learn technical skills more quickly.

Almost all of the women were single when hired, as were a majority of the men, and it was natural that some new Operations Officers would pair off over the course of the two years of training. Some married before or soon after their first tours of duty overseas. We made a special effort at the Farm to keep the place from degenerating in the way it had for a while in the 1960s, when female Trainees had been sexually harassed and one senior training officer offered to pass women who would go out for a "tumble in the woods." The ever-resourceful Trainees got their revenge by setting him up one night. As he stood in his socks in a grove of pine trees with a female Trainee he believed he had successfully propositioned, cameras flashed and his time as an instructor came to an abrupt end.

Our concern about the misuse of sexuality went beyond that specific case, however, and we emphasized in training that CIA did not want its Operations Officers jumping in and out of bed to recruit or handle agents. At the risk of being labeled sexist, we also discussed the added pressure female Operations Officers run into overseas when they meet in safehouses with macho men of other cultures who believe they have to conquer every woman in their life. Using sex to recruit for Intelligence purposes usually fails. Much of this discussion was for the few female Trainees who had not learned how to handle men without relying on their sexuality. Most of the young women had learned how to deal with all kinds of men in school and in life, especially those who had traveled outside the U.S. and had run into foreigners who believe, thanks to Hollywood, that all American women are morally loose.

The training staff also taught the new Career Trainees how to conduct clandestine Operations in a world increasingly more aware of CIA and its activities — and more hostile to the Agency as well. We also evaluated our Trainees carefully. The degeneration of American education generally, with grade inflation and a no-flunk policy, had diminished the serious weighing of student performance in U.S. colleges, and the practice had carried over into our program. In the first Operations Courses in which I served as instructor, not a single Trainee had flunked; the vast majority of them had been so carefully screened and selected that no one expected many would fail. But, with 100 percent of the Trainees making it through the Operations Course, the obligation to evaluate Trainee performance and to assess potential had clearly been neglected.

I saw some evidence of this neglect. During my second year as an instructor, before I took over Chairmanship of the main Operations Course, I was assigned as my counselee a young man fresh out of law school who looked like a Norman Rockwell schoolboy. As the Operations

Course progressed, it became clearer every week that, despite his natural talents, he was not cutting it. We had a talk. He said that he had worked his buns off in law school and had decided that he would never work that hard again. At twenty-five years of age he was not willing to put in the twelve-to-fourteen-hour days that it took to get through the training and acquire the skills necessary to keep agents alive in a very hostile world. Perhaps it was a byproduct of the 1970s beating up of CIA, but no one seemed to want to do what this young Trainee needed: that he be shown the door. Anyone worn down in his mid-twenties by a tough training course did not have the stamina for an overseas Operations career, where the demands were always bordering on the excessive.

It took a great deal of effort to see that he was not certified as having successfully completed the course, and he was assigned to one of the most tolerant Agency offices where he would not be strained and where he could use his obvious Intelligence and social skills, if not much energy. He did not perform well there either, and within six months he was dismissed altogether from CIA. Because he was a genuinely nice young man, I hope he found a niche for himself. I was chagrined that anyone so young had given up on hard work before even beginning. I had been surprised also that the Agency had become unwilling to remove from training such an unqualified individual, especially when agents' lives might some day depend on his going out in the rain in the dead of night to protect them. But we crossed that line, and the staff discovered that the world did not come to an end when a Trainee was flunked. Evaluations then became more realistic and tougher, and this young man in his own way made a contribution to the Agency's effectiveness. We had arrived at the point where we would not certify those who outright failed the training — a step in the right direction.

When I served as Chairman, I concentrated on spotting especially-talented young officers to work against the Agency's number-one target, the Russians. When I found such a young man or woman I would so advise the key officers in Soviet Operations and encourage the graduating Trainee to look into the possibility of working against our top adversary. On one occasion, I took the initiative to advise the Soviet Operations Division that one of its officers, a young Russian speaker slated to be assigned to Moscow in the following year, seemed to have difficulty in the training, not so much in clandestine skills as in attitude. The kind of person who marched to a different drummer, he could not bring himself to cooperate with other Trainees or instructors in the training exercises. Something was not right, and I saw to it that this was reflected in his final, formal evaluation, which he got to see, sign and refute if he so desired. Instead of going to Moscow, he was assigned to a Station in the Third World.

About two years later I bumped into this recruit in the DDO's office at Headquarters. I innocently asked if he was getting an award, so seldom was a junior officer on the seventh floor to see the DDO himself. He told me that he was getting no award — he was being fired. Something unsettling and confusing had happened between him and the KGB in that Third World Station; the Agency believed after its own investigation that he had accepted a Soviet pitch to spy for them. Had he been playing games again, as he had done in training, figuring he could dangle himself to the KGB and play cat and mouse? Regardless of what actually occurred, I was glad I had stuck to my guns back in training and kept him from the Soviet assignment. On their home turf the KGB would have made mincemeat of him. That same street sense that had permitted me to read Agee accurately when we first met came into play again. I certainly had my own weaknesses and shortcomings, but seeing through individuals with integrity problems was generally not one of them.

My final campaign at the Farm was to try to do something about the problem that had ruined more CIA Operations Officer careers than any other (with the possible exception of alcohol) — financial irresponsibility in handling official funds. The very latitude CIA has handling "unvouchered funds" makes the Agency extremely careful to avoid even the hint of impropriety. That ethic is true as a whole for the Clandestine Service, though individual officers have violated that trust — some have been caught while others have chosen instead to resign rather than face possible exposure during polygraph examinations.

Anti-CIA activist John Stockwell, with whom Agee recently formed the Association for Responsible Dissent (ARDIS) to attack CIA in this country, remarked in a 1988 interview: "When you're involved in a really big operation — as I was in Angola in 1975 — there's a lot of money floating around, all in cash. Say you have family problems, and one way out is a psychiatrist, or a big vacation, or a fancy Swiss boarding school for the kids. It's pretty hard not to take some of that cash, which you're handing out anyway to crooked provincial leaders or local military officers who just scribble an illegible receipt in return."

Whether a confession of sorts or a commentary on his part only, Stockwell's point is valid — Operations Officers handle cash that can easily be stolen. Those who stay on the straight and narrow do so because of honesty and integrity — personal values developed long before they ever came up on CIA's radar screen. My only contribution in a training capacity was to emphasize the obvious risk and foolishness of commingling personal and public funds — ever! I used to do unannounced cash counts of the Trainees' official funds, which had been issued for use in training exercises, to drive home the point that keeping Uncle Sam's money sacrosanct was basic in a business where the freedom to spend and even steal it was so real.

In 1981, I finished my three years in Operations Training with my spirits and my career back on a sound footing. Bonnie and I now had three children in college, another entering the following year, and my youngest completing second grade. I was ready to begin the Reagan decade, hoping that the woes of CIA and the malaise of the country in the Seventies were behind us.

14

Casey Comes to Town

WE ARRIVED back in Washington in mid-1981, six months after William "Bill" Casey had taken over as DCI. It was a time of renewed hope for the country and the Agency after the feckless Carter Administration. Expectations were often unreal as people spoke of DCI Casey "unleashing the CIA" — prompting me at the time to wish I had the talent to sketch cartoons. My first cartoon would have had Casey opening the wide doors of an enormous old barn, revealing a charging Chihuahua, yelping not growling. Such was the real state of CIA's Covert Action capability when the transition took place. As with the destruction of the Latin America Division Counterintelligence operational capabilities a decade earlier — due to Agee — no immediate turnaround was possible.

The Clandestine Service of CIA has only one set of assets — its people. Money does not produce ideas or make things happen; operational hardware is essentially passive and must be exploited by informed people. When the Agency was gutted in the 1970s, and when only career disincentives were placed in the path of Covert Action and Counterintelligence Officers, a hole was created in the officer corps that would take time to heal. It took five years from the time of hire just to take a new Trainee through training and the first two-year tour of duty in the field. By then, we had a pretty good idea whether this person was suitable for the business. A five-year employee was still pretty much a novice, with a couple of years experience in one country, usually running FI Collection agents. What was the likelihood of a five-year employee being a skilled Covert Action officer capable of going against KGB "active measures" operatives? Yet, when Congress and Carter awoke to the Soviet threat in Afghanistan and threw money at CIA for new positions and Covert Action infrastructure, they missed the point: human agent capabilities cannot be turned on and off at will. Resurrecting an effective and credible Covert Action capability that had been destroyed by Congress in the Seventies would require many years to rebuild, if it could in fact be done.

Casey was an impatient man whose expectations and demands on CIA reflected his early time with OSS in WW II, when a nationally-mobilized America managed to fight and win a two-ocean war, when Alan Dulles had penetrated the Third Reich at high levels, and when Bill Donovan's men and women ran guerrilla Operations from Yugoslavia and France to China and Malaya — all in barely three years. So when Casey came into Washington pushing hard, the flaccid response he got must have been stunning. Some think his first move was for political reasons, but I believe that it was because Casey had discovered the Chihuahua: he took the unprecedented step of bringing into CIA a Republican activist and businessman from New Hampshire and appointing him to head the administrative side of CIA and, then within weeks, moved Max Hugel to replace John McMahon as the DDO. Hugel knew next to nothing about international affairs, Foreign Intelligence or the workings of our own government, but he became the twelfth Deputy Director for Operations.

Early in his tenure, Casey ordered that more Operations Officer Career Trainees be hired and people fresh out of college be brought in as well. Over the course of the previous decade, incoming Trainees had been hired only if they could demonstrate increased *life experience*; almost none came straight off the campuses, and the average age was twenty-seven or twenty-eight. Career Trainee classes kept running behind the goals and needs of the Clandestine Service as well as Casey's directives. But nothing really changed; the Career Trainee Staff, especially its psychologists, were willing to "look at" fresh college grads, but they insisted on them having reached a certain level of maturity and life experience. That attitude blocked the DCI's plans and goals for rebuilding the Clandestine Service.

Still Casey pushed, so the staff ran more Agency "internals" into the Career Training Program, any scam that would cook the numbers and get the Director off their backs. A frustrated Casey replaced Personnel Chiefs; he found not credible their repeated assurances that the problem had been solved; Casey even circulated a memorandum in which he complained of having been misled by his managers on Operations Officer hiring. When DCI Casey went to his rest, after serving six years and a day as DCI, Operations Officer hiring was still running behind Agency needs and goals. The system, essentially, had ignored Casey's orders and applied its own criteria that discriminated against recent college graduates. There were just not enough successful twenty-five to thirty-two year old applicants to fill the classes. The Personnel Career Training Program was marching, still, to its own beat.

Casey ran into the same kind of organizational inertia on a number of important goals, from Counterterrorism to Covert Action, as I too had been running into at the Operations level. My guess, because I had no near or special access, is that this DCI recognized the Agency's internal limitations and decided to pick his external targets selectively; he would make his mark in those key trouble spots where he could have maximum impact against the Russians and their Cuban surrogates. With the Strategic Defense Initiative (SDI) upping the ante in the broad technological poker game, and with Casey going at them on the ground in South Asia, Angola and Nicaragua, the new Administration had become proactive and not reactive. For the first time since the Forties, Russian and not American soldiers were going home in body bags and in large numbers. The eventual defeat of the Soviet military in the mountains of Afghanistan, their willingness to sign strategic treaties with on-site inspection, unthinkable a decade earlier, represented a significant reversal of fortunes for the two superpowers. A good part of the credit should go to Bill Casey — especially in light of what he had to work with in a weakened CIA.

My job as Senior Training Officer for the Clandestine Service was another oddball assignment like my earlier work was on the deep cover problem. Outside the mainstream of Division line management, it offered potential to make the DDO a better organization by improving Operations Training, foreign language instruction, secretarial training and courses in management development. Part of my job was to see that DDO personnel got into the right courses. It was my responsibility also to look at the Clandestine Service and determine what training was needed. I was acutely aware of what we had been doing at the Farm, but I wanted to get fresh input from the Field Stations which, because of their chronically-hurried state, could not be counted on to forward views on training needs to Headquarters. So, I got approval to go overseas and make my own survey.

I traveled with a colleague who was running the Career Training Program at the time. We went to eight CIA Field Stations in Europe, North Africa and the Near East and interviewed thirty-nine first-tour Operations Officers, their direct supervisors, and the Chiefs of Station. This was going to be a litmus test on the direction of training, both what we had done at the Farm in the Operations Course and what we would do on other matters in the future.

My principal interest was in evaluating the adequacy of the Operations training, particularly the new emphasis on advanced tradecraft skills.

Were they appropriate for the times? Were the new skills being employed? Should we continue what was the most expensive and instructor-intensive part of the tradecraft training? Were we engaging in overkill? I had seen enough signs of sloppy operational security practices while serving as field Chief with the headhunters; cables from throughout the world presented us with agent meeting plans that meant undue risk to the agents we had recruited. But now, I would be looking at the situation three years later, after the new Trainees had gone abroad. Uniformly, we got very positive feedback from the Field Stations, especially the Chiefs of Station who privately told us that their new officers were the best trained in the Station. That was the good news. It meant also that we had a major remedial training job to do on the middle grade officers, many of whom had been rushed through training in the Vietnam era with only a smattering of tradecraft instruction.

Both I, from my time at the Farm, and my Career Training Program colleague knew all the former Trainees personally. When we learned what they were doing operationally in the field, there were few surprises. Those who had done best in training were doing best in the field. Happily, a few were even doing better than we expected. Overall, I was left with three very clear impressions, which I reported to the DDO upon my return. First, I was amazed at the level of responsibility that these new officers were assuming on their initial field tour. A few were handling sensitive Operations that were significant at a national Intelligence level for the United States and more important than those other officers might work on in their whole careers. Second, only three of the thirty-nine former Trainees were not performing well, a failure rate that was lower than one might reasonably expect. Finally, I was struck by the marked personal growth and maturity in these men and women who had assumed field Operations Officer responsibilities so recently.

These impressions reflected one of the Clandestine Service's strengths: it gives young Operations Officers tough challenges and great responsibilities and holds them immediately to high standards of performance. Later, when recruiting Operations Officer candidates in New England, I would tell them that although CIA would work them incredibly hard, it would not waste their talent by leaving it untapped. This conviction was based on the experience of many years but also reinforced by this fact-finding trip.

Ironically, the positive findings of my trip reflected CIA's habitual personnel understaffing in overseas Field Stations, which are anywhere from 15 to 35 percent below an optimal staffing level in any given situation. Everyone in a Station has to be used, even the most junior personnel, and this challenge leads to growth. Busy people do not have the luxury of sitting around bitching about perks, crummy cover or getting into self-destructive personal behavior. The challenge also forces CIA Officers to pick and choose targets and operational goals with care because time has become their most precious, finite, inelastic resource. They simply have to use it wisely to be any good.

A young, effective Operations Officer who had served earlier as a Foreign Service Officer told me that this was the key feature distinguishing a CIA from a State Department career: we used our people right from the beginning while State did not. If that is an accurate portrayal, it may explain why morale at State has been generally weak, even though the State Department never took the direct political hits CIA received in the 1970s.

Over the past thirty years, Field Stations have become very trim. There is a story about the huge Station in Germany back in the 1950s that responded to a Headquarters cable asking for numbers of personnel working there. It sent a cable back reporting 1,300 personnel. Two days later a follow-up cable corrected the first cable, reporting 1,500. By week's end the COS had counted 1,700 CIA people working in his domain. Today, the average field Station has somewhere between a half-dozen and a dozen Operations Officers. A large field Station in the Third World may have a dozen or so, and we have Stations in countries of key strategic importance to the United States with as few as two Operations Officers. As a result, each person in the field today has a vital role to play, proportionately more than in the good old days when CIA was fat, content and ruled the roost.

This trip gave me some insight into the general effectiveness of our foreign language training (adequate but not great; most had been pulled out of the instruction too early) and area studies (substantive preparation for the country of assignment was weak to nonexistent; whatever little they acquired had been on their own). I also saw that the generally slow promotion situation for Clandestine Service personnel had not changed at all.

One young GS-11 Operations Officer serving in a Western European Station for three years had been joined recently in the field by another Career Trainee, a fellow Ph.D. who had taken an analyst position in the Directorate of Intelligence, one that the field Operations Officer had turned down. The new arrival was beginning his field tour as an analyst-in-residence, and he was already a GS-13, two full promotion grades and maybe four or five years ahead of the Operations Officer who had been out meeting and recruiting agents for three years. Even the most-motivated individuals get discouraged under such circumstances.

I returned from the trip, wrote up a comprehensive report for the DDO, and set about trying to do my job. But the Directorate hierarchy was completely involved in short-term efforts to meet Casey's many demands for action, not long-term programs to strengthen the Clandestine Service.

As a young officer, I had assumed that the senior levels of the DDO and the Agency spent a fair amount of time on broad, long-range thinking and planning. At the working levels, we were usually trying to catch up with yesterday's business, putting out fires so to speak. What disappointed me most when I later got a glimpse of the top level was the discovery that procedures there seemed markedly similar; the senior managers were immersed in day-to-day, short-term responses to immediate situations or problems. There were annual planning exercises that peered into the future for budget purposes, but they too, sandwiched into the hectic workdays, were often just another chore to clear before going home. If no one is reflecting adequately at the working or senior levels, where is that necessary activity taking place?

Most similar organizations use seminars or retreats with outside consultants to stimulate management development and get people to think in a new way. Yet, when I took over the DDO training responsibility, we were often asked why we did not send our middle and senior officers to the available management courses and seminars. I knew that part of the problem was that people were chronically overworked in the Clandestine Service; most Operations Officers and their bosses were under too many immediate deadlines to take time for even a week's training. Obviously, every country and field Station in the world was not always in a crisis situation; similarly, every country desk was not continually under the gun. But being busy and working hard were marks of the rising stars, and few wanted to risk being considered a slouch by seeking a training course regardless of its good reputation. Hotshots had risen to the top of the Clandestine Service with little or no training and even boasted of that fact. The most vocal in this regard was one of the DDO's most senior officers. When I discussed such seminars with him, he said he really missed a weak officer who had retired from his staff; whenever this Chief had been under pressure to put an Operations Officer in a senior course, he proposed the name of his marginally-effective subordinate, who was not accepted but at least got the Chief off the hook until the next seminar came along.

Such was the Clandestine Service mindset I faced in taking the new position. I knew that there would be no fundamental change of attitude any time soon, but had I known just how much resistance there would be, I might have instead gone out and taken an Operations assignment instead.

Part of the difficulty in getting the Clandestine Service to address its significant training weaknesses did not come from within. The Office of Training also had its own fixed view of the world, as I would learn in time. The Office ran a course that looked like a natural for the DDO, but which had very little DDO participation — the Soviet Realities Course. Several weeks in duration, it brought in all kinds of experts on the USSR and was conducted entirely in the Russian language. I had received an end-of-course report by its Chief instructor and course organizer, who lamented lack of Clandestine Service participation. I decided to look into the matter. After determining that the course was too drawn out for the busy DDO officers, I recommended that they make an adjustment. If they broke the course into two distinct segments, I would be able to assure Operations Officer participation for the portion that really addressed Clandestine Service needs. "Forget it," they said. They would continue to run the one course in CIA that dealt with our principal adversary, the Soviets, and do it without DDO involvement.

We were also getting heavy pressure to get senior DDO officers into the sixteen-week Senior Officer Development Course (SODC), which had been put together at DCI Turner's personal direction and was supposed to be the course for future Agency leaders on their way to the top. But again, there was almost no DDO participation. Those who attended did so under duress and were not heading in any particular direction; rather, they were considered temporarily expendable by their Division Chiefs. This SODC was a hodgepodge with four segments, devoted to the four Directorates of the Agency. There were separate four-week segments on Intelligence Analysis, Technical Collection, Administration, and Clandestine Operations, with a smattering of world affairs thrown in for good measure. Now, four weeks of listening to each DDI Office Director or Division Manager talk about his or her analytical or administrative problems is the closest thing to Chinese water torture in the West. I wrote a careful, inoffensive analysis of the course, suggesting some tightening that might increase Clandestine Service participation.

The course Director's reaction must have been negative because change was never considered.

By this time, I was getting the message: the Office of Training, which was supposed to foster new ideas and change in the organization, was totally married to courses put together in a vacuum. Rather than considering adaptations that would ensure more DDO involvement, they ran them as they were constructed by training officers, and at the end of each course sent over a weak lament that the Clandestine Service was not attending. With my own DDO service not all that crazy about higher-level training and with the Office of Training determined not to make any accommodation, why not just forget the whole matter? Why not take it easy, play some golf, go home early, and spend some time with kids almost grown and gone? One predecessor in my job worked real estate sales on the side, earning more in fact in the housing market than his Agency salary, which he continued to collect of course.

I decided to give SODC one more try. I got together a team of four Operations Officers with excellent reputations, one destined to move up to the Deputy Director level within four years. We sat down and went through the course hour by hour, theme by theme, speaker by speaker to see how much of the sixteen weeks was useful and relevant for the DDO. We came up with two weeks or eighty hours altogether. We documented our case to the DDO, who had been continually harassed over SODC, and that was the end of Turner's course.

I then proceeded to examine other courses and found that more could be done in management development or executive training in crisp seminars of two or three days than in drawn-out affairs that end up attracting only slackers. I documented this for Training, but they just pulled the wagons into a tighter circle. From an office that had great leadership in the Fifties and early Sixties under Matthew Baird as well as enormous independence, it had become the weakest, least-supported office within the Directorate of Administration (DDA). It was unable to compete for power or funds with the Office of Communications, which ran CIA's worldwide message network, or with the Office of Logistics, which was supporting the Afghan war and Central American activities.

I might have taken a walk and moved on to another assignment, but there were two other areas that merited attention — foreign language instruction and training of new secretaries. The second was easy: I brought in a very experienced senior secretary who put together a course for all the newly-hired secretaries coming into the DDO, one that let them know what went on in the Agency, especially in the world of clandestine Operations. This helped them make sense of their own jobs and feel part of an important team, which they certainly were. We ran it successfully three times, and secretaries going into the other Directorates began clamoring for something similar. They too wanted to know the big picture before taking on a specific role in the DDO. Responding to the challenge and the competition, the Office of Training soon after took over all such training of incoming secretaries.

If only the foreign language training problem had been so simple. When Senator Paul Simon was still a Representative from Illinois, he had spearheaded an examination of foreign language skills and training in the United States. The conclusion reached was that there was a national foreign language crisis with national security implications. We in CIA certainly were feeling the pinch so severely that we could not make knowledge of a foreign language a requirement for entry into the Career Training Program as a Clandestine Service officer.

In fact, when I examined our own inventory of DDO language skills, the results were staggering. We had very few Operations Officers with native language fluency. Most fluent officers had come into the Agency in its infancy and had already retired or been pushed out during the Schlesinger-Turner firings of the Seventies. I found also that about a third of all Operations Officers in the field had the foreign language skills to do their job. This conclusion was based on very careful testing of officers before and after field assignments. The Office of Training was offering excellent language training courses, but the DDO was up to its old tricks of taking shortcuts and pulling officers out of courses before they achieved a working ability in the needed language.

This was rationalized by the argument that they could always strengthen it once they arrived in the field. The flaw in this thinking is that things do not work that way actually. Once in the field, Operations Officers get busy very fast and have no opportunity to take classes or study a foreign language systematically. As a result, many yield to the temptation to stay around people who speak English. Too many agents have been recruited over the years, not because their Intelligence potential was so great, but because they spoke our language.

If we are taking Operations Officers out of training too soon, why not simply decree that people cannot leave for overseas until they have reached the necessary level of fluency? This might have been fine in Genghis Khan's army, but it is not the way CIA operates. So, we tried another approach, using the Agency's Language Awards Program to try to turn the matter around, a process that would still take a decade if we were persistent and lucky. We beefed up the language financial awards program, paying monetary incentives to employees who reached proficiencies in foreign languages — more for Russian than Italian, more for Chinese than Russian. The financial inducements at least gave the officers an incentive not to cut out of language training prematurely. They helped students who spent two years in a difficult language program, such as Arabic or Chinese, and who invariably fell behind their peers promotionally as panels rewarded headhunting and reporting, not mastery of foreign languages. We enhanced the awards by thousands of dollars. Still, the language shortfall problem continued, and we may well go into the next millennium in the same state. The Agency attitude was that the rest of the world can learn English.

One of my clearest insights into the Agency occurred outside, when I took a pleasant ride up to Carlisle, Pennsylvania, to speak on CIA clandestine Operations to the class of the Army War College. I saw on their rolls that during the great wars they always closed the college and went about fighting. Between the wars, they went back to the business of training senior military officers on strategy, doctrine and history. Driving back to Headquarters I got to thinking about the Agency, especially the DDO, and why we never seemed to find time after the initial training to do anything systematic or intensive in officer development. And then it came to me: CIA, since 1947, saw itself as fighting an uninterrupted battle in one place or another — with no breaks in the battle and no armistice, just protracted struggle to match the campaigns of our adversaries. Who has time for training?

I then moved back to Operations and a Branch Chief position with responsibility for International Political and Economic Collection. The job was attractive because its scope cut across all geographic areas and dealt with significant global problem areas. We launched and ran new clandestine collection programs which, because of their recency and sensitivity, can be discussed in vague terms at best. My Branch provided a staff function on such things as Economic Summits and other matters for which economic expertise was required. Much of what we did involved the industrialized world, but we were involved also in Intelligence Collection Operations in Central America. We also addressed what the Soviet Union was getting away with in international organizations, specifically the United Nations. This assignment was, therefore, much less frustrating than trying to get Training to adapt to DDO needs or get the DDO to be serious about Officer training.

The new Branch Chief position not only cut across country lines but, very importantly in the Clandestine Service, across Area Division lines as well. An abiding feature of the DDO has been the centrality of geographic Area Divisions. Within those Divisions the Field Stations are grounded on the concept of single-country Operations. A COS's authority, and concern, begins and ends within the borders of his assigned country. Yet, the Operations my branch worked on moved across national borders and regions, targeting Terrorists, money launderers, narcotics traffickers, and those engaged in technology transfer. The multinational flavor of the job made it interesting. I knew that as long as a problem could be attacked within a nation's borders, the Agency, through its local Station, was at its best in FI Collection or in Covert Action. When problems were fluid or cut across the map to touch several countries, however, our success rate plunged dramatically. When problems spread to several regions of the globe, we lost all ability to be effective. The reason primarily was one of intra-Agency turf protection and bureaucratic stonewalling.

One day, for example, I went to see a senior Division Chief on an international Financial Intelligence Collection operation that, though sensitive and risky, offered unusual promise if successful. It was a very daring and innovative operation put together by some very imaginative people. I had come on the scene rather late, but it was my job now to cut through the Headquarters bureaucracy and remove any obstacles. As interesting as the operation was compared to most of what was going on in his area, this Division Chief had remained aloof as the operation developed. On this particular day, I bet a colleague coming to the meeting with me that the Division Chief would not once focus on the operation's target, opportunity or substance; his exclusive attention, I said, would be on the matter of turf. Almost as though it had been scripted or rehearsed, the senior Chief asked only one question: "Have you checked it out with Alan?" Alan was Chief of one of the other Divisions whose turf was also potentially affected. That was the concern of this exceptional bureaucratic survivor, who knew that mucking around in another Chief's cabbage patch was a cardinal sin. The sly Division Chief made certain also that his signature never appeared on the project's approval documents. His subordinates all signed off, but he left his signature line blank. It turned out to be a most successful operation that contributed a unique product and operational methodology in financial intelligence. If the operation is now mentioned in his presence, the Division Chief nods knowingly, winks, and lets it be known that it had its beginnings on his turf. But, conversely, had it failed, he could show he had not really been behind it — his signature was nowhere to be seen on the project documents. No wonder Casey got exasperated with the Clandestine Service!

On the international political level, we had the burden and the fun of operating on other people's turf as well, just to get to *the* collection target of the Agency — the Russians. It bewildered me always that the head of CIA Soviet Operations was not the *primus inter pares* at the Division Chief mess. I could not fathom why officers who worked Soviet Operations got promoted at a slower rate than comparative lightweights who operated against Third World targets. It seemed insane that the Soviet Operations people had to go hat in hand to the Area Division turf barons just to place their officers around the world to get at the Soviet target. Our understanding of that society is too important to be weakened by feudal arrangements built within the DDO.

What my Branch did was simply to help direct the Clandestine Service's existing collection capabilities in several regions on what the Soviets were doing in the various international organs of the U.N. Piggybacking some fine work of a Directorate of Intelligence (DDI) analyst who had been following the Soviet activities, we orchestrated some worldwide cables and meetings in Washington and New York to bring focus to the problem. The evidence of KGB unrivaled success in taking over the machinery of the U.N. system came together. By good fortune, the U.S. then appointed former Deputy DCI (and former Army General) Vernon Walters as our Ambassador to the United Nations. By our efforts, the Soviets were unmasked and the United Nations system, from which the U. S. was withdrawing in frustration, was rescued from what it had become: another KGB residentura, or Station, for the USSR.

I was now back in Operations and for a while considered getting back into Covert Action. There were few on-duty Operations Officers who had worked in CA, so the opportunities were there for the picking.

15

Covert Action Charade

WHEN I CONSIDER how I almost got back into Covert Action, I recall a saying from Latin America: Dios cuida a los pobres y los mensos — God takes care of poor people and fools. And foolish I most certainly was when I agreed to consider taking over a key branch on the Central American Task Force (CATF), set up by William Casey to fight the anti-Sandinista war in that region. My possible return to CA Operations had developed rather gradually and indirectly as an outgrowth of my Branch's international collection of political Intelligence in Central America. When not supervising the officers in the Branch, I spent the bulk of my own time and energy in the field of Financial Intelligence Operations and on my favorite activity, exposing the Soviet KGB active measures program in the international organizations. I had no personal desire to get back into Latin American matters. But the personnel situation in the field of Covert Action Operations was critical in important respects, and I was tempted to take charge of the largest branch in the CATF. The new Director, DCI Casey, was so personally and continually involved in Central America Operations that he was called <u>the</u> Operations Officer for that region. It was always a heady experience to be working on something dear to the heart of the DCI, especially one as determined and action-oriented as Bill Casey. It was also in the tradition of the Clandestine Service to go where the action was, and to think that your personal involvement would make the difference.

In June 1985, as Ranelagh researched his book on the Agency, he was told by one Congressional staffer: "There are fewer than thirty Covert Action specialists in the Agency today, and they would have trouble doing anything in even a banana republic that had more than two hundred gendarmes." This was an understatement of Agency CA capabilities certainly, but not entirely inaccurate. Although the Clandestine Service was able to draw upon its pool of exceptionally well-disposed retirees (almost all of whom remained loyal to the Agency even after public scourging by earlier DCIs), there was very little CA experience or competence among those still aboard. Working on Covert Action in CATF was for many their first Covert Action Operation of any kind. This applied at all levels, and at least one Chief of CATF had no experience whatsoever in Latin America when he was selected by Casey to run that major program. Was the Agency as impotent as the smart-ass staff guy from Capitol Hill had suggested to John Ranelagh? How could it be that an organization constantly vilified and portrayed as CA Cold Warriors by the American and international Left should have so little actual talent still on board?

To begin with, the 1967 *Ramparts* flap, which cost CIA its international CA network, was followed by several years of Southeast Asian Covert Action, which had little to do with genuine CA or anything transferable to another region. Vietnam was a real, hot war even though undeclared. Schlesinger's cuts in 1973, the fall of Vietnam in 1975, and then the DCI Turner cuts of 1977 and 1978 had left the Agency a shell of its former self, especially in Covert Action. The failed Iran hostage rescue mission of April 1980 highlighted not merely the diminution of DDO human agent collection capabilities within that strategic country; it showed that the Agency's unconventional capabilities in the action field had also reached rock bottom. In former times, no such desperate action would have been required; the United States would have had discreet ways to pressure the Iranians into respecting not only international law on the treatment of foreign diplomats, but their own holy writings, which are quite explicit in this regard. The Agency had no real agents or Operations because it had no CA officers. Nor had it been hiring or training any for more than a decade. Covert Action instruction and exercises had been taken out of the Operations training altogether. In fact, there was no Staff or Division office specifically charged with developing new officers in the arcane business of Political Action. The Career Training Program, for its part and unconsciously, was also seeing to it that most of the CIA Applicants with the temperament for CA never had a chance to get into the organization. Screening out potential CA Officers was built into their psychological testing.

The Career Training Program psychologists had done a study to help select future Operations Officers who would have the best chance of being "successful" in the difficult matter of clandestine Operations. Their methodology was relatively simple and, on the surface, seemingly reasonable: they identified those Operations Officers who had moved up most quickly in their careers in the 1960s and 1970s and isolated the personality traits that they felt should be used to screen and select the next generation of Operations Officers. As the hiring of new officers expanded to fill the many holes left by DCIs Schlesinger and Turner, the Psychological Staff "success profile" served as the template for new officer selection. Those who fit were in; those who did not were out.

What skewed the results was that most of the rising stars in the DDO, during the sample years, were FI Collection Operations Officers who had competed best in the numbers games of recruiting agents and submitting large numbers of written Intelligence Reports.

The more studious, patient, and inquisitive candidates — who may have been suitable for Counterintelligence careers — never had a chance of being hired for Operations.

The creative, imaginative, and offbeat applicants — who had the requisite flair for Covert Action — failed also to fit the template for the extremely-selective Career Training Program.

What Congress and the other enemies of Agency CA were doing from above and from outside the Agency (to damage CIA staffing) was being complemented from the bottom by the organization's own Career Training selection officers and their Psychologist allies. In time, a certain common thread could be seen in the new officer corps: a generation of FI Operations Officers had been created.

As basic and central as the FI mission might be, it left the DDO stool with one leg. What a terrible state to be in when the United States was trying to show the world's radical elements that, notwithstanding Vietnam and Iran and Lebanon, democracy would be protected — at least within our own hemisphere. On an emotional level I was inclined, therefore, to get into the fray. I knew that this would certainly be my last Operations assignment if I took it; I had long ago decided that, at age fifty and with twenty-eight years service, I would retire from the world of Intelligence. By 1988, I would take Bonnie home again to Massachusetts, as I had promised twenty-five years earlier in El Dorado. So, it was really a matter of now, or never again, for me in Covert Action.

Emotion finally surrendered to reason, however. After weighing the situation carefully, I decided to pass on the CATF job offers. There were just too many things riding against it. For all the things DCI Casey was doing to the Russians and for the Agency, I concluded that he was setting up the Agency for a fall in Central America. He *did this by acceding to groundrules the U.S. Congress designed purposely to prevent success.* In this respect, Central America was another Vietnam for the United States — Congress, again, was assuring Marxist security and subversive threats to neighboring states from Nicaragua.

From the standpoint of goals, we were locked into a no-win policy, one made explicit in the December 1982 Boland Amendment, which ruled out an overthrow of the Nicaraguan Communist government by CIA-supported forces. Imagine back in 1776, and what the American colonial leaders would have told the French if Paris had insisted that the Americans pursue not true independence but instead settle for tying the British down for a few years or decades. That was what Congress was now requiring of CIA in Congress's on-again, off-again, funding of the Nicaraguan freedom fighters.

From the standpoint of Covert Action basics, we also had little to no secrecy. This fatal operational security flaw was the basis of our 1974 Management Advisory Group paper to DCI Colby recommending we seek relief from Covert Action. It was as valid on Central America in the 1980s as it was a decade earlier. The newspapers carried articles presenting detailed reports on strategies and tactics, on funding levels for military as well as nonmilitary items, on the Congressmen supporting or opposing the President, on those Administration leaders fully behind the Contras and those tepid in their support. The Sandinistas and their supporters in the U.S. were able to measure the extent and direction of American commitment. They were able to target their defamation campaign also against the handful of officials who were carrying the Central American torch. Our lack of secrecy on any level was one of the Communists' greatest strengths.

On a governmental level we had no consensus. The President bullied Congress into going passively along with his Contra support program. The Congress tried to sabotage the program by raising red herrings over whether the mix of approved lethal and non-lethal aid funding had been violated. For example, was the Defense Department charging CIA enough for military weaponry? The Democrats hoped to use Central America to help regain the White House. At the same time, the shrewd Republicans were poised to use any setbacks in the region to whip up hysteria at home and make inroads into Congress. All in all, Central America was already a political football. Bipartisanship was dead.

As a result, there was no coherent overt American foreign policy for Central America in spite of the Kissinger Commission's effort to fashion a long-term, broad strategy. There was no possibility for major funding along the lines of the Marshall Plan. On the American priority list, Latin America fell behind Europe, Asia and the Middle East and ahead of Africa only. Clearly, the Agency Covert Action program would not have a properly-funded overt USG program leading the way.

Around the time I decided to turn down the Covert Action job, I lined up an assignment in New England, not to run clandestine Operations, but to recruit officers to fill the Agency's many holes. That was a challenge I welcomed, made extra sweet because Bonnie and I would be going home for good, at last. At the same time, I felt bad about Central America because we could win there under the right operating conditions. All we needed was to look at our own history and Covert Action record.

Successful Covert Action by CIA historically met five tests:

First, it operated in tandem with a defined overt foreign policy program. Covert Action was in the trailer and public policy was driving in the cab up front.

Second, Covert Action by CIA was necessary. Otherwise, it was a game played at the expense of others. Offsetting Soviet or Cuban "active measures" Operations, or dislodging Terrorists, called for CIA — not some social service group or even Marines in uniform.

Third, we were able to protect foreign governments, foreign officials, Intelligence services, agents, mechanisms and techniques that were part and parcel of the Covert Action program. Since Vietnam, the U.S. Congress has shown utter disregard for our commitments to others who agreed to support America internationally.

Fourth, the assigned Covert Action objectives were realistically attainable by covert means; i.e., they were reasonable and sufficiently limited in scale to protect CIA security and operational equities.

Fifth, if exposed publicly, the Covert Action did not undermine the U.S. Government by being seen as morally repugnant to our citizens. Program goals and means were viewed by normal citizens as principled, honorable, and correct — not unprincipled, dishonorable, or corrupt.

COVERT ACTION LITMUS TEST

CIA Program	Tests for CA Success					Results
	Supported overt policy?	Necessary for success?	Secrecy was possible?	Practical and reasonable?	Principled means/ends?	
Early Cold War: Europe & Japan Political Action Operations	Yes	Yes	Yes	Yes	Yes	Smashing success by early 1950s
CIA-led Invasion at the Bay of Pigs	Yes	Yes	Weak	No	Yes	Smashing defeat for U.S.; a victory for Castro
Paramilitary Operations Vietnam/ Laos in 1950s	Yes	Yes	Yes	Yes	Yes	North Vietnam checked for years
Southeast Asian war support 1960s – 1975	Yes	Moot — goal was not victory	Weak	In places	Yes — in a war situation	Mixed for Americans; disastrous for Hmong, Vietnamese, and Cambodians
Chilean Election Operation-1964	Yes	Yes	Yes	Yes	Yes	Solid win for Democrat Eduardo Frei over Marxist Salvadore Allende
Chile 1970 "Track Two" coup attempt	No	Moot — if it succeeded, civil war	Yes	No	No	Failed miserably; undermined CIA and Covert Action
Afghanistan 1980s	Yes	Yes	Yes	Yes	Yes	Soviet defeat; Afghan and U.S. victory
Anti-Sandinista Operations in Nicaragua, early 1980s	Yes	Yes	No	No. Too little, by design of U.S. Congress	Yes	Communists held Nicaragua 10 years; other nations placed at risk

As we can see in the facing chart, when the essential criteria were met, successful Covert Action was conducted. When this was not the case, the losses and damage were considerable and contributed to a weakening of American confidence in its ability to lead the Western alliance. Luckily, on the grand scale of Cold War competition, the Soviet system ran out of energy before the U.S. ran out of public will.

Over the past two decades, Covert Action has been employed frequently in place of a positive, focused, bipartisan foreign policy program. The idea that our nation can solve major international problems purely by covert means defies both common sense and our own experience. For a time, over-reliance on CA was clearly a result of some early successes. It also was used by some Presidents unwilling to deal squarely with difficult issues and hammer out an overt policy with Congress and the American public. When FDR bent the law to keep England afloat as Hitler's armies marched across Europe, he was clearly dealing with a terrible threat to Western civilization itself. More recent Presidents turned to Covert Action, at times bending the law also, to deal with nuisance situations and not great perils. Some fell back on Covert Action as Presidential power has dissipated relative to an obstructionist Congress; rather than help, poorly-conceived and poorly-executed Covert Action further weakened those Administrations.

Unfortunately, as the Presidency itself has been losing vitality, two other negative developments have occurred. First, CIA has been steadily losing its capacity to conduct Covert Action. Second, problems that do require some Covert Action resolution — narcotics trafficking, Terrorism, proliferation of exotic weapons — pose significant new threats to the United States.

So, while we bask in the temporary glow of *glasnost*, we delude ourselves into thinking that the world is now a safe place because the Russian Bear is back in the cage. Meanwhile, the snakes and scorpions have escaped from their containers, and we have virtually abandoned the one tool appropriate for dealing with small, poisonous critters: Covert Action by a professional Intelligence organization. Now Americans can be held hostage for years, servicemen and college kids are blown up on the ground or in the air, our cities approach virtual calamity from a drugged citizenry, whole regions in the Third World are returning to barbarity, and the dominant arbiter of power is now the law of the jungle. No wonder the alarm business is thriving. We no longer have the tools for our own defense, one of which happens to be a Covert Action capability that can be applied with swiftness and with certainty. But the CA charade continues. We pretend that we have it. We talk about it. We have a system of Presidential "findings" to channel its use and legitimize its existence. Congress even funds it much of the time. But, unfortunately, it's an illusion. That is why I walked away from CA. I enjoyed always the parlor game charades, but not the lethal version played at the expense of Cubans left on the beach at the Bay of Pigs, Hmong and other tribesmen left in the mountains of Southeast Asia, or Contras recruited and then abandoned in the hills outside Sandinista Nicaragua. In 1961 and again in 1975, I saw men and women crying in the halls of CIA after so much hope for freedom. I just did not want to end my career telling other freedom fighters that America was walking away again.

Lingering in the back of my mind also was the mid-1970 period, when the Department of Justice Attorneys went for CIA blood after Chile. I knew that, after Central America played itself out to an unsuccessful end, the long knives would be back across the Potomac again in search of those who had worked the CA program. Anyone found who had crossed even a procedural line would be drawn and quartered, the American left's revenge against the last Cold Warriors. That premonition was borne out and vengeance came even more swiftly than I had anticipated. The best-known victim was Ollie North.

Imagine a country retreat where a gathering of illustrious Washingtonians have come together to discuss, let's say, Terrorism. Congressmen are there along with lawyers from Justice and maybe even a bigwig from the *Washington Post*. They have also invited Ollie North, still on appeal from his conviction, to liven up the guest list. Part way through the evening the power is cut, and in due course they discover that both Abu Nidal and "Carlos" are out in the garden, the guards having all been neutralized. Phone lines have been cut. There is one AK47 assault rifle on the table, there as a conversation piece on Terrorist weaponry. There is one magazine of bullets. They see the shadowy figures darting about and conclude that their building is being prepared for demolition. Plastique explosives are being wedged along the foundation.

They have only minutes before they will be meeting their Maker. All eyes turn to Ollie North. The Congressmen tell him they never meant anything personal; they just thought they could get Bush and not have to face an incumbent Vice President. The senior lawyer from Department of Justice says he is personally willing to help on the Appeal. The *Post* manager tells about a human interest piece he was just thinking about, one which shows Ollie's family enjoying a cookout. Ollie picks up the rifle and heads out into the night. That is the kind of person who always seems to get hurt in the Washington power games — not the slick power broker, lawyer, or opinion-maker — *just the decent, brave, unsophisticated men and women who love their country and are willing to take risks for freedom.*

Just before heading home to New England, I bumped into another such fellow who would find himself within months facing prosecution after being forced into early retirement from CIA. It was a Sunday and I had gone over to a neighboring town to catch the last Mass. On the way to the parking lot I encountered Joe Fernandez, a Latin America Division officer, and Joe was his usual happy self. He was especially pleased to have been selected for assignment to Costa Rica as CIA Station Chief. I asked him why, with so many children, he would go into that quagmire, that confusion. I had already taken myself through the mental process of sorting out a CATF job. I thought back to officers who were treated like criminals after Chile "Track Two" and of the words of warning from the old veteran CA officer who had told me not to stick my neck out. I knew also that Joe Fernandez was going into Central America to help win a war that was already lost. I knew that he was not a cover-your-ass type. He was precisely the kind of guy, like Ollie North, that would take the rifle and slip out into the garden after Abu Nidal. Why was he going into Central America? Because, he said, that was where the action was and where he could have the most impact. So much for heroes and so much for Covert Action under existing groundrules.

16

CIA Recruitment Game

S TANDING in the elevator as it descended to the lobby, I could feel my anxiety rising. I was getting ready to meet the other conference guests in my new role. When the doors opened, I felt completely exposed, as if I had left my room in nothing but my socks. A career in Clandestine Service behind, I was now beginning an overt role as a CIA Personnel Recruiter. After years of hiding my Agency affiliation, I was wearing a conference name tag with the blazing words: Tom Gilligan — Central Intelligence Agency.

As I moved about the conference hall and met new people, I found myself very conscious of their reaction when they glanced at my name tag. Some were warm and accepting; they obviously had no "dirty tricks" view of CIA and, I would learn, had excellent personal dealings with earlier Agency recruiters. Others were cold and unresponsive; they too had a view of the Agency that was reflexive and negative. Fortunately, the warm reactions outnumbered the icy ones by a wide margin, and I knew that things would not be as difficult as I had expected. Even the less friendly college Career Services reps, while not soliciting an Agency visit to their campus, at least made polite noises about "working something out," which usually meant sending their interested students to CIA offices on a discreet, informal basis. No one was gauche enough to ask, "What are you killers doing here?" In time, I became more comfortable; these sorts of conferences became routine. And bringing my experiences to the outside world gave me an even clearer view of how the outside world saw CIA.

Shortly before Christmas 1985, we arrived back in New England. Our eleventh major move in twenty-five years was bringing us home; by then, three of our parents had died and three of our five children were married or engaged. The second youngest was still in college and the youngest was halfway through seventh grade. I can remember watching Alex Haley's "Roots" and sharing some of his people's loneliness; we often felt disconnected from our roots as we moved nomadically through an Agency career. For Bonnie and me, the Boston area had remained home, the place we would return to some day. Our children had been born in five separate cities and lived in fifteen houses or apartments during their formative years. Their occasional trips to see relatives in New England provided the most solid reference point in their lives.

There is some genuine loss not having a place of your own, in not having grown up in one place and gone through school and early life with the same childhood friends. For the Gilligan children, the friendships had all been temporary, intense at first and then broken by the next move. Bonnie and I felt a similar sense of loss. The professional need to break off from former agents and colleagues, including deep cover associates, may be the highest price paid by an Operations Officer in his or her career. I can remember arriving at my first assignment and being told by a local citizen that she no longer made friends with people from the American Embassy or U.S. business community because the pain had been great when they transferred in a couple of years.

As I prepared to deal with young Americans considering careers in secret Operations, I had the confidence of my experience, of having lived the life and made the moves — serving in Washington and overseas, operating under official and deep cover, being both a Trainer and a Trainee, managing single-country and multi-region Operations, and engaging in FI, CI and CA Operations. I could give them a broad, and I believed, an unvarnished picture of the Clandestine Service. That was my perspective and purpose as I got started in the beginning of 1986, the dead of New England winter when a college senior begins getting serious about career search after being badgered over the Christmas Holidays by mom and dad to find a job.

In the Office of Personnel, we were feeling DCI Casey's pressure to resolve the Operations Officer hiring problem once and for all. The DCI was starting his fifth year as head of American Intelligence and was still disgruntled over this unresolved issue. He was determined, before the end of President Reagan's final term of office and his own as CIA Chief, that he would transform the Clandestine Service and fill functional holes in all of the major missions: FI, CI and CA. Figuring that someone from the can-do Operations side would do the job, he appointed a senior Clandestine Service officer to head Personnel. In addition, the Office of Personnel's advertising budget for new hires grew to a million dollars a year. Still, the holes in Career Trainee classes continued. Casey appointed as Personnel Chief another senior manager from the

Operations Directorate, a man with a reputation for being incredibly dynamic. Yet, hiring continually fell short of the mark.

Casey knew that the solution was to hire younger officers, but the system went along in its own usual way — few recent college graduates were making it into the Operations Officer ranks as Career Trainees. A handful were hired on an extended training basis, which meant they would spend an extra year in a Trainee capacity and would reach their first overseas field assignments four years after being hired.

DCI William Casey might be the boss at CIA, but bureaucrats down in the pickle factory were having the final word. We may recall President Kennedy saying how little even the President can make things happen in the Federal Government, even though he is its elected Constitutional leader, Chief Executive, and Commander-in-Chief.

It seemed unlikely that fixing this major weakness in U.S. Intelligence could be accomplished from the top. I was hopeful, nonetheless, that I might be able to help from the bottom — at the beginning of the recruiting line. I knew all too well how important it is that we bring excellent young men and women into the Clandestine Service, individuals with superior Intelligence and street smarts, with a heroic blend of courage and prudence, and with an integrity that would endure in a career with considerable pressures to compromise one's values. That goal, under any circumstance, was ambitious because young Americans meeting all Agency standards were precisely the promising men and women sought after by the nation's top corporations, financial institutions, law schools and graduate study programs. Everyone wants the best, and CIA was no different. Few competitors, however, placed so many obstacles in the path of applicants as the Agency.

Before leaving Washington, I was disgusted to learn that, despite Bill Casey's railing from the pinnacle, a colleague of mine had recently taken over a key CIA Recruitment Office and discovered tens of thousands of unopened resumes and letters from interested, potential applicants who had responded to alluring Agency ads for exotic careers in secret Operations. The resumes were too much to deal with and they were simply sent to the shredder, never to be considered by CIA.

When I got to Boston, I learned that my predecessor, the seasoned Operations pro who had taken the lead in transforming Operations Training at the Farm, had simply given up on the hiring system. By the end of his recruiting assignment, he concluded that young people fresh out of college simply could not get hired for CIA Operations — so unbending had the Headquarters selection process become in recent years. Imagine! The U.S. Marine Corps gives a college graduate, after training, responsibility for a platoon of fighting men; the Navy trains him or her as a fighter pilot. Yet, CIA had become unwilling to bring in men and women who would, after Agency training, be twenty-seven when they arrived at their first overseas Station. The problem, again, was the "life experience" requirement discussed earlier. There were other obstacles as well.

For one thing, the field Personnel recruiters were being evaluated strictly by the numbers and, therefore, they were concentrating their attention on personnel needs in the other Directorates, not in Operations. Even the simplest had figured out that it was twenty-five to fifty times easier to get an engineer hired for the Science and Technology Directorate than to get a Clandestine Service Operations Career Trainee into the Agency. Similar odds applied for Finance Officers or Security Officers for the Administrative Directorate and for Political or Economic Analysts for the Directorate of Intelligence.

CIA recruiters got performance reports that focused on the gross number of hires they had brought in. To skew things further, a cash bonus incentive system passed out money to Agency recruiters based on number of hired only. Some clever recruiters, therefore, advised young men and women interested in Operations to go for some other Agency career track first and, once hired, shoot for a lateral transfer to Operations as an internal employee.

To add to the problems, the security disaster cases of the mid-1980s were making the bureaucrats very wary in their approach to hiring: no one wanted to hire the next Phil Agee, now in bed with the Cubans and the Central American Terrorists, or the next Ed Howard, whose defection to Moscow had broken publicly in 1985. As a result, the Career Training Staff was using several additional filters in the selection system. Every time they introduced an additional person to interview a prospective candidate, the chances of that person getting hired sunk further, especially if this were an exceptional individual. I am totally convinced that the way to keep an organization from hiring anyone outstanding is to have candidates judged by more than five people, or offices, and that each have an absolute veto power. By the late 1980s, applicants for Operations were going through as many as six to ten filters when all stages of the hiring process were considered.

The reason multi-layer screening works particularly against the outstanding candidate is that excellence strikes many people the wrong way — they often perceive the superior candidate as arrogant or self-centered, possibly threatening, and unlikely to persevere in a career. The odds that a solid, though less impressive, candidate will make it through multiple screens are greater. The more familiar I became with the system and the results we were getting, the more I doubted that Dick Welch, Dave Phillips or many great Operations Officers from the Agency's early years would make it into today's Clandestine Service.

Unrealistic standards were guiding the Office of Security processing, also. The first thing that happens after a defection (whether of National Security Agency officers William Martin and Bernon Mitchell in 1960 or CIA's traitor, Ed Howard, twenty-five years later) is that senior managers start asking a lot of questions on how a Mitchell, Martin, or Howard made it through the security clearance screening system — did the Security Office do a bad job in the field of investigation? Was something missed on the polygraph? Was full clearance granted in the face of damaging prior conduct? Who made mistakes of omission or commission? The chilling effect of such post mortems cannot be overstated. They make CIA screeners of applicants very uncomfortable with any person or incident outside the norm. Unfortunately, an outstanding individual may fall outside norms in several aspects of personality, background, and sometimes pre-Agency behavior. Less stellar individuals, by contrast, have seldom done anything either truly outrageous or marvelous, shifting odds of being hired in their favor.

Regardless of the unbelievable obstacles to being hired, I went about my job of recruiting with a great deal of passion. I knew that we field recruiters were the only ones selecting people *into* the Agency. Everyone else along the processing line thereafter was selecting people *out*. That made our job all the more important because, if we failed to channel a first-rate individual into the system, there was virtually no other way he or she could even be considered.

New England had more than its share of potential first-rate candidates. Many good students from around the country come to this area that boasts so many excellent colleges and universities — Harvard, Yale, Dartmouth, Brown, Williams, Amherst, Wesleyan, Bowdoin, Colby, Bates, Tufts, Boston College, Boston University, Kennedy School of Government, Fletcher School of Law and Diplomacy, Brandeis, Wellesley, Smith, Mt. Holyoke, Holy Cross, Clark, and Trinity, in addition to several solid state universities and lesser-known private colleges. An education mecca, this region had proportionately more students interested in international affairs than any other section of the country. Yet, Agency hiring had been shifting away from New England in recent years and towards areas like Utah, where lifestyles were more conservative. I was not looking at the shift from a parochial standpoint because, more often than not, it was not a New Englander at all whom I would be interviewing but, rather, a college senior or graduate student who had come here to study from some other part of the U.S.

Because I soon agreed with my predecessor that Operations candidates fresh out of school had virtually no chance of getting hired, I tried to give them a perspective and information on the Clandestine Service that would be helpful two-to-four years later when they were working somewhere else and getting hit by *first-job-itis*. First-job-itis is a condition that seems to hit most young men and women a very few years after they have entered the job market. After the freedom of academia and the sense of self-importance they are given upon completing college, they eventually figure out that commerce is a matter of carving out a niche and of doing a specialized thing very well. Unless one has started a business or joined the wheeler-dealer world of Wall Street, the tedium of most first jobs eventually gets to many individuals. By waiting a few years to hire college graduates, CIA seeks to avoid this phenomenon in the hope that new CIA hires will have gotten this out of their system before they come into the Agency. I tried, therefore, to convey information that was balanced, not recruitment hype. I also countered the attacks CIA was under from the radical left. The most effective psychological Operations are based in truth; the best recruitment process is grounded also in accurate portrayal of what it is like to serve in the world of secret Operations.

To do that, it was necessary to open up the recruitment process and stop hiding or obscuring things from the potential applicants. The hiring process itself was relatively murky to potential applicants, so I wrote a letter that explained to all applicants, whether for secret Operations or not, what was involved in getting into the Agency. Anyone calling in or responding by mail to an ad was sent an outline of the hiring process, the first time in four decades that we were telling potential applicants what they would face if they continued with the process. I then penned a couple of letters which told Operations Officers what they should know and consider as they decided whether to apply for entrance into the Career Training Program and a Clandestine Service career. This was also a first, and soon the letters were in use by other Personnel Recruiting Offices. (*Additional guidance on the CIA Applicant Process is provided in the Appendices to this book.*)

What we were now telling them was by no means anything secret or classified. In fact, from turncoats Agee and Howard, the Soviet KGB had learned all about the Agency hiring process in the 1970s and again in the 1980s. My own reasoning as CIA recruiter: why not tell our own prospective applicants what they needed to know to make intelligent decisions when we could do so without compromising secrets?

I also got in a supply of *Night Watch* by Dave Phillips, and set up my own lending library, as this was the best book available on what it was like to work as an overseas Operations Officer. Finally, in the information sessions at the college campuses, I tried to let candidates know what an Operations Officer overseas generally did when first arriving to a field Station. It was meant to let them know that they would indeed be working on very interesting things, and that the work itself would be very hard. The unstated message: dilettantes need not apply. The goal was to put the potential candidates in a position to decide for themselves. Operations were certainly not for everyone. But Clandestine Service did offer a chance to make a difference as few other walks of life offered — again, for the right person and if he or she could make it through the hiring obstacle course.

Making Personnel selections at the initial screening level can be a humbling experience. Some people have an incredible ability to package themselves in the most attractive, often deceptive, ways. We have all heard parents righteously proclaim, "My child never lies to my face about important things" or "I always know whether my child is being perfectly truthful." God help the poor CIA recruiter who thinks he or she can look a candidate in the eye and tell whether that person has used drugs, stolen things of value, or engaged in other disqualifying conduct. I have seen many young men and women, who I would have bet would make it unscathed through the Agency clearance process, crash in flames at the moment of truth — the session on the polygraph, or lie detector. This may be an imperfect instrument in the hands of imperfect people, but it is far and away CIA's principal defense against hostile penetration, the Agency's main concern. As is the case in virtually every organization, disgruntled employees are the main cause of stolen secrets. An enemy agent working inside an Intelligence organization, along the lines of Kim Philby of British Intelligence, can do continual harm for a whole career. Thus, there is a great emphasis on, and need for, screening new hires thoroughly — for this purpose, the polygraph is generally the toughest screen of all.

The Office of Security people who run the polygraphs do not share results with recruiters. So, most of the time, we were left in the dark about the specific problem that prevented someone from being hired.

Occasionally, however, an unsuccessful candidate would recontact the recruiter after a security rejection and plead his or her case, revealing to the CIA recruiter things that had been hidden during the early stage of the applicant process. In these circumstances, I found out how gullible I had been, believing that things were well with that candidate.

It did not help candidates that Washington was in the midst of a spy mania that was equaled only once before — during the atomic spy cases of the late 1940s and early 1950s. In 1985, the Agency was suffering the twin pummeling of the Ed Howard defection and the ostensible redefection of KGB officer Vitali Yurchenko. The Agency also discovered that it had been penetrated successfully by the People's Republic of China since the early 1950s through Larry Wu-Tai Chin, arrested in November 1985. The John Walker and the Jonathan Pollard spy cases only reinforced the obvious conclusion that American Counterintelligence was somewhere between disarray and nonexistence.

The polygraph, naturally, was a major concern to the prospective employment candidates, some of whom had heard bad things from college friends who had gone through the testing and had not fared well. My basic advice about this disagreeable procedure: be absolutely candid and straightforward in the initial process and thereby avoid the polygraph problem altogether. It was better, I advised, that they clarify their situation before getting hopes too high, before taking a trip to Washington for testing, before getting their parents thinking they were getting a job with the Agency, only to have it all come crashing down because they were hiding relevant information.

One of the main disqualifiers was the widespread use of drugs, suggesting an illicit substance epidemic in the country and on the college campuses. A remarkable number of applicants in New England colleges were either recent or current users of very dangerous substances. Experimental usage of cocaine was at a surprisingly high level, one reason the Agency was clearing and hiring proportionately more applicants from the conservative South and Midwest than from either coast, where the lifestyles were less disciplined and the drugs more plentiful.

Sexual preference was another concern. One of my first confrontations on the campus circuit was with homosexual activists who showed up at Amherst College and tried to use CIA's tough hiring policies, which they called discriminatory, to interfere with my scheduled interview of Amherst seniors. After I outlined the Agency's "whole person" clearance standard (which means that the hiring decision is made by looking at all of the information and no single matter or incident in isolation) it became clear to me that the group was not interested in that issue at all. I asked them how many would apply to CIA for employment if the Agency, by internal decision or court order, had an affirmative action program to hire homosexuals. When the laughter subsided, the activists acknowledged that their opposition was more basic than the question of hiring gays, and none of the protesters indicated even a theoretical interest in working for the Agency. Despite their feigned concern for principle, they were willing to engage in deception and exploit a sensitive personal issue for political purposes.

Their real agenda, it turned out, was the war in Central America and CIA support for the Contras. When I tried to assure them that their fears were unfounded — that Covert Action was effectively dead — they didn't believe I was telling them the truth. I did not want it to be dead, I also told them, but that was the way it really was. Ironically, the radical activists were giving us more credit than was warranted.

One of the points I made, when confronted in such sessions by gays, was that homosexuals had often been accused unfairly of disloyalty because some of the early major spy cases (Americans Martin and Mitchell, Britishers Burgess and MacLean) had involved homosexuals. The many heterosexuals who betrayed Western Intelligence services were often conveniently ignored, or their betrayals were not linked specifically to promiscuity, which often was in fact the case.

I did make the point, also, that homosexual activity is considered and treated as a criminal activity in many countries around the globe where CIA Intelligence Officers must serve.

I would then explain the standards that apply for granting access to what is classified as Sensitive Compartmented Information (SCI), information that is critically important to our national defense. Every Agency employee must meet that SCI standard to be hired, and on "sexual considerations" the following applies:

- "Sexual promiscuity, prostitution and extramarital relations are of legitimate concern to the SCI adjudicator where such conduct reflects a lack of judgment and discretion or when the conduct offers the potential for undue influence, duress or exploitation by a Foreign Intelligence service.
- Deviant sexual behavior can be a relevant consideration in circumstances in which it indicates flawed judgment or a personality disorder, or could result in exposing the individual to direct or indirect pressure because of susceptibility

to blackmail or coercion as a result of the deviant sexual behavior. Such behavior includes, but is not limited to, bestiality, fetishism, exhibitionism, necrophilia, nymphomania or satyriasis, masochism, sadism, pedophilia, transvestism and voyeurism. Homosexual conduct is also to be considered as a factor in determining an individual's judgment, discretion, stability and susceptibility to undue influence or duress.

- In examining cases involving sexual conduct of security significance, such as those described above, it is relevant to consider the age of the person, the voluntariness and the frequency of such activities, the public nature and the recency of the conduct, as well as any other circumstances which might serve to aggravate or mitigate the nature or character of the conduct. A recommendation for disapproval is appropriate when, in view of all available evidence concerning the individual's history of sexual behavior, it appears that access to SCI could pose a risk to the national security."

- Those are pretty strict standards, and the Office of Security is required on the close calls to deny approval: *"Any doubt concerning personnel having access to SCI shall be resolved in favor of the national security."*

One fundamental reason for the great care CIA takes in recruiting is that the Agency lacks the compartmentation of the KGB. Also, if under suspicion, the CIA mole will get a lawyer and protect himself with the standards of the American judicial system. The KGB would take him in a room and punch him silly until they had their "confession." The Israeli Mossad would kidnap and go to secret trial, if needed, to deal with a spy in their midst. The French Intelligence service might quietly send him the way of Louis XVI.

The sad paradox in America, where we prize individuality and the human person, is that a citizen's potential to harm the country often exceeds the individual capacity to help it. This is particularly true of those employed within the Intelligence Community, where their leverage to do harm is great. It is this reality that hovers over our Counterintelligence officials, including the CIA Office of Security, which is responsible for protecting the organization from penetration through the employee recruitment process.

As the KGB continued its own clandestine attack on American Intelligence, campus radicals swung into attack in 1986. It was the year Abbie Hoffman returned to the campuses. It was the year former Agency Officers spoke to college audiences about the alleged evils of their former employer. One retired officer even discovered how evil CIA is, once he qualified for pension after twenty-five years of service!

A constant theme of the campus radicals and the ex-Agency types: CIA should not be allowed to interview and recruit college students because they were too young to decide for themselves. Amy Carter — whose father, as President, had appointed one of CIA's least effective DCIs, Stansfield Turner — got back into the news, getting arrested for protesting my recruitment trip to the University of Massachusetts.

The themes and tactics were remarkably similar from place to place. Some were undoubtedly drawn from an "Anti-CIA Organizing Manual" put out that year by a leftist group at the University of Wisconsin at Madison. Among their suggestions:

- "Make appointments with recruiters in order to debate, harass and/or take up their time. This is also an effective means for carrying out a citizen's arrest of the recruiter for violations of international law.
- If you can get in to see the recruiter, try dumping blood or a cream pie on him or her, or maybe handcuff the agent to a table or yourself. Be creative!
- Hold obstructive sit-ins at recruiting sites to actually prevent recruiting. Tip over recruiting tables, or spill coffee, or seize their literature and leave.
- Remove recruiters and or police from campus by force or threat of force. Call the recruiters the night before their appointment and give them misinformation about the location, place, time; etc. Throw smoke bombs, stink bombs, and burning cow manure into the ventilation ducts at recruitment sites and/or at the recruiter."

This leftist guidance more or less set the stage for a campus incident that occurred in October 1987 at the University of Vermont. Precisely thirty minutes into our meeting, the college senior I was interviewing glanced at his watch, which had just emitted a faint bleep. He also looked expectantly at the conference-room door leading to the outside corridor. When he finally concluded that his game plan had gone awry, that no one would be arriving to witness and photograph the spectacle, he reached into the pocket of his finely tailored suit — radicals of the left, it seems, virtually always are the wealthier little snots, I found. The feigned innocence of job applicant turned instantly to the glare of committed foe of CIA and supporter of the Nicaraguan Sandinistas. He gingerly withdrew a plastic bag of blood.

"This is the price being paid for U.S. Government national security activities in Central America," he said, balancing the squiggly mess in his right hand and glaring at me across a divide of three feet.

The sanguinary blob seemed to convulse and, even though this event erupted in an instant, time itself seemed to have come to a halt as my mind raced through a range of thoughts, from the unlikelihood of him missing his target to the hideous specter of AIDS. Had I nicked myself shaving that morning? What about the scrapes on my fingers from the weekend's sanding, chiseling and plastering? What about the cuts I will certainly get on my knuckles when I hit that chameleon and bagman in the mouth at the moment he launches his bloody package?

My confrontation with the student did not come as a complete surprise. An Agency colleague and I had begun our day over coffee with some officers from the Federal Protective Service who had traveled from Boston to give us a hand as we interviewed for CIA careers in Burlington, Vermont. We had expected protests and even unlawful disruptions. Though, up to then, most of the campus trouble had involved more legitimate measures, this was the fall of 1987 when the whole Central American issue was being hotly debated in Washington. Since the 1960s, Vermont itself had served as a magnet for anti-establishment individuals who had managed to convert this mountainous state from a traditional bastion of Republican Yankees to one in which its largest city, Burlington, elected a Socialist mayor (later a Member of Congress). Vermont voters also sent the angry Senator Patrick Leahy to the U. S. Senate where he was running his own campaign against CIA from the protected perch of the Intelligence Committee. The University of Vermont, a haven for leftists of the Vietnam era who rallied against Vermont defense contractors, came to be labeled "Berkeley East" or "Moscow on the Lake" for its far leftist, Marxist orientation. Feelings and emotions were clearly running high.

As Chief of New England Recruitment for the Agency, I was making every effort to carry out the responsibility in the least provocative manner. Throwing gasoline on a fire seldom produces good results. So, rather than exercising strictly our right to conduct the interviews on this public university campus, I had acceded to a request of the University to do the interviewing at the Federal Building in downtown

Burlington. The school, in turn, agreed to provide direct assistance for the process — announcing the CIA job interviews, collecting the resumes, and providing transportation to any student who needed it.

The resumes had arrived the previous week at my office in Boston, and UVM seniors began calling in to get their names on the interview schedule. Even at this early stage, the bagman called attention to himself by phoning a second time to assure that his interview was at midday, rather than first thing in the morning, as originally scheduled. There is a neat *Wizard of Id* cartoon in which a spy is hauled before the king, who wants to know how he was identified. The spy, it seems, gave himself away by arriving first to the courtyard to hear the king's speech — violating a rule of Intelligence Operations: blend in with the masses.

There had been reason to scrutinize this young bagman whose resume exhibited academic achievement and special interest in Central America. When he arrived early for his interview, it did not take high-grade Intelligence analysis to figure out that he was up to no good. His early arrival, it turned out, was meant to allow him to case or check out the building from the inside and then tape open the rear basement doors so his cohorts could enter unnoticed and be on hand to see him douse the CIA recruiter in the name of the Sandinista Revolution. An alert building guard had removed the tape. Protective officers had escorted out of the building members of the local media who had been found wandering the corridors just before the planned dousing hour, their cameras ready to capture the incident for replay on the news. As a precaution, I had locked the conference-room door from the inside as I escorted the young man in for the noon interview.

As he held the bag of blood in his grip, we both knew it was just the two of us; none of his allies had made it inside and my colleagues were covering the lobby and basement, in no position to give me a hand. The Sandinista and the CIA man and the wobbly bag of blood.

Totally unprepared for blood, I had no considered plan or script. In fact, for the first thirty seconds, I was not a CIA career officer with twenty-seven years experience, fifty years old and father of five children, four of whom were older than my adversary. All that had been stripped away and I felt a rush of emotions overridden by rage. For an instant, I reverted back to adolescence and warned in street language that somehow, fancy dress and all, he seemed to fully grasp: "If you do it, I will put your f'ing teeth in the back of your f'ing mouth."

As he tried to measure my commitment, it occurred to me that the bureaucrats back in Washington would leave me hanging, but at that point I could not care less. In fact, I went on to say to the bagman, "This may be my last act as a government employee, but you better know that you will not walk out of here in one piece." He sat quietly for a few minutes weighing his options, then lay the bag unopened on the conference-room table and left the room. Outside, he told the media that he had just been threatened by the representative from CIA. Naturally, his self-serving version of events was carried the next day in the Vermont newspapers.

This was just one incident of a single Agency recruiter, but illustrative of the anti-Agency climate that the American Left was promoting on the nation's campuses in their efforts to destroy CIA from below. The Agency was taking it on the chin both in the American hinterlands and in Washington with Sandinista allies in Congress.

Meanwhile, Agee was back in the States, no longer fearful of Federal prosecution. Ollie North and Joe Fernandez would face trial, but not the former CIA Officer who violated his Secrecy Agreement, traveled to Communist Cuba several times, and exposed all that he could, with Cuban assistance. He got together with Agency dissident Stockwell to form the Association for Responsible Dissent (ARDIS). In November 1987, Agee appeared on the television program "Crossfire." He called ARDIS a "new association of former CIA officers against foreign intervention," but said his problem was really with America, not only CIA. "The argument is not with the CIA. That is only an instrument. The argument is with every Administration since Truman ... In fact, it is an ideological conflict with the United States."

Stockwell, for his part, tried to make the abolition of CIA part of the 1988 Presidential campaign. He said, in May of the following year, that "CIA poses the ultimate threat to democracy, and should be dismantled for the good of the United States and the world."

Why are some former employees of CIA bent on revenge? Is there a common thread running through the corps of defectors and detractors which would explain their crusade against CIA years after resigning, retiring or being fired? Unfortunately for the Agency, the reasons seem to be varied and many. There is no single thing that can be done to remedy a situation entirely incompatible with the organization's need for confidentiality and a properly informed American public. Some of the dissidents are creatures of CIA itself, individuals who, mistreated by the Agency, left the organization embittered by incidents that caused personal or career damage. Revenge, again, is powerful, abiding and not of recent vintage.

Two millennia before there was an America or a CIA, Aristotle recognized the power of revenge in human motivation, making the point
that one so inclined derives pleasure from the mere contemplation of
inflicting harm on the object of hate. Obviously, if simply thinking
about getting even gives joy to the avenger, imagine how much greater
the satisfaction when actual damage is achieved. The anti-CIA avengers have, in fact, united in a new organization in an effort to attract
more former employees to their cause — a cause, by the way, without
risk as the Agency is in no position to defend itself, domestically, in an
effective manner. It cannot really enter into a public discussion of its
former or present clandestine Operations. It cannot prove negatives
either: how can CIA prove that it did not murder Allende — which it
did not? Although it can lawfully protect classified information from
unauthorized disclosure by former employees, it is powerless to do
anything about outright fiction and distortions. The avengers can say
and print anything they wish so long as they do not publish classified
information. This leaves a very broad opening for anti-CIA former
employees, and they have been taking advantage of that gap with impunity, spreading disinformation that paints CIA as the villain of the
post-World War II period.

Other dissidents come from the ranks of the true believers and
zealots who could not adapt to U.S. Government policy reversals which
undermined CIA programs, Operations, or agents. The Bay of Pigs
debacle, the loss of Vietnam, Laos and Cambodia to the Communist
invaders, and the abandonment of allies in Africa were too much for
some. Even though CIA itself may not have been calling the shots — it
was the U.S. Congress that ruled out continued support for freedom-
fighting Angolans in the 1970s and Nicaraguans in the 1980s — some
of the dissidents have directed all of their anger at CIA alone.

A few of the dissidents are outright sociopaths who, by the way,
are extremely difficult to screen on a polygraph — their utter lack
of conscience makes them immune to detection of their deceptive
responses. Such individuals abused their office while employed at
CIA, were hired under false pretenses in the first place, and attacked
the Agency in the end with the same unprincipled skill that had char-
acterized their Intelligence years. Too often, having made the error
of hiring a sociopath such as Ed Howard, the Agency compounded
that mistake by abruptly firing him rather than moving him first
to a non-sensitive area until the risks were no longer great for CIA
or its field agents. Somewhere in the hinterlands of America, CIA

could have found a quiet sinecure for Howard, one that would have given the CIA's Soviet agents a chance to escape before they were executed.

The 1987 anti-CIA protests were dramatic and spreading in number and intensity around the region's campuses. The short-term activists were eager to use the CIA target as an oblique way to attack the Reagan Administration policies and actions in Central America. Their goal was to keep the heat on the U.S. Congress, not merely in the nation's capital but, more critically, back in the Congressional Districts as the 1988 election year got underway. I was not concerned that the protests or even yet another cutoff of funds to the anti-Sandinista forces would affect Marxist consolidation in Nicaragua or the threat posed to its democratic neighbors. My own Latin American and Covert Action experience had convinced me already that, under existing groundrules for Operations, CIA could not substantially affect the outcome of events in that region. The Marxists, at that moment, were winning anyway.

As we saw in Chapter 15, Agency activities in Central America fail four of the five tests for a viable Covert Action program. A surgeon operating in a poorly lighted room, and with no nurse or sterile instruments, is not likely to pull off open heart surgery and have the patient live to tell about it. That surgeon would be missing three of his essential surgical supports. CIA's situation in Central America has been even less satisfactory and more perilous. In fact, had the CIA program to strengthen the anti-Marxist forces by some miracle become wildly successful, Congress would surely have applied the brakes so completely that the whole enterprise would have come to a halt.

Concerning me more than the protests, however, was the more subtle sense I had had in the quieter campus information sessions and in the privacy of several hundred job interviews with prospective career Intelligence candidates. Few of the interested individuals had read balanced information on Agency careers because most of the books on the library and bookstore shelves dealing with CIA as an employer were written by the disgruntled. Books written by former Directors of Central Intelligence have dealt with national Intelligence issues and provide a personal perspective at the highest level only.

An exception is David Phillips's excellent book, *Night Watch*, which was so difficult to find that I had resorted to buying it in fifty-book lots and running my own lending library with prospective applicants who may have thought, initially at least, they really would like to have a career in CIA Operations. As expected, most of the young men and women would conclude, after reading about the real world of Agency Operations, that this was not for them, at least not fresh out of school.

At only two New England schools, Yale University and Williams College, was there a course specifically dealing with the Central Intelligence Agency. Not surprisingly, these two institutions had provided proportionately more and better-informed applicants than similar schools. Their students had long before been systematically able to examine the business of Intelligence, its strengths and weaknesses, its relationship to American and world situations, and were able therefore to make informed judgments regarding career choices. Former Agency radicals would prefer, naturally, to make such decisions for them.

The challenge of recruiting the next generation of Operations Officers for CIA is affected by what would broadly be termed a "communications" problem. Yet, it is certainly more than that, involving some fundamental factors rooted in the Agency and, more broadly, American society. Even if library shelves were not dominated by negative books written for the specific purpose of harming CIA, even if the Agency were able publicly to reveal its full record, there are elements at play in the post-Cold War period that did not exist decades ago when the Agency was going through its post-WW II expansion.

Lifestyles have altered considerably. It is unrealistic to expect that family mobility and responsiveness to organizational needs will be the same in this generation as they were among those who experienced Depression and WWII. There have been shifts of values, including a higher demand for materially-rewarding employment and a reduced commitment and willingness to place employment responsibilities before individual creature comforts. International careers have lost some luster, in part because Terrorists have had their impact and in part because America no longer perceives itself as having broad solutions to the rest of the world's problems as was the case as recently as 1961 when Kennedy launched the Alliance for Progress in Latin America.

The foreign language shortfall for America has reached crisis proportions. The conversion of America in the last ten years from the world's largest creditor to the largest debtor nation, the reduction of U.S. automobile production from 75 percent to 25 percent of the world's output and the dramatic weakening of the U.S. dollar are stark macro-indicators of an economic freefall that portends calamity for the economy overall unless checked very soon. Meanwhile, a career in Federal service, especially one that demands a single income for most of its overseas families, is increasingly marked by significant economic disincentives. The chance that things will improve in light of the massive national debt and chronic budget deficits of the Federal Government is not good. Recruiting and retaining a professional corps of Operation Officers who can work effectively under these circumstances, and do so for the next thirty years, will be hard indeed.

The crisis is made more serious by the nature of the mission. The new recruits will be going against the highly elusive and vile targets of Terrorism and the international narcotics syndicates. These dangerous forces have not only joined together in various parts of the world, but they have increased their own penetration and corruption of elected governments as well. The most important traditional target of American Intelligence, the Soviet Union, enjoys the active collusion of Agency turncoats, both in Moscow and here, with a profoundly damaging effect on U.S. security. The foreign adversaries of America and CIA will, on their own, be presenting a formidable challenge in the decades to come. The domestic anti-CIA forces make the job more difficult as they seek to sow disinformation among prospective applicants, attempt to drive CIA into narrower recruiting circles, and deprive access to the broadest cross section of young Americans. They are assisted greatly in this effort by former employees whose accounts of their Agency careers are exceedingly loose with the truth and often bear no resemblance to reality. Is CIA the perfect organization and employer? Not by a long shot. But neither is it villainous in nature or entirely unrewarding either.

In the course of my final assignment in the Agency, I made special effort to explain CIA's Clandestine Service in realistic terms. Quite often, college seniors reacted with surprise to my demystification of the organization and my avoidance of the temptation to paint a rosy picture of an Operations Officer career. I wrote materials that forthrightly explained what prospective applicants needed to know to make informed decisions, but which previously had been cloaked in unwarranted secrecy. I have written this book in a similar spirit. It is the story of one person's journey from college applicant in 1959 to overseas Operations Officer to recruiter of new talent for CIA. I hope it effectively shares personal views and insights on the business of Intelligence while raising some questions and shedding light on others.

- Is it still necessary to have a CIA — established in the Cold War, when the USSR was ruled by Stalin and his Terror — in the new era of Gorbachev and his glasnost?

- Within that framework, is Covert Action dead and, if not, should it be?
- Can CIA under existing groundrules make a difference in the problems of narcotics, international economic survival, Soviet challenges of an overt military and political nature, covert subversion by several nations and their Intelligence services, ad hoc as well as government-sponsored Terrorism, and technology theft?
- How successful is the Agency likely to be in recruiting and retaining its next generation of Intelligence Officers and assuring it gets good people who are up to the technical and the moral challenges of the 1990s and beyond? "Good people" in the world of Intelligence have what is implied by the term "the right stuff" in the world of space exploration: superb competence and personal courage along with impeccable integrity and values. A lot to ask for government work!
- Finally, what about accountability and the non-negotiable requirement that an essentially secret spy organization operate properly in our own open, democratically-governed society?

If this book sheds light on these five questions for citizens in general, and for prospective employees in particular, it will have been worth the year spent reflecting and delving more deeply into my own career memories than I may have liked at times. Playing neither cheerleader nor cynic, if I help others understand CIA and put a balanced book on library shelves so that citizens are not reliant solely on the works of anti-CIA avengers, it will have been worth doing.

On a macro level, the Agency never did solve the recruiting problem during DCI Casey's tenure at CIA. He died in January 1987 and was replaced by Judge William Webster who had headed the FBI for almost the full ten-year term of that office. This was the period of the Congressional hearings into Iran-Contra, an example of how the virtual destruction of the Agency's Covert Action capability had driven some in the Executive Branch (notably DCI Casey and Ollie North, among others) to attack tough problems in the Middle East and Central America outside the framework and groundrules established in the National Security Act of 1947. Congress, effectively, had done to the Reagan Administration what the KGB had done to its dissidents: Capitol Hill beat CIA Covert Action warriors *until* they defecated in their pants and then beat them *because* they defecated in their pants.

On a better note, it was the year the Soviets announced their intention to withdraw from Afghanistan and acknowledged both the practical failure of their system and inability to compete internationally without major internal reforms. This may well turn out to have been Bill Casey's legacy — he helped tame the Russian Bear, despite Congress. On the matter of Operations Officer selection and hiring, however, he never could tame his own bureaucracy.

As the post-Casey era got underway, a whole new personnel leadership was in place with some now-familiar orders on recruiting: "Fix it once and for all." Recruiters out in the field were ordered to send in more applications, at a rate in fact three times faster than had ever been the case. Soon, CIA Headquarters became deluged with applicant files; however, the high quotas for more applicant files were maintained. Field Recruitment offices were soon getting inundated with phone calls from applicants who had heard no feedback for months.

Then, miracle of miracles, a very simple adjustment was made at Headquarters: rather than send candidates with inconclusive polygraph exams back home for later recall to Washington for re-testing, they kept the applicants in town until the matter was settled one way or the other. The results were astounding: the polygraph "success rate" instantly increased by a whopping 50 percent! Within a few months, the Agency was not merely up to its authorized personnel ceiling, but surpassed it by the legal two-percent maximum cap. The so-called "recruitment problem" turned out to have been a Headquarters recruitment processing problem after all, at least in terms of hiring needs of the Agency as a whole. Operations Officer hiring continued to lag for reasons described earlier, but DCI Casey was now gone from the scene, and that pressure disappeared entirely.

The administrators now had a new problem: many hundreds of CIA job applicants had been told that, if they got through the polygraph successfully, they had a job in this or that Directorate. But, the Agency was now up to its personnel ceiling, could hire no more people in 1987, and had thousands of applicant files in the pipeline. The quick-fix solution of the Headquarters bureaucrats: they set up a register, or waiting list, with the intention of hiring people off that list at a controlled rate. Order had replaced disorder, or so it seemed. But, who waits longest for employment to open up, the best and the brightest, or those with the least attractive alternatives? My experience, which does not seem counter to common sense, has been that outstanding applicants tend to have other job opportunities in the private or public sector and are under the most time pressure to make an early decision.

Did the pressure to send in massive numbers of new applicant files diminish now that there were no openings, now that thousands of applicant files were already in the hiring queue, and now that thousands of applicants had just been sent vague turn-down letters despite having perfectly-acceptable credentials, experience, and skills? Nope! We were told to keep sending in new applicant files, beyond the rate one would expect from a functioning field office. The numbers game still was the only game in town. Young, well-disposed applicants were earnestly going through the process in the false belief that they had a chance of getting hired. September came, I turned fifty, and decided it was time to escape beancounters and numbers guys who had made a mockery of the CIA Recruitment process and jerked young Americans around callously and unnecessarily. I decided, after talking with my wife of 29 years — 28 spent in CIA together — to move on and call it quits as 1987 came to a close. I called Dave Phillips and suggested we meet for lunch.

17

CIA and the Threats Facing
America in the 1990s

I N MID-JANUARY 1990, the U.S. Senate began assessing the reduced
threats facing the United States in the wake of what seemed to be
the impending collapse of the Soviet empire. The review opened with
the testimony of Director of Central Intelligence William H. Webster,
who provided as sober a portrayal of the world situation at that time as
one could expect to obtain on so broad and dynamic of a subject. His
statement discussed the matter of Gorbachev's own political survival as
well as the status of *perestroika* and *glasnost*. In contrast to most of the
Western giddiness which greeted changes in the Communist world, DCI
Webster spoke of the continued Soviet vigor in modernizing their nuclear
and other strategic forces. He mentioned that the ABM system around
Moscow had become operational in 1989.

Moving into some of the side theatres, DCI Webster referred to
the significant dangers from North Korea, the considerable instability
within China, the governmental weaknesses in the Philippines, and the
resurgent Khmer Rouge forces in Cambodia. Looking ahead to the year
2000, he predicted Western dependence on Middle Eastern oil would
reach 40 percent; American reliance on oil from that region would rise
from 10 percent to a strategically-significant 25 percent. He signaled
great risk from nuclear and ballistic weapons proliferation. He spoke of
the Cubans and the drug cartels in terms that made clear the enormous
difficulties facing the U.S. within its own hemisphere. Finally, he spoke
of the continued need for good Intelligence and a strong CIA in order
to stay abreast of world developments.

How well can CIA do its job now and in the years ahead? Does it
make any difference? After all, "the Cold War is over" — or so suggest some of the most knowledgeable international commentators. Is
it really over? The cataclysmic events at the end of 1989 suggest that
it has ended with respect to the four-decade-old conflict between the
Western partners of NATO and the Eastern members of the Warsaw

Pact. One would be hard pressed to suggest a credible scenario that would produce the same Soviet Bloc unity, belligerence and threat which existed previously.

At the same time, it would be historical amnesia, if not outright foolishness, to ignore the dangerous threats which persist despite the many favorable developments which occurred in 1989. It would, moreover, be prudent to remind ourselves of some unpleasant realities, taking a devil's advocate position on occasion, to make certain we do not get caught with our collective heads in a hopeful trance — spending peace dividends before real peace has been bolted down and without durable protections based on solid Intelligence.

Unpleasant realities? Let's look at just a few, starting with the Soviet Union itself. Starting, in fact, with Gorbachev — "Gorby" to his many admirers in the West; *Time* magazine's own *Man of the Decade*. For openers, Mikhail Gorbachev did not launch the reform process in the Soviet Union to create a democratic, republican form of government. He did the *perestroika* economic restructuring move to strengthen a crumbling, corrupt Soviet Union. The openness game plan, *glasnost*, was fashioned to attract international support, including trade and credits, for the benefit of the USSR and for it alone. His chosen instrument for maintaining power, neutralizing opposition and carrying out this program, was not Russia's equivalent of our citizen groups, Common Cause or the League of Women Voters. Rather, his instrument was the KGB, the Committee for State Security, Felix Dzerzhinsky's creature for the *Red Terror* and the group responsible for more political murders than any other secret police — ever. And the USSR under Gorbachev? In addition to the continued strategic threat described by DCI Webster, we had the following report:

CIA reported that KGB activities were increasing in the 1980s on a worldwide scale. The USSR still spends close to one seventh of GNP on military weapons and forces, primarily of an offensive nature. They provided in recent months advanced fighter aircraft to Fidel Castro. Their submarines have been penetrating Scandinavian waters with a new aggressiveness. They have recently sentenced to death a Soviet citizen who allegedly spied on them for the West. With openness, what secrets require such life-and-death protections? Internally, the link between current Soviet leader Gorbachev (and his mentor, Yuri Andropov) and the KGB was last matched on a sustained basis by one other leader of the USSR, Joseph Stalin, who used the Soviet secret police also to remain in power, neutralize all domestic foes, and carry out his own ambitious policies and programs. The scale on which Stalin carried out his terror outstrips anything done since by his successors, but the principle instrument of that terror, the KGB, remains in place.

And how have Americans responded generally to the Soviet Union in recent months? With characteristic openness. With hearts full of hope. With a willingness to put behind past bad feelings and fears. With even a special commitment to help Gorbachev succeed because the Soviet leader is credited with permitting all of these positive changes to take place, if not having willed them in the first place.

What is to protect us from our own trusting ways and from falling into the trap of confusing the real and the illusory? By having an unvarnished handle on what is genuine in the outside world. By solid Intelligence coming in good part from a CIA that is adept at the craft of spying.

For there will be no peace dividend any time soon unless CIA can document both where the Soviet military is now, and where it is heading. We cannot expect the Pentagon to champion defense spending rollbacks any more than we can expect Congressmen to offer up for closing military bases in their own districts. The U.S. Military, after all, has to do the fighting if again we miscalculate.

The Central Intelligence Agency studies the world and does as good a job in its analytical role as any branch of the U.S. Government. It hires good scholars, bestows on them considerable intellectual independence for a government bureaucracy, compiles information from around the globe and, finally, tries to steal as many strategic secrets as possible from foreign armies, governments and groups for the benefit of Agency analysts. CIA officers from the analytical Directorate of Intelligence give a daily world briefing to the President of the United States, the American Intelligence Community's number one consumer and boss. The Agency annually provides thousands of Intelligence reports and studies to the rest of the Executive Branch and to Congress. When it comes to dealing with the outside world, CIA probably has no American equal in terms of knowledge and credibility. What it cannot collect freely and openly, it may go after through remote technical means, if the subject matter merits the high dollar costs of S&T collection. If neither approach yields positive results, it may then assign the collection mission to the Agency's Clandestine Service, the Operations Directorate.

The Clandestine Service continues to do a good job collecting Intelligence on traditional political and government targets of specific interest to American Ambassadors and to those policymakers in Washington concerned with individual country relations and situations.

Unfortunately, the human agent side of CIA is hurting in other arenas and is not up to many of the newer challenges and threats facing us in the world. Some of the weakness arise because the new Intelligence targets are so difficult compared to what CIA previously has faced. Part comes from wounds inflicted on the Agency from the outside. A good portion is simply a matter of bureaucratic old age as CIA, heading for fifty, looks and behaves increasingly like every other tired department of government. The weaknesses show up in an examination of the Agency's primary missions and the results it has achieved.

Within the Agency, Counterintelligence, or CI, has never been ranked with either the collection of Foreign Intelligence (FI) or its Covert Action (CA) Operations. The low priority for CI was reflected in assigned manpower, budgets, formally-defined requirements and, since the mid-1970s, bureaucratic clout. Yet, even astute critics of our nation's CI capabilities had to be dumbstruck by the colossal CI failures that hit in the 1980s. America's defenses were severely damaged in such critical areas as Naval communications (compromised by the Walker spy ring for well over a decade), CIA Operations in the USSR (due to the Howard defection to Moscow) and with regard to China (the Larry Wu-Tai Chin case), to name only the more notable public examples.

When it became clear in the mid-1980s that even a D-minus grade would be overly generous for the Agency capability in CI, a Counterintelligence Center was created. One of its main features was bringing together both the Clandestine Service operators and Intelligence Directorate scholars. That course had been charted by William Donovan back in 1942 when creating OSS. However, having the operators and scholars working in unison was lost within CIA, an American institution long on action and short on reflection. Beginning essentially over again in CI has proved a difficult process for the Agency because the painstaking, shadowy world of CI demands that one take a long and patient view of things. That runs against America's cultural grain in a most fundamental way. Agency CI suffers also because, offering as it does a very slow career path, it has not and will not attract the Operations Directorate's best personnel. Finally, within what is essentially an overseas field service, Counterintelligence activity, by its nature and necessity, is centered in Washington. Spycatching involves pulling together many seemingly-unrelated threads to form a single tapestry, one that reveals purposely-hidden secrets of our most determined adversaries. Again, CI calls for a patience and reflection that is scarce indeed within such a characteristically-American institution as the Agency, especially its active Clandestine Service bent on meeting numbers goals each quarter.

For all these reasons, America and CIA cannot expect over time to earn more than a passing grade in this arcane craft. The good news in CI is that the upheavals within the Soviet Union and Eastern Europe, combined with strains in their relationship with the more radical states and groups, promise to produce superb windfalls for U.S. and other Western Intelligence services. Indeed, one may be sure that the Agency has been receiving offers aplenty of cooperation from former adversaries within hostile Foreign Intelligence services. Thus, it is undoubtedly a bad time to be a Communist anything, especially one of their spies. The penetration programs of the disintegrating Communist powers will unravel in a few key defections, if not in a landslide.

The error now would be in confusing such instant fortunes in spycatching with lasting improvements in American CI. Unfortunately, even the least sophisticated Terrorist groups know CIA's methods, understand how to block S&T collection against them, and have developed highly-effective ways to frustrate American Intelligence efforts at penetrating their organizations. From the standpoint of CI, America remains an open book to many of its most dangerous enemies.

CIA's Foreign Intelligence collection capability mirrors, and is on a par with, the performance of the rest of American society: short-term views and programs producing useful, if shallow, results. The Intelligence effectiveness test or question is not whether the Agency could or could not locate General Manuel Noriega during the initial hours of the U.S. invasion of Panama in 1989, as some have suggested. An invasion is a chaotic event and not ordinarily subject to perfect planning or pinpoint human agent Operations. Instead, to weigh the Agency's FI Collection capabilities against more legitimate criteria, one should examine current strategic problem areas and see how well CIA is doing against more enduring targets associated with these problems.

Apart from traditional "hard targets" against which the Agency has operated since the Forties, specifically the Soviets and their allies, it now faces new foes that are qualitatively different for CIA to attack in an Intelligence collection sense. Terrorists, narcotics traffickers, money launderers and weapons proliferators join the terrorist nations of Iran, Iraq, Libya, North Korea, Cuba and Vietnam in presenting formidable challenges to United States Intelligence. Yet, as the 1980s drew to a close, there was very little in the way of Operations Officer or clandestine agent capability to deal with such hostile, nontraditional and transnational target groups or countries. These critical problem areas were not reflected in CIA recruitment of new personnel in recent years — not in their ethnic origins, their linguistic skills, their temperaments and lifestyles, or even their specific academic preparation.

The Middle East is an extremely critical arena; there are very few Clandestine Service officers who speak Arabic, have studied the region's history and culture, or want to serve there for a career. We live in an S&T age, but virtually none of the Operations Officer candidates has a background in science or engineering; in fact, were such an applicant to come along, the hiring system would drive him or her in the direction of either the Intelligence Analysis or the S&T Directorate — away from Operations for certain.

Also, the common denominator linking these target groups is often financial; but you could count on one hand the Agency Operations Officers with more than a smattering of knowledge on international finance. The new highly-violent groups can be attacked successfully only by streetwise officers who deal effectively against unconventional operational targets. Because of 1980s security flaps, however, the tendency is to hire squeaky-clean Joe and Jane College, "team players" with highly conventional experience, even by American standards. With two-thirds of CIA field Operations personnel unable to speak the host country language at even an intermediate level of comprehension, and with almost no native foreign language speakers coming into the Clandestine Service, CIA's ability to operate against the most lethal targets is substantially limited overall and nonexistent in a number of critical areas.

So, although the world has changed and the Agency's penetration targets have increasingly hardened, shifted and become more elusive, CIA does business as it used to be done. For starters, it continues to hire an officer corps for the 1950s, when political science was deemed sufficient for international careers, when the Agency still had a solid cadre of immigrant linguists, and when the nation's top Intelligence targets were genteel enough to work in embassies, attend cocktail parties and observe Marquess of Queensbury rules. It is much tougher to work in CIA Operations at this time than it was in the organization's early years. But you would never know it by today's personnel and bureaucratic disincentives.

If the personnel situation "on the inside" has become stultified, CIA's deep cover Operations Officer or NOC program is floundering again and the Agency is dealing with it in typical bureaucratic fashion — where denial fails, try scapegoating. In the heartland of America, hundreds of miles from Washington and CIA Headquarters, I recently attended a trade convention and bumped into a young man I had worked with in the Clandestine Service in the early 1980s. He was exceptionally motivated for a career in Intelligence, was tough, and had previously served as a combat infantry officer. Within six years of being hired he resigned, joining the legion of former Agency deep cover officers who quietly take a walk because CIA mishandles them so badly. His inside contacts probably explain away his resignation by glibly remarking about "his limitations." One would need no less than Los Angeles Coliseum to host a reunion of Agency NOCs who quit in frustration over the years! And how do CIA's bureaucrats deal with the latest deep cover program failure? This time blame goes to late DCI, Bill Casey, who, they say, "made deep cover service expand too fast so that the wrong people were hired."

So CIA conducts its business as usual. Rather than doing a thoughtful, thorough review to learn why CIA historically has failed to recruit, lead, support and make productive use of the American Intelligence deep cover corps serving out in the cold, the organization assigns all blame to those who have silently departed.

The Central Intelligence Agency suffers from the same short-term numbers myopia from being on a short budget-and-reporting leash which impedes long-term programs of any kind. Rising stars within CIA foolish enough to take on one of the intractable problem areas, such as Counterintelligence, Counterterrorism or Counternarcotics Operations, are likely headed for career oblivion if they remain with such activities more than 18-24 months. It is not by accident that the Agency recently created a "Center" for each of these tough target areas; that is and has been the Clandestine Service's proven method for isolating these viral fields from the main body of the spy organization. It did the same type of thing with "Task Force" creation — one for Cuba, another for Vietnam, then Angola, next Iran, soon Central America, and finally the only seemingly successful one, the Afghanistan Task Force, which helped drive the Russians back over their own borders. On the surface, these units were supposed to get a specific job or "task" done by strongly concentrating Operations Officer talent and logistical resources to produce the required "force" for success. What was most often at play was that Operations Directorate managers wanted to separate these pain-in-the-ass, no-win causes from the "real work" of the Clandestine Service. The real work? Running conventional FI Operations out of Field Stations in pursuit of large numbers of recruitments to yield even larger numbers of Intelligence reports. That was how careers were measured and made, by the numbers. Thus, to a great extent the very mission of CIA came to reflect the part of the business that best lent itself to beancounting: FI Collection on soft political targets.

Finally, besides FI Collection and CI Protection, CIA's Clandestine Service was, by statute, assigned responsibility to "perform such other duties as the President may direct" — CA or Covert Action, to use the trade name. Loss of genuine CA options since the early 1970s severely weakened the last five Presidents.

Most recently, President Bush was forced reluctantly to don his Commander-in-Chief cap and send thousands of American combat troops into action in tiny Panama City to remove from power the unelected General Manuel Noriega. Twenty-three young Americans paid with their lives because the U.S. President had little in the way of Covert Action options between diplomatic handwringing and sending in the military. The one billion dollar aid package to Panama is just the first installment in a process that will cost the American taxpayers (and other allies whose own U.S. aid will be accordingly reduced) far more than should be paid to deal with a Noriega. Even the diplomatic flack throughout the hemisphere from the open invasion exceeded whatever negative repercussions might have followed a Covert Action coup by CIA. The Panama invasion increased the President's popularity at home. It made Americans feel good. And it came at a price — material, political and, especially, human. Great stuff, that "overt military action." Well, I'll take old-fashioned Covert Political Action any day.

Why is Covert Action effectively dead? Is it because CIA simply cannot run such Operations due to poor management, lack of CA officers, or some purely internal shortcoming? Why does one President have to watch helplessly as American officials are held hostage, why does his successor have to send in jet bombers from an American carrier to tame Qaddafi, and why does the current President have to send Americans to die for "Panamanian democracy?" Why are warships off the coast of Colombia and why are we weighing the use of U.S. troops to battle the cocaine-producing forces in the Andes of Colombia, Peru and Bolivia? And when growing coca leaves and processing cocaine becomes too hot in those nations, will the U.S. then have to send still more troops to Argentina, Paraguay, Chile, Brazil, Mexico or wherever the drug-growing activity inevitably shifts to, so long as the U.S. appetite for drugs is high and lucrative? How will our military forces be able to distinguish drug cartels and allied insurgent Terrorists from peasants trying to make a simple living from the land? If the very fabric of American society is at risk and demands that we directly attack the foreign supply bases for illicit drugs, is not that precisely why one would have and use Covert Action? Are not the stakes high enough, in that we are talking about what we treasure — the nation's youth?

The absolute necessity to identify why Covert Action has been paralyzed affects our whole foreign policy and, ultimately, the safety and quality of life for Americans here and abroad. We continue to hemorrhage as a society, major cities are crime-ridden and effectively in ruins, American youth has been scuttled in the hundreds of thousands to a drug culture that delivers disease, crime, and death. Around the world, only Americans are targeted by sundry groups for indiscriminate kidnapping, airline bombings and assassination — merely because they are citizens of this particular country.

Why is Covert Action dead, America's international options so feeble? The technical reasons CIA cannot perform CA effectively under current conditions have been discussed earlier. The underlying cause goes much deeper than just the technical problems in Covert Action. It is rooted in the lack of cohesiveness within American Government, a disorder that undermines departments and programs throughout the whole Federal Government, both internationally and domestically. The Federal Government is less able in the 1990s to do well the required job with a trillion dollar budget than it was able in 1960 with dollar outlays less than one-tenth that amount. The Central Intelligence Agency is similarly handicapped, not because it is inherently inept or its foes so smart. Nor is it because the American people desire a weak CIA? Then why? The answer rests on Capitol Hill where bipartisanship in foreign policy was abandoned twenty years ago by politicians who put party ahead of country.

"Congress wants preeminence over the Executive Branch. America is witnessing a classic internal struggle, a revolution going back to the Constitutional foundation of the Republic. These are strong words, but Congress has launched a powerful attack. That is why some basic understanding of American Intelligence is important. This apparatus is now at the center of a battle at the highest levels of our national leadership". So writes, from his retirement perch, long-time Washington insider Senator Barry Goldwater, who served with distinction on both the Armed Services and Intelligence Committees of the Senate.

But it is not just the memoirs of this conservative Senator that show the spoiler role Congress has chosen to play in American foreign policy.

All foreign adversaries, including the Nicaraguan Sandinistas and their Marxist comrades-in-arms in El Salvador, learned well the lesson of Southeast Asia. They freely cultivate elected Members and unelected staffers from Congress, looking to them for help (Amendments such as Hughes-Ryan, Clark, and Boland, to name the more egregious examples where the legislature usurped Executive Branch power). They look to them confidently for harassing oversight of CIA, making even the most serious Covert Action Operations unworkable. A weakened, less flexible President is what the Congress wants. That is what we now have. The Presidential decline results in part from CIA's diminished CA capabilities, in what it can and cannot do to resolve messy international problems discreetly, without committing the national flag and without unnecessarily losing American lives.

Can CIA make a comeback? First, can America? Certainly, each has the underlying potential for excellence and a legacy upon which to build new capabilities to meet the threats of the 1990s and beyond. America can be restored to vibrancy — if it draws upon strengths in its people and rebuilds infrastructures, not the on lines of the post-World War II period, but of the Information Age, which had so much to do with collapsing the Soviet empire with barely a trace of violence and hardly a whimper.

Whether and when the U.S. digs itself out of its deep hole depends basically on one overriding factor — leadership of and by whoever occupies the Oval Office. The President is free either to "manage" the U.S. decline along comfortable lines or "lead" us into painful recovery. The political numbers folk show that the President can do quite well in the polls, even assure reelection, by gently managing the erosion of America. This is especially so if he makes us feel good despite the realities. Making the citizenry feel good is, after all, the new civic opiate. And if the problem areas are like the 600 pound gorilla, too imposing to deny? Then there's always scapegoating.

Why not blame the Japanese for our trade problem and weakened dollar? Obviously, America has problems because Japanese and other Asians work hard and save, produce quality goods, invest in long-term R&D, stress education, get more S&T doctoral degrees than the U.S. (even in the U.S.!), register more patents than we do, aggressively attack open markets and protect their own weaker ones, reach "understandings" with American former government officials, attend all important scientific conferences and carry home every high tech secret they can find, foster cooperation between their public and private sectors, and have the nerve to take a long view in their world trade strategy. The challenge is quite clear: either we start competing just as aggressively on each and every level, or we start the American nursery school kids learning Asian and European languages, because they will end up working for one or the other by the year 2010.

And what is Congress doing while America crumbles? Swapping unethical outside income and "fund raising" for pay and retirement bonanzas that will, simply, make them wealthy, one and all. It's just as though the crew on the Titanic snuck away in the night in lifeboats, taking banquet goodies, balloons and party hats with them. After all, how much of an added dent can 535 Congressmen make to a national Federal debt, of their creation, which now surpasses three trillion dollars? That's right: a million dollars, three million times — $12,000 for each and every American. So, if anyone is going to lead America out of its stupor, it must be the President of the United States.

The Agency can also be led back to excellence, first by a President determined to restore his rightful, unrivaled primacy in foreign affairs. At some point, the President will have to draw some lines, telling Congress to stick in its ear its many un-Constitutional amendments circumscribing Executive Branch foreign policy prerogatives, and be prepared to go to the Supreme Court, and to the people, to restore the Presidency to its proper position. The nation should not pay eternally for Presidential failures of the Johnson-Nixon years which opened the way for the Congressional power grab. When would be the appropriate time to make some waves and get things back on track? Probably 1993. By then the Congressional hogs will have max'ed their feeding at the public trough under the latest pay-retirement arrangement. Many in Congress will be heading for greener pastures and not seeking reelection in 1994. They will have too little at stake personally to carry the Constitutional battle all the way. And if they do, the Legislature will lose before the Supreme Court by any rational reading of the separation of powers. In the court of public opinion, the outcome is even more certain: any President who draws the line with Congress on the conduct of foreign affairs will win. And so will the country.

What specifically can be done at CIA to restore its ability to keep Presidents wise and America able to deal clandestinely with its future foreign subversive threats? For openers it needs to develop a sense of history and perspective, reflecting on how it arrived at its feeble state and then charting a path to viability. It will have to recommit itself to basic secrecy without which Intelligence Operations really do get reduced absurdly, and lethally, to playing Russian roulette. The Agency will have to approach the new challenges to American Intelligence and American Security with a commitment which exceeds what was brought to the Cold War itself. After all, a nation in decline needs wisdom, protection, and flexible response more than does a nation on the rise.

Two things that are not required are more money or more legislation. There is not an entity in the Federal sector that could not withstand, and probably be strengthened, by a cut of 5 percent in personnel and 10 percent in operating funds. The Clandestine Service of CIA, as government departments go, is lean. That said, several decades of numbers games and bureaucrats have padded the budget to the extent that needed reforms could be accomplished within current budgets.

Another reason for staying within current funding levels is that the Congress misuses the budget process, particularly when there are brand new authorizations, to wrest ever more power from the Chief Executive on the conduct of foreign affairs. The budget process is the Trojan horse by which Congress is able to move in, overstep its bounds, and hamstring the President. The less Capitol Hill has to do with the renaissance of American Intelligence, the more likely that some degree of successful transformation will occur. The correlation could not be more direct: the stronger the Congress, the weaker is U.S. Intelligence, the Presidency and the country itself.

On the need for new laws to strengthen U.S. Intelligence, existing national security legislation is sufficient for any President and DCI genuinely willing to lead. Internally, the Agency needs to do a number of things to be able to meet the new threats effectively. First, it will have to shoot for at least a passing grade in Counterintelligence, in fact expanding the CI focus to include the newer targets such as Terrorists and the international drug syndicates. Traditional CI emphasis on government-owned-and-operated Intelligence services will not suffice in a nontraditional age where old rules no longer apply. CIA also must knock off the numbers games in Foreign Intelligence Collection, giving Operations Officers the incentive to go after difficult new targets. It has to restore a solid Covert Action capability and hire new officers with the requisite imagination and adventuresome spirit required of this discipline — and training them while CIA still has older officers and retirees who recall what CA is about. In sum, for the first time in years the Clandestine Service will have to bolster fundamentally all three of its basic missions. How can this institution undertake such renewal?

CIA can start by administering to itself a bureaucratic enema and reducing the hoard of administrative power brokers, bean counters and supporting legal confederates to their proper roles. The current revolution in Eastern Europe and the USSR was as much a revolt against institutionalized bureaucracy as it was a formal abandonment of the precepts of Marxist-Leninism. Ideology long ago ceased to play a major role in the subjugation of these peoples. But apparatchiks in the Party and government grew in power, perks and prominence until, at last, they brought the whole Soviet system to gridlock. America's bureaucrats have also been accruing power, perks and prominence the past forty years. And they have undermined the effectiveness of institution after institution, sector after sector, of the American society.

Our national education system is scandalously weak, unable to produce excellence at the top, competence in the middle, literacy in the lower quartile. The medical field is no longer equipped to meet our medical needs. The criminal justice system is a disgrace and protects few of us from crime. The country's transportation network is in an advanced stage of disintegration. And our national security establishment is as porous as Swiss cheese, saved only because the Soviets and the KGB ran out of gas before America and CIA did.

Finally, the Central Intelligence Agency needs to recognize that morale is low throughout much of the Clandestine Service, not only due to recent firings over Central America and Bill Casey's war there, but because of anti-CIA actions of Congress and certain DCI's going back two decades. The covenant of two-way loyalty needs to be restored so that lower ranking employees are not left in the lurch to face every Congressional and political witch hunt that comes along. CIA's own Inspector General and Office of General Counsel have to develop a new relationship with the personnel out on the line, supporting them rather than serving only as wagons circling around and protecting just the DCI. Rewards for service in clandestine Operations should be commensurate with the risks, keeping in mind that this is still public service and few came to CIA for either recognition or tangible benefits. Nevertheless, it is simply fair that the Agency's spies receive pay parity with those working comfortably in other Directorates of the Agency. At present they fare the worst of all CIA employees. They merit pensions at least equal to other dangerous occupations in Federal Government. It is an outrage, one far more "criminal" than Iran-Contra, that Congressional pensions use the much superior law enforcement formula of 2.5 percent per year while CIA's overseas operatives get treated, in retirement, little better than had they been passing out highway maps in Hawaii. Deep cover NOCs should have overseas premium pay of 25 percent, not 10 percent, and retirement should be based on 3 percent per year of service, in recognition of the value and sacrifice of Nonofficial Cover Operations and the people who run them.

And the most important thing that can be done to re-motivate CIA Clandestine Service personnel: challenge the dickens out of them, and then provide the means to get on with the job of penetrating international drug rings, identifying the foreign political and financial leaders supporting the drug trade, getting inside Terrorist groups that target American and other innocent civilians, getting a fix on hostile economic and technology targets, and carrying out covert Operations to neutralize the effectiveness of all such groups and governments.

It is time this country put behind the post-Vietnam and post-Watergate barnacles which became attached to the ship of state. The U.S. Congress, like a heavy anchor, has the American Presidency dead in the water, notwithstanding wonderful events that have occurred in the East. In 1989, fortunately, the breezes were warm and gentle. But what do we do when the winds turn cold and violent, as they surely will in a world with 25 wars during this period of "peace", so-called? We better have a U.S. Government that has the knowledge and power to chart and take correct action. We need a new CIA, one that is well-led, well-staffed and well-used to keep the world's barbarians at bay.

APPENDIX A
Tips to Applicants

EACH YEAR tens of thousands of Americans interact with the Agency, most of them as applicants for employment in one of CIA's four Directorates: Intelligence (Analysis), Science and Technology (Technical Collection), Administration (Offices of Finance, Logistics, Communications, Personnel, Training, and Medical Services), or Operations (the human spy world). The way things were going during my time as personnel recruiter, I used to quip that by the turn of the century the Agency will have rejected practically every man and woman in America. CIA was throwing out the bait and net broadly to attract as many fish as possible, then throwing most of them over the other side of the boat. The Office of Personnel had decided that it would not even bother responding to most who had sent in a resume or letter; it instead responded now only to those considered of possible interest. Of course, in large institutions the majority of employment applications and resumes eventually end up in the shredder. But individuals applying to the country's spy agency generally give the matter more thought than they would when applying to yet another private sector firm.

Do not assume, because you have not received a response, that CIA has carefully examined your credentials against the available openings. The resume may have been screened by a new recruiter or a secretary who hasn't the foggiest notion of what talent is really needed. Don't be afraid to send another letter and resume — even to a contact in CIA Headquarters — until satisfied that your credentials have been seriously reviewed. Visiting a CIA recruitment office can be helpful too.

Getting hired by CIA is a capricious business; good people, even fully-qualified people, get turned down every day. This can be very disappointing and frustrating for those who apply and for those who recommend someone for employment, especially into Clandestine Operations. A senior Operations Officer, just back from assignment as Chief of Station in a most important country, told me he had given up on suggesting that the young people he knew apply to CIA. In fact, the Agency effort to resurrect its spotter network on American campuses in the 1980s collapsed rather quickly. Its demise had little to do with changing attitudes among American academics. Instead, most who agreed to cooperate got dismayed as young graduates they respected got turned down, and turned off, by the CIA applicant process. Like that experienced Chief of Station, the university professors wanted no part of subjecting young associates to such an ineffectual hiring process.

Part of the problem, admittedly, is the simple fact that tens of thousands of applicants for merely hundreds of Operations Officer positions means a high rejection rate anyway. Not making this clear from the start is part of the Agency hiring problem. This is aggravated by the trauma of the polygraph — many "fail" when they have done nothing that should disqualify them on security grounds but were unable to so persuade the polygraph operator. Many have been turned down when they were confident, correctly so, that they really could do clandestine Operations work on a career basis and do it well; they simply had been screened out by one of the organization's many filters.

The capriciousness of the applicant process was poignantly illustrated one day in 1986 at the Farm. I was having lunch with "George," an Operations Officer who was in charge of the Career Training Program. We were seated at a table among a class of fresh new Operations Officer Trainees just beginning their careers (as he and I had done about three decades earlier) and starting to learn the arts of clandestinity out in the Virginia woods. "George," I asked, "if we threw the whole bunch of these qualified, security-cleared, fully certified Operations Officer Trainees out the door right now and had them all reapply, how many do you think would make it through the process?" He thought for a while and then responded, "About half." Yet, every one of them had already successfully passed every conceivable hurdle to get in! At that moment, ironically, the Agency had not recovered from its Operations Officer personnel losses of the 1970s, a matter of grave concern to CIA Director Bill Casey. So we really needed new Operations Officers badly.

How is it possible that we would continue to turn down suitable young men and women willing to take the risks and pay the price to serve in America's "peculiar service" — as it has been accurately called? I will not try to answer that here; I have tried to do so already in *CIA LIFE*. I tell the story to make a point: if you have applied to CIA and done everything legitimately possible to get hired, you should in the interim go about your life as though CIA has turned you down (except do not tell one and all that you are an applicant, certainly). Do not put your life on hold; do not turn down another job offer or a graduate school program. The odds against getting hired by the Agency are so great that, until you receive a formal letter from the CIA Director of Personnel offering a specific position at an acceptable pay level and a precise starting date, you are not across the finish line.

In fact, no matter what anyone may say, you may not even be close either. This is true no matter what encouragement you may be given by the CIA recruiter, a member of the Career Training Staff, or even an acquaintance within the Agency. They may like you, they may want you to make it, they may think as I often did that someone like you "has it made." But no one you talk to has a handle on the whole process.

Do not think either that a letter or resume, or even a formal application, is going to result in some kind of CIA security investigation of you or create a permanent file somewhere in the Agency archives. Under current groundrules, no background investigation is done unless the applicant has made it through the whole process and successfully gone through the polygraph. The written application form itself is kept only two years and then destroyed unless the individual has been hired or rejected after taking the polygraph. If someone has done something he or she would prefer not be made a matter of permanent record in the files of the Federal Government, it would be advisable not to go through the Agency hiring process, especially the polygraph. *More than anything else, it is the polygraph that creates the permanent record on an Agency applicant.*

If you are accepted into the Agency and have no independent source of income, take a hard look at the career during your first five years. You will be on probationary status for three years anyway, which means your superiors can fire you without having to go all the way up to the DCI for approval to show you the door. At the five-year mark, make up your own scorecard for viability — both for the Clandestine Service and your own career — and assess how things seem to be going. The CIA career service and how it meets, or fails to meet, your own needs and aspirations are things you can evaluate. You should do this before your thirty-fifth birthday — if you wish to have something reasonably fresh to offer another employer.

The weakening of the retirement system for government employees hired after 1983 presents a special burden to those who enter Operations Officer careers after their mid-twenties. They will have too little time to develop a retirement base adequate to avoid the breadlines when they do leave the Agency between their fiftieth and sixtieth birthdays. Experts suggest that you need around 75 percent of your final career earnings to make it in retirement. Operations Officers who begin careers at age thirty and end them at fifty-five, for example, will have only 45 percent of final CIA earnings in retirement. Recent changes in Social Security (so-called windfall earnings provisions) basically exclude younger Federal employees from accumulating supplemental retirement credits to bolster their earnings later in life. It is by no means unpatriotic to pay close attention to the trends to see what this will mean for you and your family. Because Clandestine Service spouses have few opportunities to develop independent professional careers, Operations Officer families are already disadvantaged during their careers by having to compete in a two-salary economy with one modest salary. *Post-career economic disincentives, in fact, now make CIA's Operations Officer career one of the most financially hazardous occupations in government.*

So, if you are bright and educated, disciplined and creative, risk taking and judicious, and have a piggy bank to fall back on if things do not work out, give it some thought and do serious reading before deciding to apply. If you do get hired, I hope you find that an Operations Officer career is both challenging and rewarding. For all its difficulties, which I have tried to share forthrightly, CIA remains the most effective American organization involved in international affairs. It is a necessary organization and has a solid record of accomplishment, overall. It is not up to the challenges we now face in the world and needs a ten-year renewal effort, led by a new DCI with the "right stuff."

APPENDIX B

A Day in the Life

of a First-Tour Ops Officer

A S A CIA RECRUITER, to give recruits a realistic idea of an Operations Officer career, I anticipated and answered two important questions: 1) What would the first field assignment be like? and 2) How does a typical day in the life of an Operations Officer proceed? I think my answers were forthright, insightful, and helpful to anyone interested in this career. In this spirit, I offer the following common scenario.

After two years of Headquarters desk and Operations training, and the better part of a third year getting language and cover training, you arrive at the field Station a week or so before your predecessor is scheduled to depart on his next assignment. You do not yet have a place to live and are staying for a time at a hotel. The officer you are replacing, who has been running his tail off for three years, is also living in a hotel during his final days. He is extremely worn out at the point of transferring Operations over to you.

Reporting to the Station, you meet key personnel and then get your Operations assignment, targets and ongoing cases from your supervisor — the Branch Chief in a large Station, the COS or his Deputy COS in a small Station. If your predecessor was handling ten agents and three broad categories of targets (say, Communist Party penetrations, international Terrorist or narcotics targets, penetrations of the host government's foreign ministry that the KGB has "in the bag") they may decide to give you six or seven of these agents and two of these targets for starters, perhaps holding off on the politically-sensitive government penetrations until you have more experience in the local milieu. Everyone in the world knows we go after the KGB and local Communists as recruitment targets, but they get mad as hell when we recruit agents in their own governments. Because you have shown some interest or skills in the Technical Operations area, the COS wants you to take over operational responsibility for a technical-penetration program that involves getting into a foreign diplomatic installation and bugging their code room or their Ambassador's conference room. Outside technical support is available for the actual entry and installation of the transmitters; your job is to serve as inside Station coordinator. The operation will reach its zenith in about ninety days.

Your immediate responsibility is to become familiar with the area around the target installation and to find an apartment to serve as a listening post close enough to receive the signals if we succeed in the installation. As a newly-arrived officer without a place to live, you have a good cover for checking out apartments in all parts of town. If you do find a place that would serve as a listening post, we will get someone else to rent the apartment, someone less likely to attract attention than an American official. The COS hands you some photos and maps of the area and suggests you take one swing around the target embassy just to get your bearings, but be careful not to get exposed as we do not want to alert them that we are up to anything unusual.

At this point, I would take the Operations Officer candidate on a detour — a scenario in which, on the first drive past the embassy, his view is poor because he had not been prepared for it. He drives down the road a while, does a U-turn and comes back from the opposite direction. As he gets to the embassy the light turns red, and he has to stop. As he glances in through the gate, out walk a couple of embassy security men, and one of them looks him over carefully and jots down the license-plate number. My question: Do you say nothing or do you tell the COS you screwed up? If you are honest the COS will scream at you, probably hate you for days and even take you off the operation — but at least he can make any necessary adjustments in the operation. People make mistakes when they take risks, or they get unlucky, *but the only unforgivable thing is to be dishonest in your CIA Operations or Intelligence reporting.* Then, little flaps can grow into big ones, and we lose the trust essential for CIA to operate effectively. Though the officer must use deception and cover with outsiders in Operations, the Agency demands complete honesty in his dealings with the organization itself.

Assuming everything does go well, you get a glance into the target installation undetected and even find a couple of apartment buildings within two blocks. You will check these out over the course of the next week to see if any available apartments are elevated enough to be unobstructed by other buildings or trees. Having a well-located listening post is critical.

Now it is time to get busy with the departing Operations Officer and take over Operations and agents that are now yours to handle. You read the Station files on the cases you will be taking over. The files are pretty thin because "burn time" in this volatile country is kept down to a couple of hours so all CIA files can be destroyed quickly in the event of riots. Turnover time is always tricky because the clandestine agents and contacts are comfortable with your predecessor, and you are an entirely unknown quantity to them. You may be delighted and eager to meet them directly, if personal meetings are the way the cases are handled. However, the agents are concerned, possibly even nervous and now having second thoughts on their relationship with CIA — maybe, they may feel that this is the time to call it quits.

Because you have done your homework on the Operations, have studied how the city works from the standpoint of running secret Operations, have a good grounding in the language, and your predecessor has done a superb job setting the stage for an effective turnover of cases, things go smoothly. You meet one agent in a safehouse, another out on a dark road at night, one under light social guise at a camera shop where he works, another in a neighboring town, and the last indirectly, as all contact with this delicate case is through dead drops, where secret writing messages are passed back and forth.

Whatever the mix of Operations, targets, agents and security threats, you have to fit the operational tradecraft to the situation — for *there is no CIA modus operandi*. Each is and has to be its own work of art, all originals and no copies. Your colleague in the final weekend is virtually inaccessible as he attends to social and family matters and you spend a good part of the weekend in the CIA Station going over the Operations, the meeting plans, any outstanding administrative matters, Intelligence Collection requirements, recent reporting from the various agents, and then you make your own work plan for the following week. Your cover duties alone will demand twenty hours a week to support that cover credibly. There will be very little spin-off during those hours that will help you get at the Communist Party, the Terrorist target or the technical target. But the cover price is one that must be paid; cover erosion will set in soon enough because of events beyond your control. The transfer of responsibility and power is not yet complete, and already you seem overwhelmed. Now, what about the average day?

You awake bright and early on Monday of your first week as an Operations Officer. You get over to the Station by 7:30 AM; you want to read the cable traffic from Washington first thing in the morning, before going to work your cover job which will take up a good chunk of the morning hours. You have a chance to chat briefly with your CIA supervisor and tell her what you have going on that day. She makes a few suggestions, for one thing telling you that if one of your agents gives you information on any traveling PLO types, this must get to Washington on an "immediate basis" because there is some indication that a Terrorist operation is being planned for this or a neighboring country and no one knows which one.

Late morning, you have put in your cover time and get ready to leave for a midday tennis match at a local sports club. You have been invited there by a young Russian Consular Officer whom you met at a reception your third night in town; you both hit it off well, he having spent some time in the States as an "exchange student" a few years before. The Station has him pegged as probable Intelligence Officer, so you are already belly-to-belly with your *opposite number* — another ops officer out trolling for scalps. On your way to the sports club, you walk through the market district and, precisely at 11:45 AM, you turn a corner. As you do, you place a capsule in the hands of one of your agents, who slips just as quickly back into a busy shop and emerges seconds later from a second door leading to a side street. You have passed him some questions on the possible traveling PLO types and made arrangements for a late-night meeting, if he comes up with anything worthwhile. How did he know you would be there at that moment? You had sent him an electronic burst message, similar to the device that opens up your garage door in the States, that stopped a clock in his house at a coded time. When deciphered, it means you will be seeing him at 11:45 AM.

You play tennis for forty minutes, grab a quick sandwich and Coke, and say good-bye to your new Russian acquaintance after agreeing to go hiking in the next couple of weeks in the nearby mountains. He has promised to bring along some pretty women from his mission. Already they are ganging up on you. You cross town, getting out of your car and move through the shopping district again. After making sure you are clean and not being followed, you enter a hotel, where you take the elevator to the seventh floor, get out, and then go down the stairs to the fifth floor. You enter room 507, where a deep cover officer is awaiting your arrival for a 1:45 PM meeting.

This NOC officer is handling some of the preparations for the Technical Operation, and you spend an hour going over what has been done so far, what still needs to be done, what problems exist, and what specific tasks each of you will be doing to make this thing work. He is an old pro and you are a newcomer, but he couldn't care less because he assumes that, if the COS gave you inside responsibility, then you must be up to the job. You are out of there before 3:00 PM, and then arrive back to the Station where you really have some follow-up things to do.

You need to get down some notes and thoughts on your tennis companion while they are fresh in your mind — does he look like a consular officer or does he display any traits that might suggest he too is an Intelligence Officer? If you write them down today, you will have vivid detail and a thousand words. By tomorrow, you would be writing generalities and maybe three hundred words at best. By the weekend, you would have a couple of sentences that would be more impressionistic than descriptive. For that is the way the mind works: it filters all the time, shedding details that, if not lost, would permit you to really describe and assess this individual, your relationship with him, the possibility of moving toward his recruitment, and include any Counterintelligence matters to be recorded for future reference.

You report to your boss that you passed the PLO questions to your agent and may have something on it later tonight. If so, she says, come right in and send the message regardless of the hour; a communicator will be alerted to be on hand, if needed. You shoot over to your cover office to check for any messages or phone calls, spend an hour there shuffling papers, and head for your hotel a little after 5:00 PM to shower, change clothes, and get over to a diplomatic reception, where you hope to trawl for contacts and possible recruitment targets.

You especially want to meet a couple of young foreign ministry types whose names you saw on the guest list. You know the Technical Operation will not last forever; it will either work or not work in three to four months. It is your goal to get into the business of handling the local government penetration program, after another officer is transferred later in the year, because that is the most important Intelligence target at the Station. One step in that direction would be to make some progress in developing sources for the Station. Then, you may be asked to take over the whole program when the COS finds out that you can cut it.

At this point you are still an unknown quantity to him, and your direct boss has given no indication, one way or another, how she feels about your professional skills. Rather than waiting for the target to come to you, therefore, you have elected to go to the target. One of the foreign ministry types may be the key after all.

The reception gets underway at 6:00 PM, and you spend two hours moving about, meeting people, and engaging in the inane chatter that characterizes get-togethers of more than ten people. You manage to meet one of this evening's targets, exchange cards, and open the door for re-contact based on an aspect of your cover job. Maybe the cover job will not be down-time, if it can be used to meet people of interest.

At about 8:00 PM, people start to leave and you join some American colleagues to go to a nearby restaurant for dinner — no Agency stuff, just a social meal with a couple of new acquaintances. At 10:00 PM everyone heads for home, but not you; you drive across town and up a quiet road, opening your car door after turning a corner. In jumps your agent with the PLO collection requirements, and he has something hot to report. You drive around for ten minutes, making certain that you have gotten the information straight that he has to report, dropping him off on another side street, and head to the Station, arriving at 11: 15 PM.

You signal the CIA communicator to come back into the Station and start typing a report that tells Washington, and Stations in neighboring countries, that the PLO types, in fact, turn out to be part of the PFLP (Popular Front for the Liberation of Palestine), a more radical and violent splinter group than the PLO umbrella organization. You report their arrival in town the previous weekend. Since arriving, they have been planning an operation that will take place within two weeks in a neighboring country. CIA's agent has just been asked to line up some safe haven for a strike team coming into town within two days. The message gets sent at midnight. You go back to your hotel. It takes an hour to get to sleep because you are hyped up by the day's happenings.

You set your alarm for 6:00 AM; you have arranged to go running in the park with another new arrival at the hotel, and you cannot bow out by saying you were out all evening running Agency Operations.

Thus ends a day as a field Operations Officer. Although it may seem like a lot has happened in one day, it may understate what takes place in many ops officers' workdays; the world of a CIA Clandestine Service Operations Officer is very demanding, when all is said and done. But that's okay; the pay stinks too.

Notes on Sources

For general purposes I relied primarily on two works, one written by the quintessential insider, David Atlee Phillips (*The Night Watch*, Ballantine Books, New York, 1987) and the other by outside observer John Ranelagh (*The Agency: The Rise and Decline of the CIA*, Simon and Schuster, New York, 1986).

Spying in the American Revolutionary period was the subject of an Agency unclassified monograph (*Intelligence in the War of Independence*, Office of Public Affairs, Central Intelligence Agency, Washington, D.C.) and mirrored in *John Jay: The Making of a Revolutionary*: Unpublished Papers 1745-1780 (Richard B. Morris, Editor, Harper and Row, New York, 1975). The role of Intelligence in the War Between the States was revealed in short stories in *The Eyes and Ears of the Civil War* (Criterion Books, New York, 1963). On World War II, *The Secret War Report of the OSS* (Anthony Cave Brown, Editor, Berkeley Publishing, New York, 1976) provides the declassified official version of Office of Strategic Services Operations. A personal glimpse of OSS and one of its (and later CIA's) most illustrious operatives is contained in *Dulles: A Biography of Eleanor, Allen, and John Foster Dulles and Their Family Network* (Leonard Moseley, The Dial Press/James Wade, New York, 1978).

The New KGB: Engine of Soviet Power (William R. Corson and Robert T. Crowley, William Morrow & Company, New York, 1985) provides the most persuasive case that the spies are now the rulers in the Soviet Union, a view that is continually reinforced as Gorbachev uses the KGB to consolidate power and to effect change within the failing empire. KGB Intelligence history would be incomplete without two John Barron works (*KGB: The Secret Work of Soviet Secret Agents*, Bantam Books, New York, 1974, and *KGB Today: The Hidden Hand*, Berkeley Books, New York, 1983). In *This Deception: The Story of a Woman Agent* (Duell, Sloan and Pearce, New York, 1951), Hede Massing describes her years with and break from Soviet Intelligence. Chapman Pincher describes the KGB success in penetrating Western Intelligence in *Too Secret Too Long* (St. Martin's Press, New York, 1984). Pincher takes a special look at turncoats in *Traitors: The Anatomy of Treason* (St. Martin's Press, New York, 1987). George Leggett takes us back to the origins of Soviet Intelligence in *The Cheka: Lenin's Political Police* (Oxford University Press, London, 1981). Former KGB officer Peter Deriabin provides an inside view of his former employer in

Watchdogs of Terror (Arlington House, New Rochelle, New York, 1972). A compendium of Soviet Intelligence operatives and activities is contained in *Famous Soviet Spies: The Kremlin's Secret Weapon* (U.S. News and World Report, Washington, D.C., 1973).

Jean-Francois Revel contributes to an understanding of our Soviet adversary and ourselves in *The Totalitarian Temptation* (Doubleday, Garden City, N.Y., 1977) and *How Democracies Perish* (Doubleday, Garden City, N.Y., 1984). C. S. Lewis's linkage of bureaucracy to evil appears in *The Screwtape Letters* (Bantam, New York, 1982).

Secret Armies, James Adams, 1989, Viking Publishers.

The Agency's own reading list for prospective applicants includes the following additional sources and annotations:

HISTORY OF THE AGENCY

Ray Cline, *The CIA Under Reagan, Bush and Casey: The Evolution of the Agency from Roosevelt to Reagan,* Washington, DC., Acropolis Books Ltd., 1981

William Colby, *Honorable Men: My Life in the CIA*, New York, Simon and Schuster, 1978

Thomas Powers, *The Man Who Kept The Secrets: Richard Helms and the CIA*, New York, Alfred A. Knopf, 1979

Allen Dulles, *The Craft of Intelligence*, New York, Harper & Row, 1963

Thomas F Troy, *Donovan and the CIA: A History of the Establishment of the CIA*, Aletheia Books, University Publications of America Inc., 1981

William M. Leary, *The Central Intelligence Agency: History and Documents*, Huntsville, University of Alabama Press, 1984

OPERATIONS

David A. Phillips, *Careers in Secret Operations: How to be a Federal Intelligence Officer*, Frederick, Maryland, University Publications of America Inc., 1984

William Hood, *The Mole*, New York, W.W. Norton & Co., 1982

ANALYSIS

Roy Godson (Ed.), *Intelligence Requirements for the 1980's*,
 Washington, D. C., National Strategy Information Center,
 1979-86 (Distributed by Transaction Books, New Brunswick,
 NJ)
Walter Laquer, *A World of Secret: The Uses and Limits of
 Intelligence*, New York, Basic Books Inc., 1985
John Prados, *The Soviet Estimate: US Intelligence Analysis and
 Russian Military Strength*, New York, Dial Press, 1982

GENERAL INTEREST

Scott D. Breckinridge, *The CIA and the US Intelligence System*,
 Boulder, Colorado, Westview Press, 1986
Cord Meyer, *Facing Reality: From World Federalism to the CIA*,
 New York, Simon and Schuster, 1978
Viktor Suvorov, *Aquarium: The Career and Defection of a Soviet
 Spy*, London, Hamish Hamilton, 1985
Christopher Dobson and Ronald Payne, *War Without End: The
 Terrorists-An Intelligence Dossier*, London, Harrap Limited,
 1986
R.V. Jones, *The Wizard War*, New York, Coward, McCann &
 Geoghegan. Inc., 1978

NEW BOOKS

Milt Bearden and James Risen, *The Main Enemy: The Inside
 Story of the CIA's Final Showdown with the KGB*, NY,
 Random House, 2003
Richard Helms with William Hood, *A Look Over My Shoulder:
 A Life in the Central Intelligence Agency*, New York, Random
 House, 2003.
Elizabeth P. McIntosh, *Sisterhood of Spies — The Women of the
 OSS*, Annapolis, Maryland, Naval Institute Press, 1998

Acronyms and Abbreviations

ABM......................... Antiballistic missile
ACLU .... American Civil Liberties Union
ARDIS...................... Association for Responsible Dissent
AWACS .... Airborne Warning and Control System
CA .... Covert Action Operations
CATF .... Central American Task Force
Cheka...................... Extraordinary Commission to Combat
                            Counterrevolution, Speculation, and Sabotage.
                            ("Cheka" derives from the names of the
                            initial letters [che + ka] of Chresvychainaya
                            Kommissiya, 'Extraordinary Commission.')
                            Established 1917 by the Bolsheviks. Reorganized
                            as OGPU in 1923, NKVD in 1934, and finally,
                            after a series of other names, as KGB in 1954.
CI .... Counterintelligence Operations
CIA .... Central Intelligence Agency
COI .... Coordinator of Information
Comintern .... Communist International. (Also spelled Komintern.)
Comsomol............... Communist Youth Organization. (Short
                            for Kommunisticheskii Soyuz Molodezhi,
                            'Communist Union of Youth.' Also, 'Komsomol'.)
COS.......................... Chief of Station
CPCh .... Communist Party (of Chile)
CT .... Career Training or Trainee
DCI .... Director of Central Intelligence
DDA......................... Directorate of Administration
DDO .... Directorate of Operations
DS&T....................... Directorate of Science and Technology
FBI........................... Federal Bureau of Investigation
FDR......................... Franklin Delano Roosevelt
FI .... Foreign Intelligence Operations
FSLN....................... Sandinista National Liberation Front (Frente
                            Sandinista de Liberación Nacional)
FSO .... Foreign Service Officer
GNP......................... Gross National Product
GRU .... Chief Intelligence Directorate of the Soviet
                            General Staff (Glavnoye Razvedyvatelnoye
                            Upravleniye)

HHD .... Headhunter Division
IG .... Inspector General
IOD .... International Organizations Division
KGB .... Committee for State Security (Komitet
                                     Gosudarstvennoi Bezopasnosti). Given this
                                     name in 1954, upon the death of Stalin and the
                                     execution of Lavrenti Beria. (See Cheka)
LAD .... Latin America Division.
MAG .... Management Advisory Group
MBO .... Management by Objectives
M.O. .... Method of Operation (modus operandi)
NATO .... North Atlantic Treaty Organization
NKVD .... People's Commissariat of Internal Affairs. KGB
                                     Forerunner.
NOC .... Nonofficial Cover (deep cover Operations and
                                     operatives)
OAS .... Organization of American States
OGPU .... Unified State Political Administration NKVD
                                     forerunner.
OMB .... Office of Management and Budget
OO .... Special Department (Osobye Otdel; system
                                     of political commissars and the commissars
                                     themselves)
Ops Fam .... Operations Familiarization Training Course
PDC .... Christian Democrat Party of Chile (Partido
                                     Democrata Cristiano)
PFLP .... Popular Front for the Liberation of Palestine
PLO .... Palestine Liberation Organization
R&D .... research and development
RIF .... reduction in force
S&T .... Science and Technology
SCI .... Sensitive Compartmented Information
SDI .... Strategic Defense Initiative. (Also known as "Star
                                     Wars".)
SODC .... Senior Officer Development Course
UAW .... United Automobile Workers
U. N. .... United Nations
USSR .... Union of Soviet Socialist Republics

Index

Dekanozov, Vladimir, 42
Dickinson, John, 30
Directorate of Administration (DA) /
  Deputy Director for Administration
  (DDA); 158, 179, 218, 283
Directorate of Intelligence (DI)/ Deputy
  Director for Intelligence (DDI), 178,
  215, 217, 222, 236, 257
Directorate of Operations (DO) and
  Deputy Director for Operations
  (DDO), Prologue (1-12); Chapters 13
  and 14 (197-222), 88, 152, 168, 169,
  171-172, 174-175, 180, 184, 190, 193-
  194, 224-225, 283
Directorate of Management and Services
  (DM&S), 179
Directorate of Science and Technology/
  Deputy Director for Science and
  Technology (DS&T), 8, 177, 198, 236,
  269, 283
Director of Central Intelligence (DCI), 3,
  6, 7, 8, 11, 87, 105, 195, 267, 271, 272.
  Also see DCIs Bush, Colby, Dulles,
  Helms, Hillenkoetter, McCone,
  Schlesinger, Smith, Souers, Turner,
  Webster, Woolsey.
Disinformation, 33, 35, 40, 58, 66, 108,
  174, 247, 250
Donovan, William J. ("Wild Bill"), 7, 8,
  36, 37, 38, 212, 258, 280
"Double dippers", 193
"Drops", 31, 187, 188, 202, 204, 275
Drucker, Peter, 142
Drugs. See narcotics.
Dulles, Allen W (DCI), 7, 17, 25, 38, 49,
  51, 58, 59, 66, 93, 152, 212, 279
Dulles, John Foster, 58, 279
Dungan, Ralph, 118, 120
Duran, Julio Senator, 126
Dzerzhinsky, Felix E., 39-41, 46, 127, 256

Eisenhower, Dwight David, President,
  3,7,18, 22, 29, 45, 46, 58, 64, 67-68
"Either-or" syndrome, 3
El Dorado (fictitious name of country),
  Chapter 6 (79-101)
England/English/Britain/British, 7, 30-35,
  36, 37, 38, 39, 44, 55, 67, 77, 93, 114,

115, 134, 153, 154, 174, 226, 229, 239,
  241
Espionage, 17, 37-38, 50, 51, 56, 86, 94, 153

"Falcon and the Snowman", 150
"Family Jewels" (Colby report), 172-173,
  178, 195
"The Farm", Chapter 3 (49-61) Chapter 13
  (197-209).
Federal Bureau of Investigation (FBI), 2,
  7, 8, 10, 12, 22, 38, 55, 58, 72, 138, 174,
  251, 283
Females/women (in CIA Operations), 50,
  96, 97, 186, 189, 190, 205-206, 214,
  231, 235, 236, 279
Fernandez, Joseph , 231, 246
Field Station (CIA), 9, 17, 18, 52, 73, 74,
  80, 81, 82, 87, 89, 90, 95, 96, 98, 100,
  104, 105, 106, 128, 129, 131-132, 141,
  157, 158, 167, 177, 178, 179, 203, 213-
  215, 221, 239, 261
"First Principles", 5-12
FitzGerald, Desmond, 17, 180
Ford, Gerald R., President 173-175, 177, 192
Ford, John, 38
Foreign Intelligence Collection (FI
  Operations), 1, 2, 4, 9, 17, 34, 37, 52-
  56, 75, 78, 81, 98, 105, 141-142, 177,
  203, 211, 220, 221, 225, 234, 235, 261,
  262, 266, 275, 283
Foreign languages, 11, 17, 24, 56, 60, 71,
  73, 95, 154, 188, 213, 215, 218, 219,
  220, 249, 260, 273, 275
Foreign Service/Foreign Service Officer
  (FSO), 12, 34, 128, 145, 163, 174, 184,
  215
Fort Pitt, 32
Four Power Agreement, 77
France, 30, 33, 35, 36, 53, 71, 77, 212
Franklin, Benjamin, 30-33, 169
Frei, Eduardo President, Chapter 8 (113-
  135), 109, 110, 111, 228
"Fronts war", 54

Galvez, Bernardo de, 32
Germany, 7, 23, 36, 39, 44, 46, 73, 114,
  198, 215

Kennedy, John Fitzgerald (JFK), 3, 7, 29,
    46, 49, 50, 51, 54, 58, 59, 64, 66, 68,
    77-78, 106, 110, 118, 235, 249; and his
    administration, 22, 45, 54, 63, 65, 67,
    97, 99, 117, 119, 125, 128, 192
Kennedy, Robert F., 63, 66, 120
Khmer Rouge, 127, 255
Khrushchev, Nikita S., Premier 67, 77
Kissinger Commission, 226
Kissinger, Henry A., 130, 132-133
Kobulov, Bofdan, 42
Kosovo, 3

Labor Operations, 75, 76, 77, 103, 145-146
Langdon, John, 30
Laos, 99, 201, 228, 247
Latin America Division (LA or LAD),
    Chapter 4: (63-69); 59, 61, 72, 75, 82,
    96, 98, 103, 124, 147, 148, 149, 151,
    157, 167, 168, 173, 174, 179, 197, 211,
    231, 284
Lawyers (in CIA), 3, 11, 157, 158, 190,
    195, 204
League of Nations, 36
Lee, Andrew Daulton, 150
Lee, Robert E., 35
Lend Lease, 23, 36, 37
Lenin, Nikolai (orig. Vladimir Ilyich
    Ulyanov), 39-41, 46, 58, 279; and
    Allen Dulles, 58
Life Experience, 212, 236
Lowe, Thaddeus S., 35
Lumumba, Patrice, 64, 173
lysergic acid diethylamide (LSD), 172

MacArthur, Douglas General, 38
MacLean, Donald, 241
MacLeish, Archibald, 38
Madison, James President, 169
Magneto, 35
Management by Objectives (MBO), 178,
    179, 284
Mao Tse Tung, 64, 125; Maoist(s), 69, 121
Marshall, George C. General and
    Secretary of State, 47
Marshall Plan, 44, 46, 226
Martin, William, 237, 241
Massing, Hede, 42-43, 73, 279
Massing, Paul, 42

McCarthy, Joseph R. Senator, 21, 49, 59, 63
McCone, John A. (DCI), 7-8, 78, 99, 198
McMahon, John (DDO), 197-201, 204, 212
McNamara, Robert Strange, Secretary of
    Defense, 8, 63, 99, 142, 180
Media Operations, 104
Menshik, Pavel, 42
Merkulov, Vsevolod, 42
Message intercept, 35
Meyer, Cord, 59-60, 75, 76, 281
Mig-23, 199
Mineral deposits (Chile), 118-119
Mitchell, Bernon, 237, 241
Modus operandi (M.O.), 187, 275, 284
Money laundering/launderers, 2, 221, 259
Monroe Doctrine, 34, 35, 64
Monroe, James President, 169
Morris, Robert, 30
Moseley, Leonard, 58, 279
Mossad (Israel), 242
Mr. Decisive, 147, 149-151, 157
Myer, Albert, 35

Naranjo, Oscar, 125
Narco-Terrorism, 2
Narcotics trafficking and Counter-
    Narcotics Operations, 37, 93, 167, 221,
    229, 250-251, 259, 261, 273
Nation building activities, 97, 118
National Security Act of 1947, 6, 11, 29,
    50, 173, 251
National Security Council (NSC), 9, 120,
    132, 133
National Student Association, 99
Naval War College, 192
New York Times, 11, 56, 99
Nicaragua, 14, 107, 213, 225, 226, 228,
    230, 244, 247, 248, 264
Night Watch, The, (Phillips), 133, 239, 248,
    279
Nimitz, Chester W., 38
Nixon, Richard M. President, 3, 46, 50,
    64, 133, 168, 170-171; administration
    of, 113, 265; "Nixon's revenge", 171-
    172
NKVD, 41, 42, 283, 284; See also
    Acronyms and Abbreviations Used in
    This Book.

Roosevelt, Franklin Delano President
(FDR) 7, 36, 37, 39, 76, 229, 280, 283
Rostow, Walter Whitman, 38
Rusk, Dean Secretary of State, 8, 63
Russo-German Pact (1939), 23, 42

Safehouse(s), 53, 83-84, 88, 154, 155, 156,
164, 188, 192, 206, 275
Sandinista National Liberation Front
(FSLN) / anti-Sandinista, 107, 223,
226, 228, 230, 244, 245, 246, 248, 264,
283
"Scalps" (and numbers game), 142, 179, 276
Schlesinger, Arthur, 38
Schlesinger, James R. (DCI), 171-172, 173,
178, 179, 193, 195, 199, 201, 205, 219,
224, 225
Schneider, Rene General, 134
Second Continental Congress, 30
Secrecy (Operational), 4, 10, 30, 31, 32,
63-64, 163, 174, 228, 250, 265; CIA
lack of secrecy, 3, 175, 226, 228; CIA
Secrecy Agreements, 51, 107, 150, 246
Senior Officer Development Course
(SODC), 217-218, 284
Sensitive Compartmented Information
(SCI), 241-242, 284
Sherman, William T., 35
Simon, Paul Senator, 219
"Sleeper" operations, 93, 153
Smith, Walter Bedell General (DCI), 7
Smith, Joseph, 174
Somalia, 3
Sorenson, Theodore, 192
Sorge, Richard, 43, 73-74, 153-155
Souers, Sidney W. Rear Admiral, (DCI), 7
Southeast Asia, 47, 54, 64, 97, 99, 113, 127,
131, 135, 142, 147, 165, 166, 170, 193,
201, 224, 230, 264; refugees from, 17
Spain, 114; and the American Revolution, 32
Spoiler Operations (Chile), 133
Stalin, Joseph (original name, Joseph
Vissarionovich Dzhugashvili), 23, 39,
41-43, 44, 64, 73, 74, 75, 140, 200, 250,
256, 284; daughter Svetlana defection
of, 200
Stevenson, Adlai E., 63, 66
Stimson, Henry L. Secretary of State, 37
Stockwell, John, 208, 246

Strategic Defense Initiative (SDI; "Star
Wars"), 213, 284
Sudan, 3
Summit: Eisenhower-Khrushchev, 67
Surge Funding, 104

Task Forces, creation of, 261; see
Afghanistan and Central American
Task Force
Terrorism/Terrorists, 1-12, 37, 39, 76,
81, 106, 107, 122, 127, 170, 195, 201,
221, 227, 229, 230, 236, 249, 250, 251,
259, 262, 266, 268, 273, 275, 276, 281.
See also Counterterrorism and Red
Terror.
Third World, 29, 45, 65, 89, 98, 180, 181,
205, 208, 215, 222, 229
Tomic, Radimiro Senator, 129-133, 132,
133
"Track Two" program, 133, 228, 231
Tradecraft (spy techniques),53-54, 99,
191, 200-205, 213, 214, 275; audio
operations, 54; casing, 202, 204;
clandestine photography, 204; dead
drops, 188, 202, 204, 275; recruiting
agents, Appendix A (269-72); secret
writing, 33, 81, 188, 275; surveillance
detection, 202
Training: Operations, Chapter 3(49-61),
Chapter 13(197-209), Chapter 14
(211-222); See also Foreign languages;
Soviet Realities Course, 217. See also
Office of Training.
Treaty of Versailles, 36
Trident submarine, 183
Trotskyites: Followers of Leon Trotsky;
original name, Lev Davidovich
Bronstein, 41, 74, 75
Trujillo, Rafael L., 64, 173
Truman, Harry S President, 3, 6, 7, 39, 45,
46, 67, 246
Tunney-Clark Amendment, 170
Turner, Stansfield Admiral (DCI), 184,
189, 192-195, 199, 201, 205, 217-219,
224-225, 243

Union of Soviet Socialist Republics
(USSR), 1, 22, 23, 24, 29, 39, 43, 44, 47,
50, 54, 67, 74, 75, 76, 77, 80, 108, 118,

Printed in the United States
109076LV00001B/151/A